IN THE TEETH OF THE WIND

IN THE TEETH OF THE WIND

South through the Pole

BY
ALAIN HUBERT, DIXIE DANSERCOER
AND
MICHEL BRENT
PREFACE BY
BARON GASTON DE GERLACHE

BLUNTISHAM BOOKS
ERSKINE PRESS
2001

First published in English in 2001 by
Bluntisham Books
Oak House, East Street, Bluntisham, Huntingdon PE28 3LS
and the Erskine Press
The Old Bakery, Banham, Norwich, Norfolk NR16 2HW

Translated from the original
Cent Jours Pour L'Antarctique, La Grande Traversée"
Editions Labor, 1998, Brussels
Supervised by Nighat Johnson–Amin

British Library Cataloguing in Publication Data
A catalogue record of this book is available
from the British Library

ISBN 1 85297 066 9

© Alain Hubert

Typeset by Waveney Typesetters
Wymondham, Norfolk

Printed by Gallpen Colour Print, Norwich, Norfolk

CONTENTS

PREFACE

My first encounter with Alain Hubert took place on Sunday, 2 April 1995. I remember it as if it were yesterday. The night before, at the *Palais des Académies*, in Brussels, the Belgica Prize was awarded to the British glaciologist, David Drewry. Sunday morning, Alain Hubert came to explain to me his project for crossing the Antarctic (without re-supply), starting from the old Belgian Base, the Roi Baudoin, and finishing at the American base at McMurdo Sound, via the geographic South Pole: 3 800 kilometres!

He had brought me a copy of his book "*L'Enfer Blanc*" ("Into The White Hell") which had just been published. It was based on his expedition with Didier Goetghebuer to the North Pole, which he reached on the 18 of May, after 74 days and 1000 kilometres on skis across a truly infernal ice pack.

His proposed trek across the South Pole had a mythic quality to it. It moved me, in more ways than one. Alain Hubert wanted to do the crossing in the winter of 1997–98 to commemorate, in his own inimitable way, the centennial of the *Belgica* expedition, led by my father, Adrien de Gerlache. He would be starting from the site of the Roi Baudoin Base, which was established by the expedition that I led in 1958, and above which flew the flag of that glorious *Belgica*. Hubert, the Walloon from Harsin, would be taking with him a Flemish travelling companion, Dixie Dansercoer from Huldenberg, sealing in this way the national character of his expedition.

Finally, he wanted to carry out some scientific research, within the present programme of research on the Antarctic.

The man impressed me. With his past achievements, his clear eyes, his determined chin, his athletic build, his intimate knowledge of ski techniques, the meticulousness of his preparation, he was indeed an impressive figure. His unshakeable faith in his projects alone could move all the mountains of Antarctica. I tried to give him the information and support he asked for, and I suggested that he contact the geologist, Tony Van Autenboer, who had on numerous occasions crossed the mountainous zone and the glaciers to the South of the Roi Baudoin Base, and knew them far better than I did. This first encounter left me dreaming. I didn't say it to him, but I gave him only a fifty-percent chance of success. He had all those undeniable qualities, and who knew, he might actually succeed, particularly with the use of the power kites, which he was off to Greenland to perfect. But against him was the enormity of the challenge, the sheer distance they would have to cover, the weight of the fully loaded sledges they would have to pull, the hostile nature of the terrain, with the cutting sastrugis and the fearsome crevasses, the cold, the immobilising blizzards.......

The winds, on which he was basing his hopes of success, would they be favourable? Our two countrymen, would they be able to tame those winds enough to optimise the use of their sails, flying, as they would be, thirty feet in front of them.

Well, succeed they did. In 99 days, despite terrible setbacks and tremendous difficulties, thanks in a large part to the force of their characters and their indomitable will to win.

In the telling of their exploits, they document almost each day of their advance, (a technique which accentuates the suspense), detailing their internal debates, the personal monologues, the point and counterpoint of a long campaign. Going far beyond one's capacities, to the limits of human endurance, as they did, intensifies the awareness of the "*raison d'être*". The heaven and hell of the kilometres covered made each reflect endlessly on the meaning of the cosmos. The single daily word prepared lovingly in advance by his wife, to be delivered to the meditations of the explorer, encouraged him at the start of each stage.

A third man, the essential link in the realisation of this exploit, was Michel Brent, who was in charge of the headquarters in Brussels, and of the search and rescue operations, and who took on the problems of communicating with the expedition, the families, the friends, and the public. We often shared his agonies.

Our two polar adventurers have earned a seat of honour in the long line of Belgians who have laboured in the Antarctic. They are an example to the young, whose imagination they have kindled, and whose hearts and minds they have won. For this, we must congratulate them.

By their impact on our society through the media they will surely be able to influence the policy makers of our country towards intensifying the research on The Last Continent. For this, we must thank them.

Baron Gaston de Gerlache
President of the Belgian National Committee for Antarctic Research

INTRODUCTION

On 18 May 1994, after struggling over the Arctic ice pack for 76 days with Didier Goetghebuer, I finally achieved my dream of reaching the geographical North Pole. During those last hours of dragging our heavy sledges across ice, and over channels of running water which opened in our paths, fending off the freezing winds and stumbling blindly through the fog, we should have had one idea, and only one, in our heads: end the madness, stand on that damned abstract point and, at last, to go home to our families, and to take up life where we had left off …

That is not quite how it went. Who could have believed it! With each agonising step drawing us closer to the North Pole, another idea, another image was rising to tantalise me. The Antarctic had already begun to seep into my brain. In the loneliness of the dogged, mute repetition of the mechanical movements of the march to the Pole, step by step, yard after yard, one stubborn notion was forming, becoming clearer, and more insistent. The grandeur of my immediate environment was already enticing me towards the southern continent, with a persistent questioning in my brain. What would it be like if one were to add, to these magnificent icy landscapes surrounding us, enormous mountain chains? Demented winds? The scarcely imaginable vastness of a largely virgin territory? The reminder of a once audacious Belgium? What was happening to me? Dementia in the unbridled exaltation of the final kilometres? Perhaps.

At the press conference awaiting us on our return, there was of course the inevitable question from a journalist as to my future plans, to which came the inevitable, impulsive reply: "The Antarctic!" Truly astonished, I had just come to realise that even before going home, I had already decided to pile Pelion upon Ossa. Head South!

The Antarctic. An evocative word that conjures up myriad dreams. Fundamentally, it appealed to the child in me, the one who is always off seeking adventure. It awoke vague, childhood recollections, of interminable escapades in the forests near my home, of my wondrous first discovery of mountains, followed by the Himalayan expeditions and, finally, the incursions further and further into the Great Frozen North. The Antarctic would offer new horizons, new quests and the promise of new dialogues with the wind and the earth. How could I hold out against such temptation?

For every young Belgian, this continent also denotes tales from a homespun mythology. For among the numerous accounts of adventures that are told and retold to our children, there stand out the magnificent exploits of Adrien de Gerlache and the crew of the *Belgica* who achieved the first wintering in southern waters. Reaching for the shores of these faraway mythic lands was therefore, in a sense, daring to take a tentative step into the hall of the great warriors.

On another level, for the "concerned citizen" that lurks in each of us, the importance of the Antarctic has another dimension, one of which most of us may not even be aware.

In a curious paradox, this deserted and unknown continent is at the crux of the issues surrounding the future of our planet. It has become the key observatory of our climate, in all its complexity. The anxiety caused by certain well publicised aspects of climate change, such as the increase in green-houses gasses, the worrying reduction of the ozone layer or the unusually large size of some recent icebergs, has emerged on the international arena following the convening of multilateral negotiations to combat further environmental deterioration. The role of the Antarctic underpins the importance of the Antarctic Treaty, one of the more effective international agreements. A despoliation of Antarctica would spell the beginning of the end.

The strands began to come together. The child, the Belgian patriot and the concerned citizen; adventure, tradition and science. As the origins of the long path on which I found myself became clearer, a new understanding began to dawn the further I progressed along this path, leading me inexorably towards this new endeavour.

No sooner had the seed germinated, than the brilliant idea occurred to me to have this new expedition coincide with the centenary of Adrien de Gerlache's first over-wintering in Antarctica. That still left me to come up with a project worthy of our illustrious predecessor.

To be frank, at this time, the little I knew about this first over-wintering came from some photographs and a few indirect accounts published at the time in the weekly magazine "*Illustration*". I therefore set myself the task of finding accounts of these polar expeditions so that I could immerse myself in the incredible adventures of men like Shackleton, Amundsen and Scott. I re-read several times the final lines written by Scott in his diary on his return from the South Pole, where Amundsen had preceded him by a few short weeks. He had continued to write even as he lay dying, trapped in his tent by a blizzard, hardly 16 kilometres from his last stockpile of supplies. I ran through the account of the first crossing of the Antarctic made by Fuchs and Hillary in 1957–58, and of the more recent accounts of Fiennes, Messner and Etienne.

Gradually, the idea of a complete crossing took shape. Why not leave from the former Belgian scientific base (the *Roi Baudouin* Base) and make for the American base, at McMurdo Sound, on the Ross Sea at the other end of the continent? A journey of nearly 4000 km, with some sections still unexplored, two mountain chains to cross, sledges weighing more than 180 kilos to drag up to 3,700 m altitude …. Could it be done? But more pertinently, could it be done without re-supply?

THE "FOUR"

At the end of the press conference where I had just announced my latest challenge – the Antarctic Eric Janssen, the CEO of Compaq Belgium–Luxembourg, took me to one side to suggest teaming up again. The "*North to the Pole*" expedition had taught me to appreciate and value the qualities of my sponsors. The open-mindedness and wholehearted support offered by Eric Janssen and his team in backing the venture in all its different dimensions had forged a solid, mutual respect.

To be able to count on the financial support of such a reliable partner, from the very genesis of the project, was surely a sign from heaven. This relieved me of the burden of spending many long months trying to raise the funds necessary for the undertaking. Time and again, the generosity and the understanding of the team at Compaq and their director were put rudely to the test: but never failing.

As part of the Centenary celebration we also came up with another project – "The Last Continent" exhibition. Looking for a way to *truly* celebrate the centenary, to pay homage to the Belgian presence in the Antarctic, and to raise public awareness of the crucial role that this continent is called upon to play in the next century, we decided to create a very unique exhibition in which the visitor would be able to give full rein to his imagination. The importance of this event for Belgium, coupled with the urgency of the matter, meant that I would have to hurry if I wished to see all the various initiatives come to something.

"The Last Continent" exhibition was to cover many aspects of the history of Antarctica from the early exploration, including the over-wintering of the *Belgica*, and the race for the Pole, to the present day scientific initiatives coming out of the frozen continent. The de Gerlache family was quick to assure us of their total co-operation. In addition, once more, Compaq provided the funds necessary to set up the exhibition. The Euroculture team selected to organise the exhibition was the same team behind the widely acclaimed exhibition "*I was 20 years old in 45*". Only this team, we felt, could properly capture the spirit of the Antarctic with its many facets. To our delight, Euroculture agreed to collaborate with us. The resounding success of the event led to the closing date being postponed several times, which to our minds amply demonstrates that the choice of designers was inspired.

The sixth continent began to exercise a serious fascination over me, which only intensified as the presence of Belgium in its history became increasingly more evident.

The initial exploits of Adrien de Gerlache were to have an important influence on the history of scientific research in the Antarctic. The scientific findings of his voyage were to form the basis for numerous important research projects. Under the decisive influence of the International Geophysics Year and the installation of the Roi

Baudouin Base on the continent in the fifties and sixties, Belgium developed an enviable international reputation in the field.

But the true revelation for me was the realisation of how active in Antarctic Research the Belgian scientific community is today. Budget restrictions and the abandonment of a permanent polar base would, in many cases, have confined these researchers to relative anonymity, condemned them to graft their research initiatives as best they could, on to projects of other countries. And yet, even in such circumstances, the results of their work are a reason for which to be proud.

I discovered that there were an impressive number of Belgian researchers at the cutting edge of Antarctic research. I was astonished to learn that the future of detergents was connected to fishing for low temperature enzymes in Antarctic waters, or that the removal and analysis of ice core samples were extremely useful in the reconstitution of the ancient climates of the planet. Painstaking work is carried out by each of these laboratories or universities in fields ranging from ice-dynamics to climatology and biodiversity to name but a few. Research is also being conducted into the carbon cycle in the food chain of the southern ocean in order to determine the percentage of CO_2 that could be absorbed there.

As the exhibition would only remain effective so long as it remained open, one further initiative was required. Michel Brent (who was already charged with the communication logistics of the expedition) was asked if he would be prepared to draft a work on the history of Belgium's relations with the Antarctica over these last one hundred years, concluding with the research currently being conducted. With his customary enthusiasm, he accepted.

The different encounters that I made in the context of preparing the various projects have enabled me to get to know many researchers whose precise knowledge of particular aspects of this continent contributed significantly to the logistics of the expedition. The exhibition project, the book project and the expedition project combined to create an increased interchange and collaboration within the Belgian scientific world. We were soon asked to participate in some on-the-ground research projects (ice core sampling and various other activities). It soon became clear that the expedition would need to develop this dimension. It was only the Federal Minister in charge of scientific research who failed to grasp the research dimension of the project!

With Compaq and Michel Brent, the project had solid foundations on which to build. Nothing was now lacking except a travelling companion. Didier Goetghebuer, who accompanied me to the North Pole and was a seasoned veteran of several other expeditions, was in the frame from the outset but had to withdraw for professional reasons. It was only natural for me to approach Dixie Dansercoer next. We first met in Tibet, on an expedition to climb Cho Oyu, and our paths continued to cross frequently thereafter. We were even team members for the Greenland crossing, and so he was no stranger to me. I had already learnt to appreciate the astonishing energy and strength of character possessed by this fanatic of the great outdoors. An accomplished athlete and windsurf champion, he devoted as much attention to his training as to the ethics related

to the pursuit of his passions. I was convinced that we would be able to form an efficient and cohesive team, while maintaining enough freedom of manoeuvre for the
personal development of each. He was the judicious completion of "The Four".

This team is, however, only the smallest tip of the proverbial iceberg. An endeavour
such as this, from its conception, through its preparation to its execution can only be
successful with the support and assistance of a whole army of meticulous and dedi-
cated people.

RECONCILIATION

A friend once said to me: "For you, an expedition is like drawing a bridge or designing
a Concorde, always a fabulous engineering project. Things that seem insurmountable
to us, to you appear only as a challenge, a mega-problem, which is no more than the
sum of a series of problems. And each one of them is like a collection of jumbled specific queries to which you want to be able to give precise answers." I liked the sound of
it. And that is basically how it goes. But it would be tedious to try to describe all the
choices, tests and research necessary for the preparation of basic equipment for the
expedition. From the shape and stress resistance of the tent, to the choice of clothing;
from the insulation material of the sleeping bags, to the design of the sledges and their
constituent materials; from the adaptation of the ski boots for the traction systems, to
the communication protocols established; the list is very long and the number and
variety of tests, unending.

Something that had barely been taught to me during my training as an engineer was
that, into the planning of logistical details, one must also incorporate the possibility of
changing one's mind – back and forth – on numerous occasions. This allows one to
add the finishing touches to solutions, analysing those selected, comparing new ones
with old ones, letting them develop in the subconscious mind, giving free rein to the
imagination and so, by this gradual refining process reaching the best possible solution.

Moreover, preparing such a venture in every minute detail means that you must lay
yourself open to chance encounters, as these were to provide many key solutions.

In "South Through The Pole 1997–98", the decision to make a complete unassisted
crossing was faced, from the outset, with two great challenges: Wind and Weight.

It would never be possible to do such a crossing on foot. The duration of the crossing would mean having to take along food and supplies in such enormous quantities
that it would have been impossible for a man to drag these around. We, therefore, had
to use traction kites or parafoils, as I had already done in the Northern Hemisphere, (in
Greenland) to increase the rate of advance. But commercially available kites were too
heavy and could not climb sufficiently into the wind. The perfecting of a new traction
system, and the tracing of an itinerary that would extract the maximum advantage
from the prevailing winds, became the key factors for the success of the expedition.
Two unforeseen encounters were to provide the solution to these particular problems.

In 1995, two days before my departure for Greenland with Dixie, carrying out the tests on the equipment, with the trans-Antarctic crossing in mind (already!), I needed new suspension lines for the parafoil prototype that I was trying to perfect. Searching around for a specialist, I made the acquaintance of a multimedia expert, who was also, incidentally, passionate about traction kites. His name was Patrick Nassogne. With him and his team, we were to spend most of the following year designing and perfecting the new bat wing sail. Much lighter and more efficient than the usual parafoils, it was going to open the doors of this expedition for us.

Then, one spring evening in 1996, when I was giving a speech on my expedition to the North Pole, I met Hubert Gallée, engineer and environmental physicist at the Georges Lemaître Institute of the Catholic University of Louvain-la-Neuve. He confided to me that he had developed a mathematical model on the circulation patterns of the most prevalent winds in the Antarctic, the famous katabatics. It was, finally, only after a detailed study of his mathematical model that the definitive itinerary was established.

There remained the question of the excess weight of the sledges to tackle. The necessity of keeping the weight down to a minimum meant that every piece of equipment had to be examined for possible weight saving options. Every item selected was subjected to a rigorous testing, with the main criteria being efficiency (fitness for purpose), resistance to stress, and of course, weight. We went even so far as to wrap up our photographic films in cellophane rather than leaving them in their cartons.

But the most important weight savings had to be made on the food, because this would constitute the major part of the load. The means of achieving this weight saving relied on a simple fact, namely that one gram of fat yields more than twice the calories of one gram of protein or sugar. This meant that we would, therefore, have to eat as much fat as possible, while producing a maximum output of effort. We were going to endure severe physical activity over a very long period of time, with long stretches of endurance work. It was evident that the usual diet used by expeditions would no longer be sufficient. A more thorough study of this concept had to be made.

During March 1997, whilst training in the Great Canadian North at Resolute Bay, I met the Frenchman Arnaud Tortel, a sports dietician, and a fellow lover of the Polar Regions. Together, we were to perfect a formula that would enable us to optimise our dietary intake, while eliminating all superfluous food related weight from the load. From there, with the collaboration of food technology and packaging experts, we even managed to arrive at new weight savings with thermo-retractable packaging which, for two persons daily food rations, did not exceed 14 grams in weight.

By a constant mental juggling with these problems, of turning them every which way in my head, of playing with the details to hand and conceptualising many others, the exceptional realities of this distant continent became somehow tamed. They became almost familiar. Progressively, I came to convince myself that the Antarctic environment was manageable if the logistics were sufficiently organised. From then on, it was a completely natural progression for me to actually go there.

MIND AND BODY

The scale of the venture and the physical demands of its execution required total commitment on our part to the preparation of the expedition. Dixie obtained, without too much difficulty, unpaid leave from his employer, and the financial support of my sponsors also enabled me to devote myself to it more intensively.

The efficiency of the finest logistics is never sufficient without physical and mental preparation. Training, weight lifting, running, bicycle races, and other endurance activities became daily events. These were followed with mountain races, ski treks, two crossings of Greenland, and a reconnaissance visit to the Antarctic to accustom ourselves to the southern conditions. But the training also had its more unusual components. During the months of July and August, Dixie used to go regularly to Nieuport to paddle against the tide in the mornings and to pull a loaded kayak across the dunes in the afternoons. After which, we would go for "haulage" sessions in the little hollow paths that cross the Huldenberg countryside. This consisted of tying an old tyre (which we had previously filled with concrete) along behind us, and running around in this manner for several hours under the disbelieving stares of the locals, and the bemused gaze of the grazing cows.

Testing the sails in Engadine on Lake Silvaplana.

We were, naturally, aware that an expedition of this kind would be as demanding psychologically as it was physically. And if the physical preparation is easy to programme, the mental preparation is more subtle. The process is intimately personal, dependent on each person's individual journey through life, basing itself on non-negotiable convictions and experiences, and is not transferable from one person to another. With experiences gained through the passage of time and on expedition, each one forges his own techniques and develops his own accompanying training methods. Dixie relies on yoga for working on his concentration, relaxation and mental vision. One must imagine the confined space of a tent in polar conditions to get a measure of the strength of character that drove him to perform his yoga posture sequences every single day. Nevertheless, some common markers are essential. Contacts with the Sports Psychology department of Leuven University enabled us to understand more fully the impact of emotion on sporting performance. This also motivated us to note down observations throughout the expedition, with a view to conducting a special study.

How ought one to prepare oneself for the strong and unpredictable emotions that will undoubtedly come to the fore? One can reduce their impact by endeavouring to visualise, throughout the training period, all the circumstances imaginable that may arise in the course of the journey, and, for each theoretical situation, to make a list for oneself of all the available alternative responses, whether reflex or recourse to some other means, together with their relevance. Rigorous work and intense effort, which is also mentally taxing, can increase ones capacity for resistance to stress, and can create life-saving automatic reflexes.

One of the most decisive bases for mental work was, without doubt, the eradication of all spirit of competition. An expedition is not and cannot be conceived of as a competition. It is rather a combination of dialogues, physical dialogue with the surrounds, intense dialogue with one's companion, intimate dialogue with oneself. Had Dixie not given up competing when a long distance runner had once said to him that the competition itself would always win?

The Hubert Dansercoer team in action.

The last tests undertaken in Greenland before departure.

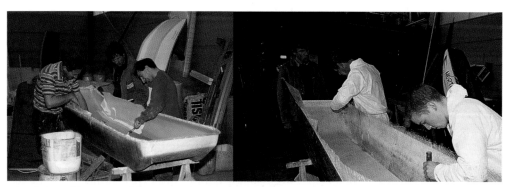

The sledges, like most of the material, were manufactured specially.

A *KOAN* FOR ETERNITY

There is a particular dream that I have had for many years. I live it, I return to it, I leave it to soak, then I come back to it almost belligerently, like with those elliptical maxims, the *koans*, that the Zen masters give to their apprentices to ponder over. But always, I resign myself to it.

How can I describe it? Pure madness? Spoilt whim? Passion? Prolonged adolescence? Dreams to fulfill? Life-journey? Spiritual quest? The list could go on and on. If the response is not as clear as I would have liked, one thing is however certain. Life has taught me that there is no perfectly clear-cut explanation for human behaviour. With Didier Goetghebuer, Dixie Dansercoer and other fellow adventurers that I have spent time with over recent years, we have shared some difficult and some exalted moments, and we have exchanged views at length on this question. Beyond our individual journeys, our respective approaches and our fundamentally indomitable and unique personalities, we share a common motivation: the intuition, intimate yet powerful, that an important part of man takes root in his original rapport with nature, and that the spiritual profile of the coming century will to a large extent consist of the rediscovery of this essential dimension.

We are conscious of the extreme fragility of our place in the cosmos. Our voyages are hardly anything other than that will to put ourselves into situations where Mother Nature will never forget to remind us of our duty of humility. Minute, fragile in a cosmos that will always and entirely outstrip us.

At the publication of "White Hell", (*"L'Enfer Blanc"* story of the North Pole Expedition) a friend remarked to me how much this title evoked the ninth circle of the hell of ice in The Divine Comedy.

Beyond the historical and theological contexts of the period, Dante had indeed offered us a slow "crossing" of the self. So perhaps one should not be surprised to see the ghost of this illustrious Italian appear in the course of this southern crossing. How many times, on the verge of discouragement in the face of never-ending obstacles, will we not aspire to cross this last circle of hell, to cross the realm of purgatory and catch a glimpse of the gates of paradise at the end of the road?

And of our families? Without their unwavering support ventures such as this would never see the light of day. Will we ever be able to repay them for the happiness that they give us in allowing us to live in this way, so that we come home full of renewed energy? The lengthy preoccupation with the preparations, and the long periods of absence on expeditions sometimes weighs heavily on them. And of course, it is they who take over the responsibilities and the rhythms of every day life.

We both know, each in his own way, the difficulties the expedition creates for our wives and children – before, during and after. We also know, above all, of the necessity for dialogue in our relationships, of opening ourselves to the other's needs, to their aspirations and their dreams, (which inspire them just as much as we have been inspired by this great adventure that we have lived).

Alain Hubert

Alain Hubert and Dixie Dansercoer training.

The writing of this book, and the success of this whole endeavour, is the fruit of the close collaboration between three men: Alain Hubert, Dixie Dansercoer and Michel Brent. The body of the work consists of extracts from the diaries of Alain and Dixie, supplemented with additional data collected and worked by Alain Hubert with the aid of Michel Brent. It is therefore the result of a concerted effort and one likes to think that it reflects a common perception. In order to preserve and to underline the individual contributions, the extracts from Dixie Dansercoer's diary are italicised and indicated by an indent.

Note: All measurements of distance are given in metric units (i.e. kilometres, metres and centimetres). One mile is equivalent to 1.6 kilometres, one yard is approximately 0.9 metres, and one inch is 2.54 centimetres.

THE JOURNAL

1 November 1997–18 February 1998

Saturday, 1 November (Day D-2)

The Third Man

Cape Town. 10 o'clock in the morning. On its way towards the immense cold of the Antarctic, the expedition opts to stay in a charming guesthouse in the French quarter of the town. Some rooms look over a garden of exotic plants, others over the swimming pool with its turquoise water and, beyond the roofs, the vastness of the Atlantic. As well as this enchanting setting, we are enjoying magnificent weather: the sun, the sweltering heat of the tropics and a frequently blue sky. As far as atmosphere is concerned, not at all bad either (here ends the picture postcard that I'm sending to you all). Not only has the owner literally abandoned a part of his house to us, but we also have the good fortune of sharing the guesthouse with a bevy of young South African beauties who have come to the capital to flirt with fame. The only elements out of keeping with this idyllic décor are our polar sledges which, because of lack of space, have had to be parked by the pool.

When Dixie told me a month beforehand that he had found a nice motel for housing the expedition, I was a million miles away from imagining that this great adventure would begin in such a charming manner, and that these days would have the appearance of a kind of surrealistic episode between the feverish preparations of the preceding few weeks and what was waiting for us in the next few days. A temporary immersion in a holiday atmosphere.

Beginning in such an agreeable manner, that's quite a send off! The atmosphere is, however, not one of complete idleness. The great departure is now closer than ever. In addition to the final imponderables to be settled with Brussels, there is the wait and the many unresolved factors of the flight to the Antarctic. It was envisaged that we would leave as early as possible, but the flight depends on the weather conditions at the landing site, that is to say at the tourist base Blue One, which is, it would appear, a fairly well developed encampment on a blue ice area free of snow.

We have now, in fact, been waiting for two days. And for two days, Anne Kershaw, the head of Adventure Network International (ANI) who have organised our transportation to the Antarctic, has been bustling back and forth between our hotel and hers to keep us up to date with the situation. Sometimes it's "Yes, we can go in a little while". Then it's "No; the weather down there has got worse again". The decision is all the more difficult to make because, due to the distance which separates us, the weather forecasts coming from the continent are naturally not as accurate as those to which we are accustomed in the Northern Hemisphere. (This is further complicated by the fact that the Hercules flight requires 7 to 8 hours to reach Blue One.)

Then, there is the point of no return. That is the point at which the C130 has to decide whether to continue its flight, or not, as it cannot make the Cape Town – Antarctic run and back without refuelling at Blue One. So already, a few shivers are running gently up and down our spines.

There are a few more reasons for worrying. At daybreak, we learn that the plane (which we have partially chartered) and which is supposed to transport the expedition to its initial starting-point is still operating in the Central African region. I suddenly have the feeling that our departure is to be put off indefinitely! As for the Twin Otter, the twin-engine plane that should be waiting to take us on to the final departure-point (the site of the former Belgian Roi Baudouin base), has not even arrived at Blue One. They are apparently blocked by bad weather somewhere between Patriot Hills and Blue One.

In short, if we make a quick assessment of the situation on this Saturday morning, we quickly realise that we have no chance of leaving today. Tomorrow morning, per-haps, announces "La Kershaw" by telephone at midday.

No doubt, without really wanting to, I cannot stop myself thinking about all these minutes, hours and days lost, here, in South Africa, while waiting to leave. I know that for polar expeditions things can go completely wrong from the start, because of a too long wait for favourable weather conditions for flights from the world of earth to the world of ice. For expeditions to the Antarctic, the favourable time gap that opens each year is very short, running from the beginning of November to the end of February. If one proposes to cross the whole of the continent, a distance of some 3 900 km, in such a short time, you get the overwhelming conviction that every minute counts.

But we cannot allow such considerations to depress us. We will instead trust in the latest news, which arrived after lunch. In any case, if we don't leave this evening, we will in any event leave tomorrow.

Patience …

We are in the process of making plans for our evening – the Chinese in the little street opposite or the Italian close to the sea? – when Anne Kershaw calls to tell us that we have only two hours to prepare before the pick-ups arrive to take us all to the air-port. *"I've had Blue One on the line"*, she tells me, *"We must make the most of the favourable climatic conditions. It's beginning to turn fine down there, the blizzard stopped during the night. Take-off planned for 22.00 hours!"*

Is this finally it? Nobody knows. But given that the information seems pretty precise, we decide on the final rush to get everything ready. As we are almost ready anyway, all that is left is to put the frozen rations into their refrigerated containers (they had been stored in the guesthouse refrigerators). Last check on the sledges and sails, last dive into the pool, last phone call to our loved ones, one last shower... Good luck, girls!

Circumstances such as these always make one reflective, be it on the eve of a great adventure such as ours, or before any other departure. You need to be alone for a moment of inner reflection, to look yourself in the face, to gather all your energies, to link the past to the present, to make knots in your memory, to take leave of a part of yourself... In short, like a cat, to coil yourself up, all the better to leap. That is what is happening to us now, to Dixie and me. He has gone to meditate in the area by the nearby hill: I'm sitting under my parasol by the pool, a place of which I have become particularly fond and where, incidentally, I have installed a sort of make-shift campaign office.

Quickly, write a few lines. I call this operation *"inaugurating the ritual of the log-book"*. This small notebook will have three principal purposes: Firstly, to note the progress of the expedition day by day: positions, distances, temperatures, wind speed and direction, etc. as a lasting reminder of the individual days. Secondly, to serve as confidant during difficult moments, allowing me to give free rein to my emotions, preserve what I had not been able – or had not wished – to express to my companion, organise the questionings on the purpose of my adventure and, beyond that, of my life. In fact, writing is for me a matter of survival. If one has no outlet, for the outpouring of the overflow of the mind, it would be better not to leave at all. With this each morning, the will can be unshakeable, the mind clear, alert and strong. And finally, to bear witness to the experience of my adventures, to revive the brightness of various visions, to re-awaken doubts, to re-ask questions, to recreate the moments of profound joy.

Throughout the years, these little logbooks of my expeditions have piled up on a shelf in my office. It is only very rarely that I leaf through them. But when at times the waves hit the soul, I know then that I only have to look at them in a different way to open immediately the flood gates of memory to my finest adventures: the demanding paths, the dangerous days, the moments of despair, encounters that left their mark, childlike happiness, flashes of confidence...

The telephone rings: another set back? No, it's my son Martin. Normally so reserved, he is ringing to wish me *"bonne route"*. Will he ever know the inestimable gift that he gave me that evening? To be the last to call, to be the only one to guess that there were only a few more minutes before we finally leave the guesthouse for the airport... Such are the coincidences of life!

Suddenly I hear the noise of car doors. The pick-ups that are to take us to the airport have arrived. The reality of the departure takes shape. Piling the two sledges and the rest of the baggage into these vehicles is not so easy. At last, it's OK, but only just. The drivers must however take care not to lose anything on the way. Half an hour later, we arrive on the tarmac.

It is 21.30.

Without wasting time, we make the acquaintance of the captain and his five crew members. From that moment on, it seems to me that everything happens very quickly: loading the sledges into the C130, the final good-byes and the backslapping for those who arrive to send us off. One hour later, here we are in the cabin of this hulking great machine. It never fails to impress me, especially when I think of the service that this very same Hercules provides on a daily basis to the needy and underprivileged in Africa. Already, the engines roar. The next time we set foot on solid ground will be in the Antarctic!

Although it is our expedition that has chartered half the plane for this flight to Blue One, we find that there are more than thirty people in the belly of this monster. Apart from the crew, our cameraman Remy Révellin, a local team from the BBC and some fellow countrymen, we have been joined by a number of South African technicians who are going to travel to the new base at Sanae, and in addition some Indian scientists who are also on the way to their Antarctic station. A few friends also wanted to make the journey with us. Among them Ida Verlinden, the Belgian consul at the Cape, and Frank Tyga, a former surfer friend of Dixie's and owner of the guesthouse where we stayed. Frank is what you could call a colourful character: a Belgian, expatriate doctor, a great sportsman and a sports car fanatic, he never misses the chance of throwing himself into crazy schemes. When he heard that there were still some unoccupied seats on the plane he immediately offered to join us, paying for his own place. One of the passengers on the flight is a rich American tourist who "collects" countries he visits to try to be included in the *Guinness Book of Records*. He has paid the trifling sum of £12,000 for the return trip from Cape Town to Blue One for the sole purpose of walking on Antarctic "soil" and thus being able to add the continent to his trophy cupboard.

I cannot list the passengers on this flight Cape Town / Blue One without mentioning Michel Brent. I met this journalist for the first time at an interview, after I had climbed the East face of Ama Dablam in Nepal (a "first" that I achieved in 1983 with the Swiss mountaineer André Georges). We almost "stayed there", as they say in the jargon, and I suspected him of being interested only in the more spectacular aspects of our saga. At the time I couldn't have guessed that behind his outwardly staid demeanour was hidden an old jungle hand who had lived for three years in Sumatra. He knew a lot more than I did about adventure. He had been the second white man to stay with the Sakuddei, a clan of 26 tribespeople living as though in the Neolithic age, recluses in the deepest Indonesian jungle, resisting all evangelisation. We saw each other again during my Himalayan adventures, for drafting the press folders and finalising the "communication" aspect of each of my expeditions. In him I discovered an exacting and meticulous man, fired with a passion for travel, for the sea, for music, as well as being a total workaholic. Driven by an all too rare sense of what is ethical, this journalist, photographer and writer has been fighting a relentless struggle for several years against the pillaging of the ancient archaeological sites, an infamous practice that often destroys large chunks of history in less developed countries. I have come to recognise his passions, his outbursts, to love his foibles, and his booming telephone calls in the small hours.

The winter of 1989 reunited us on the south slopes of Cho-Oyu in Nepal. Only just arrived at the base camp, he nearly died there of a cerebral oedema. Lord knows how frightened I was! In short, this old moaner has over the years become my trusted friend and confidant, the indispensable companion in all my adventures. When I spoke to him for the first time about the Antarctic, Michel threw himself with enthusiasm into this somewhat crazy venture: he especially succeeded in the huge task of writing the book "The Antarctic and Belgium".

Because I have absolute confidence in his many talents, I have decided that he will be the sole point of contact with the world of men. Michel will be the "third man" of this adventure.

While everyone is struggling with greater or lesser success to catch a few moments of sleep in this bare and empty cabin, Michel and I are putting the hours to good use by going over once more all the instructions that we have assembled these last few months. The Argos satellite codes [1], for example, the frequency of communication, their nature (telephone or e-mail), the emergency procedures, the possible help organisations, the list of people to be contacted for such and such a necessity, the press communiqués, the web-site, useful addresses of people that I had been unable to talk to during the preparations, the final things to be done, dealing with the ANI situation…

We discuss for the umpteenth time the eternal problems of money. (I always fume whenever I hear people suggesting that I "make a lot of dough" from my expeditions for nothing could be further from the truth). Michel will have to make all the important decisions on his own.

But I have to admit that this night, at 28,000 feet above the Indian Ocean, somewhere between the southern tip of Africa and the shores of the Antarctic, financial preoccupations, which normally haunt me, slowly fade. In any event, what can I do about it now? Nothing, if not to trust in my guiding star and to tell myself that clearing away my debts on my return would certainly have more to so with speleology than with alpinism.

Around us, passengers and friends are falling asleep one after another. I should of course do the same and sneak in a few hours' sleep. But I want too much to see, at first hand, the flight over the ice field. I slip into the navigator's seat to watch for the first signs of the continent.

The madness of this fateful rendezvous should have worried me. But I had no feeling of anxiety. On the contrary: locked up in this infernal machine, enveloped in a deafening racket, I feel fine. Ready for the great encounter.

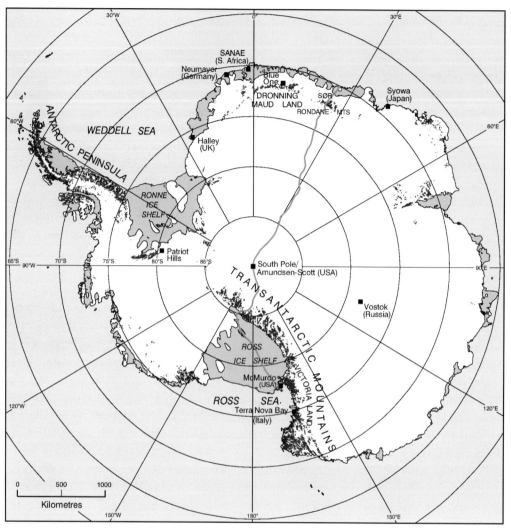

The route taken across the Antarctic Continent.

Sunday, 2 November (Day D-1)

The Blue One Tourist Base

I spoke yesterday of the point of no return. We now know that the decision to continue, and therefore, eventually, to land, has to be taken two hours before arrival. At 4
o'clock in the morning, the captain informs the passengers that the weather is fine and
that the flight will continue. This time there is no doubt, the Antarctic continent is
looming on the horizon.

Flirting with the first glimmers of dawn, we fly over the blue ice fields. Superb
mountains smooth as mirrors and never-ending waves of ice presage the Blue One

base. After Patriot Hills in the Mount Ellsworth region, it is the second tourist station on the Antarctic continent. Situated in Dronning Maud Land, it was opened in 1996 at the time of the National Geographic Magazine expedition organised by Adventure Network International (ANI). This station consists of a mess tent, several private tents, crates of supplies buried in the snow, a row of sledges, a couple of twin-engine planes and an impressive number of petrol tanks. Everything is set out on the ice, about 10 km from the nearest mountain slopes.

We land at Blue One at 6.30 a.m. on a blue ice field: seven and a half hours were needed for the South Africa – Antarctica flight, a distance of 4 326 km.

After a relatively soft landing, we savour our first impressions in a relatively gentle climate: minus 25° C, an 18 km/h wind, sun … On account of the sudden moods of the Antarctic weather, our stop has to be as short as possible. No question of the C130 being blocked on the ice because of a sudden storm.

But before the people who accompanied us this far return, a few photographs must be taken. We get out the traction sails; and for the first time, we get to feel how hard the ground is. For a moment, we lose all control. A few falls lead to prudence. But it is good finally to be ready to get down to the job, to breathe the cold air, to let oneself be overawed by the vastness, to begin the dialogue with the surrounding mountains, to hear the sliding of the sledges and the crunching of the snow under the skis. Those who know Alain will recognise that particular jaw movement and the gleam in the eye. There can be no doubt: we are there.

When the departure of the C130 is announced – more or less around noon – the crew offer us small, signed, flags, as is the custom. One small problem: Dr Frank Tyga is nowhere to be found. In fact, as soon as he was on Antarctic ground, he had not been able to resist the call of the wilds and, wearing skis borrowed from Remy, he went off on his own towards the mountains which he thought were only two or three kilometres away, little realising that over open ground and in bright light there is a tendency to underestimate distances. A search is made, but without success. Suddenly, the captain of the C130 decides to leave; one doesn't play around with the flight programme of a C130, especially if you consider the hourly costs involved. The engines are already revving. This means that poor Frank will be stuck here for a month, at Blue One, until the next ANI round trip. He has no luggage and a crowd of patients waiting for him back home.

Everybody bustles about. A last sweep with the binoculars… *"Alain, I can see him, over there, near the mountains, a little black speck, far away…"* The captain agrees to delay the departure and a skiddoo goes off like a whirlwind to collect the imprudent medic. Amongst us once more, Frank smiles a winning smile, without the slightest idea of the trouble he has caused for the whole group. He is unceremoniously bundled onto the plane under the disapproving glare of the other passengers.

A few moments later the Hercules passes in front of us, throwing up a huge powdery cloud. Again that familiar sensation, that overwhelming emotion, welling up in the throat. After so many departures like this, one should be used to it by now. But it's not so. In the end, I have even come to like it: I think of it as a good sign of motivation. The day when it doesn't happen any more is the day that I should beware.

I realise now that the real point of no return has been reached.

We are only a Twin Otter flight away from the final departure.

Calm restored, we must get organised. In order for him to be able to take back with him some pictures of our first moments on the continent, Remy, our photographer, has agreed to accompany us as far as the site of the former Roi Baudouin Base, which is to be the departure point. Because no other Hercules is expected for another month, he must remain and share the life of the four men who are living out here. He told me later about the indelible impression made on him of those few weeks spent in sharing the ordinary daily existence of the station.

This is one of the stories that Remy told me about his stay. A few days after our departure, a violent storm struck Blue One. There were still ten or so South African technicians at the base – people well acquainted with the harsh Antarctic climate – who had come from Cape Town to work for four months at the South African Sanae base. They were waiting for favourable weather conditions before boarding the Twin Otter to fly there. One of the technicians went to the latrine tent, which was less then ten metres from his own tent. When he stepped outside to return, the blizzard was blowing so fiercely that he couldn't find his way to his own tent again. Nobody noticed his absence until his colleagues, who were preparing to go to the mess tent, noticed that he had disappeared. The staff at the base immediately began a search. Roped together, they searched in ever-increasing circles around the latrine tent and the tent of the missing man. They searched for four hours, in whiteout and found him 250 metres from camp. By some miracle, the lucky man was still alive. What had happened? After realising that he couldn't find his tent again, he followed his training and stayed where he was, huddled up to wait for rescue. He remained in that position for some 14 hours. That's a taste of Antarctica for you!

Tuesday, 4 November (Day 1)

Flying over the Moon

Shortly after breakfast, Mike Sharp, the camp supervisor at Blue One, announces that the weather is getting worse: we must leave as soon as possible. In two hours time, in fact.

We just have time to unpack the crates containing the one hundred daily food rations. In order to keep them frozen, they have been stored in special insulated packaging. In just ten minutes or so, the 362 kilos of equipment have been arranged on the sledges: a routine affair because this procedure was meticulously rehearsed before we left. Then, the equipment is loaded on board the twin-engine plane.

The departure is announced. I realise that it's the last chance for me to write home. I set myself up in the mess tent, sitting with my elbows on the table, where the overwhelming odour of sausages from our last meal is still hanging in the air, wafting over from the pan swimming in grease on the stove. The canvas flaps in the wind. I'm overcome by powerful impressions. These images will stay with me for a long time. A personal confrontation, suddenly to understand the seriousness and the scope of this adventure, to be torn from everything which is part of this world, to understand our good fortune.

"…I would like to thank you for your support … I'm feeling great strength and harmony… I would like to be able to send you these emotions in this letter… emotions from an extraterrestrial world."

It is 12.00 GMT when we board the Twin Otter; 2 hours 20 minutes flying time towards the east, first flying over the Gruber Mountains situated to the south of the Russian scientific base, Novalazarevskaya. The two pilots make themselves comfortable, feet up on the control panel, headphones from the CD player plugged into their ears. Pure and simple rock 'n roll! A little

A Twin Otter transports Alain and Dixie from Blue One to Roi Baudoin Base.

Flying over the Sør Rondane Mountain chain, which the Expedition will have to cross to reach the polar plateau.

later, they offer us champagne: a good moment. The first impressions are so intense, so calming! I let them overwhelm me and I enjoy them.

Bewitched by the enormous expanse of these almost lunar landscapes, I had not realised that we were already in sight of our final objective. Between Blue One and the Roi Baudouin Base (70°S, 25°E) there is only some 450 kilometres and the flight is pretty rapid.

We are now flying over the Sør Rondane; and thanks to the altitude, we have no difficulty in making out the gripping sight of the majestic flow of the glaciers in their slow progress towards the coastline.

Unforgettable… I'm going to be able, at last, to compare the photographs shown to me by Professor Tony Van Autenboer (one of the most accomplished Belgian Antarctic scientists) with the spectacle unravelling beneath the plane. I recognise the rocks that appear to have been sculpted by the wind, the scoops – kinds of ice circus giants that form upwind of the obstacle that the wind buffets against areas of unbelievably blue ice…

On the right of the cockpit I think I recognise Mt Romnaes, a nunatak[2] of characteristic shape, which was mentioned hundreds of times in the accounts of the Belgian Antarctic expeditions of the sixties. To the south, I can even make out the beginning of the entry into Gunnesstadt, the glacier that we have to cross to reach the polar plateau.

The Twin Otter is now flying over Breidbay where some polynyas[3] have appeared – proof that the ocean is not far away. It approaches the area of the former Roi Baudouin Base that is no longer visible today[4]. Two hours after leaving Blue One, the Twin Otter at last does some wide circles looking for an appropriate place to land; the greatest possible prudence is essential in the Antarctic. Finally, after finding an area of flat ice, we touch down, in the place we have so often dreamt of. In my mind's eye I look back to 40 years ago, to December 1957 to be precise. I can see the motorised vehicles, snow-cats, going back and forth carrying equipment between Breidbay and what was to become the first Roi Baudouin Base. I can see two far away ships berthed alongside the ice, I see a group of enthusiastic young researchers, bustling about like ants, setting up pre-fabricated buildings, transporting waterproof partitions, laying the first insulation material, unloading machines and equipment of every kind, looking after the dogs… In short, participating in one of the great scientific exploits of our age, the construction of a research base in Antarctica.

It is 14.20. The weather is clear and the sun is still low on the horizon.

First reflex: listen to the wind.

The wind is too weak; even though it is constant from the northwest, we cannot leave by sail. So we have to start off on skis. Here is the moment for which I have been waiting two years for; to find myself suddenly confronted by the implications of the inevitable, to finally allow all my desire for adventure to be realised, to depart towards and within an immense unknown, and to plant my senses in another world. It is not surprising that I feel a strange serenity invading me.

It is 3 o'clock in the afternoon and, at last, the moment for the great departure has arrived.

I fill my lungs; it's incredible how the purity of the Antarctic air lashes the lungs. I feel well, deeply serene, and without the slightest apprehension for the future.

While we are making our initial adjustments and already marching in the direction of the South Pole, I see the Twin Otter flying overhead, dipping its wings. It's a farewell salute from Greg and Al, but also our final visual contact with the outside world.

We put aside nostalgia and make room for serious matters.

The first immutable rule of the Polar Regions; one must depart slowly. And so, we depart slowly.

A second truth to lodge firmly in one corner of the brain, and as quickly as possible: here we are no longer the masters. We are up against something stronger and more powerful than we are. It is quite clear, a conviction only reinforced by the in-depth study I have immersed myself in over several long months. If I were not convinced that the Antarctic is the stronger, I would have to be a complete idiot. Last precept, a corollary of the previous one: one must learn to bend one's back, to let the light, the wind and the cold gradually insert themselves into our very beings. That too, is clear.

I would even say that it's partly to be able to engage in a dialogue with these obscure forces of nature that I put myself at risk in such endeavours.

Already, we remove a layer of clothing, so mild is the temperature and so strenuous the effort. The terrain is relatively flat; the surface of the ice is just dotted, here and there, with little uneven dunes.

Far away, due south, we can see Mt Romnaes; from here it is merely a black speck on the horizon. But it is, in fact, the first visual point of reference in this race to the ends of the earth. It is as if one was about to sit an examination and the teacher, in a burst of magnanimity, decided to give you the beginning of the answer. It is clear that, as we are confronted with this world without colours, without shapes, without smells and without life, plunged so abruptly into a space of almost cosmic proportions, this nunatak presents a psychological support which comes at just the right moment at the beginning of the expedition.

Moreover, the memory of the Belgian scientists and field workers who have walked over this frozen ground, and who also went to the Sør Rondane by the same route, is in itself very reassuring.

As if waiting for us to be finally alone before welcoming us, the wind suddenly picks up, coming down from the mountains to the south-east. Time for the kites, which will enable us to proceed at more than 15 km/h.

This evening, we have covered 26 km. For the first time, we put up the tent. Because of all the practice, these actions have become second nature to us during these last three months. The sun, still low on the horizon, is not sufficiently warming: we set to brushing our frozen clothes. It is −15°C, the wind is blowing at 30 km/h: I'm cold and I feel tired. It's the tension of these last few days, almost certainly…

As I go to sleep, I see a whole year's work go by, as if in an accelerated dream. Although I have managed to arrive here in perfect physical shape and well rested, I realise that I'm going to have to get rid of the nervous tension that has built up in the course of the last few weeks. I feel that I am far away from everything, far from this civilised land, this "*little platform that makes us so fierce*", as Dante wrote.

I feel calm, very calm, and above all determined to give this attempt whatever it may cost, even the ultimate price.

Wednesday, 5 November (Day 2)

Sharks on the Ice

An excellent night's rest. Fortunately we have brought along earplugs in the luggage or the flapping of the canvas in the wind would have prevented us from sleeping. In the background is an incessant noise, which conjures up wild dreams and strange images, filled with strong impressions and crazy fantasies jostling each other.

Julie has come to find me in my sleeping bag. She has lit some candles. Everything is calm all around us. She slips her body alongside mine, little by little I feel the softness of her hands win me, invade me.

Whatever am I doing here missing such things?

06.00h: To work! How I would like to sleep a bit longer! Two hours are all we need to be ready. I think I have already lost one of my outer mittens while folding the double roof of the tent. I look for it everywhere. Perhaps it's fallen behind a sastrugi? In vain I search…

"Alain, be careful, you have only one spare pair, and you have hardly begun. Calm down, you are in a life or death situation here, don't forget."

(Thankfully, I was to find it that evening, stuck in the folds of the double roof).

The wind is blowing at 30 km/h. We unfurl the sails for the second time. Very soon it has reached more than 50 km/h and we must continue on skis. We each have two pairs of skis. The first are wide mountain skis, for maintaining good lateral stability with the kites. The others are a narrower, "back country" type, with a self-adhesive skin stuck to the central part of the sole only and not, as is usual, to its whole length. This trick was discovered by Børge Ousland, the first man to have crossed the Antarctic solo (1997), from Berkner Island to McMurdo. Leaving the front and back parts of the ski in contact with the ice allows for better sliding; so for crackpots like us who were going to have to take thousands, no millions, of steps on the Antarctic ice-cap, this was an excellent way of saving energy.

Marching allows us to adopt a regular forward rhythm: when I'm on an expedition, I usually stop every hour for 5 to 10 minutes at the most. Time to drink a mouthful of tea and to have a bite to eat.

After six hours progress, the sky covers over, and the wind drops. We spot two Antarctic petrels. These birds, resembling seagulls, glide by on the katabatic wind, as if to remind us that it is time to take to the sails again.

A south-south-easterly wind picks up to around 30–35 km/h. Despite the lateness of the hour (it's about 4 o'clock), we can't resist the temptation of gliding. But since this morning the terrain has changed and sastrugis have appeared. These are dangerous waves of ice formed by the wind; they are streaked across the Antarctic ice cap and take on the most bizarre shapes. When we get to the plateau, Dixie finds that some of them look like sharks, because their contours often remind us of the jaws of those predators when they burst through the surface to grab their prey. The victims on this occasion were our sails, of course…

The sastrugis follow one another in successive bands that we have to zigzag across to find the best trajectory. A little like kerbstones, the only difference being that here the kerbs can reach 70 cm in height. We have not yet found the right method for using sails on terrain such as this.

Still a little like beginners we proceed. Dixie snags his sail, and then it's my turn. The sail turns on itself, inflates like a spinnaker, and there I am, being dragged along the ground. I pull on the rear suspension lines and succeed in stopping. No way of untangling these knots in the wind, so I take out the spare sail. In fact, we each have three kites of different sizes, (6 sq.m., 12 sq.m. and 21 sq.m.) and, for the team, a spare of each size in case of problems.

We're losing a lot of time. Would deploying the kites be harder than we thought? The low sun leaves a filtered light on the banks of drifting snow. This phenomenon is unique to the Antarctic. As soon as the wind blows hard (above 50 km/h), it carries along horizontal storm banks of snow crystals that sweep along the ice at a height varying from 20 cm to several metres. When the pale Antarctic light is added to this gripping sight, it's as if a conveyor belt was passing with great speed before your very eyes. Magic!

Everything is white all around me. This time, this is it: I have just put my toe into another world...

21 km, 47 km in less than two days: we're off to a good start!

This evening, fatigue and a headache. I have not digested my daily rations properly: I don't tolerate the excess fat very well, despite the fact that since the end of September we have both been following a diet designed to get us progressively more accustomed to eating more fat[5].

On the evening of this second day, we find ourselves already re-stitching the sail that I snagged this morning; and I really believed that we would be able to start without having to face technical problems! *"Don't worry, Alain, you're a pro, it'll get better, you'll see..."*. I recall the final words of Mike Sharp at Blue One to cheer myself up. While this old polar fox (he was the first to fly over the Antarctic at the time of the aerial reconnaissance flights of the eighties) was watching us packing the equipment into the sledges, he said to me: "There are many ways of doing it wrong, but you are doing it right..."

Thursday, 6 November (Day 3)

Huddled up

Get up at 7 o'clock despite an irresistible urge to go on sleeping. The weather is bright but overcast. Like yesterday evening, the horizon is darkening in the south and the wind is blowing hard from the south-east. I measure it: 47 km/h. While it rages, we quietly get ready. "Quietly" is not quite accurate, because as I take down the tent, I break the junction of one of the supporting arcs. In ten years of expedition, that has never happened to me before.

What is going on?

As the weather doesn't appear to be improving, I decide that it would be better to repair it now than in the evening. I get into a large transparent nylon bag, which acts as

At the beginning of the Expedition, during the southern spring, the sun is still low on the horizon.

shelter from the driving snow, to carry out the repairs. Luckily, it doesn't take long and we are ready to leave at about 9 o'clock.

Already chaotic, the terrain is now beginning to get steeper, forming a succession of valleys. It's hard, almost to the point of being unbearable. We are labouring like beasts of burden but suffice it to say, we are hardly making any progress. To accelerate matters, we try the small sail that ought to make us go faster in this strong wind. But the technique is not up to scratch, our suspension lines get tangled up and we end up with rags. I realise that we are going to have to improve our technique to avoid wasting time, and especially to avoid premature damage to our equipment.

We start off again on foot, and decide to try gliding an hour later: this time I choose the 12sq.m. sail. As it fills, I'm tugged off the ground and the sail falls back on to Dixie's lines, turns around on itself and breaks half of its 28 suspension lines. I can't believe my eyes!

In view of the strength of the wind, we try to use only one sail for both of us; I hook my sledge to Dixie's and follow him as if we were advancing with a team of dogs. At the end of the morning, after this chain of small mishaps, our clumsy actions and attempted variations, I suddenly realise that we are behaving like true novices of the ice and the sled. *"But what am I doing? Why this impatience? What crazy dream am I hoping to fulfil? We'll never cross the Antarctic like this… I know for a fact, that our new sail system is the only way we have of succeeding in this great adventure, and so…"*

Like kids who can, at last, play with a much-coveted toy, we were being too feverish, too impatient, no doubt hurrying to meet, as quickly as possible, this immense challenge.

During a pause, we put the counters back to zero. Each of us deploys the size of sail that he thinks best adapted to the conditions. But quickly, visibility drops to almost nothing. We can no longer make out the contours of the ground and so we decide to stay where we are for the remainder of the day.

It is 2 o'clock and we have barely covered 3.5 km. Two hours of effective progress for five hours of struggling with the elements. We must get used to such limitations. Get used as well to the conditions of Antarctic progress because, at the moment, we have not found the rhythm, the sledges being so heavy and the terrain so difficult. And then I ask myself what are all these sastrugis doing here. When I visited the scientists who were working in this part of the Antarctic – particularly Tony Van Autenboer – to ask their advice and counsel, I don't remember hearing them talk of sastrugis..... Or perhaps I wasn't paying much attention as I was convinced that the first part of our journey, as far as the Sør Rondane, would be flat and easy.

During the afternoon the wind blows at more than 50 km/h: 5.30 goes by with us in the tent repairing the kites. They've really taken a battering already!

This evening, the barometer drops and I begin to tell myself that the task waiting for us is quite simply e-n-o-r-m-o-u-s. Just the fact of reaching Sør Rondane, this chain of mountains that we are obliged to cross for access to the polar plateau, seems from here like a gigantic challenge. And to think that after that obstacle there are at least 3,500 kilometres still to cover…

This evening, I listen to a little music. For the first time, I think of those that I have left behind. Of all those who have helped me to get ready for the start of this crazy undertaking.

Friday, 7 November (Day 4)

Like Oxen in the Antarctic

The wind wakes us at four in the morning. The racket made by the tent canvas flapping in the wind is so deafening that it's not surprising to be dragged from our sleep in this way. But, apart from the din, something else is niggling at me. Even though I'm still huddled up in my sleeping bag, I'm aware that something is very wrong. The noise of the wind is unusual. Quickly I wake my companion and we are outside. While we are making a tour of our property, I realise that the roof-flaps have been badly covered and that they are letting in the wind. These flaps, unique to polar tents, are pieces of fabric of about 50 cm long sewn into the lower part of the double roof, which one covers with ice and snow to stop the wind creeping into the gap between the double roof and the inner tent.

There was not enough snow piled onto the flaps. I was annoyed. You can never, I repeat never, compromise on what some might think is an unimportant detail. Because all it need is one godawful blizzard to sweep into this gap while we are sleeping – in fact, just what has happened tonight – to cause a total catastrophe. We only have one tent, and it must be protected and attended to with the greatest possible care.

After putting some more snow on the flaps, I go back to sleep.

What a wind! We are frightened that the tent will be blown away in the storm; the ice screws guarantee that it's solidly anchored but one can never be too careful.

I have to laugh at myself because when we go out at four in the morning to retighten the canvas the wind blows me over. A violent headache prevents me from going back to sleep.

I have breakfast on my own, like some antisocial creature. Is there any point in continuing to pull like this? There certainly is.

8.15: the wind is blowing just as strongly, 52 km/h. Even so, the sky is calm. Small banks of drifting snow – we leave on skis.

God, it's hard! These sastrugis that we have to step over all the time, this sledge which is getting heavier and heavier, these hips already in agony from being struck by the harness with unbearable regularity. How we must resemble those oxen harnessed to the plough that I see during my expeditions in Nepal. Of course, we aren't ploughing any furrow in the hard and rock-strewn ground, but it sure feels like it…

As the ice is getting harder and harder, we have to fit the crampons to our boots. The grip underfoot is better, the hauling more regular and more efficient. But we have to take care not to push too hard: the tendons would chafe and blisters would appear. That could be classified as hell. That kind of persistent nagging pain, a bit like a burn, is enough to break even the most hardened spirit. We snake our way between these waves of ice, each taking the lead in turn.

16.15: the wind continues to strengthen. We put up the tent with extreme care.

Six hours of incessant effort to advance 7.8 km. Not bad, considering. This evening we have reached our first degree; 71°S and there are only 32 degrees remaining before we reach the other side of the continent. A mere trifle…

The essential, I can feel it, is to concentrate on each step, especially during the long ascent to the polar plateau. The sledge is decidedly too heavy, nearly 200 kilos as against the 160 of Dixie's. This is not a question of chance: being taller than him, and probably stronger, I had offered to take more weight from the beginning so that our relative effort would be distributed equitably. One consolation of size: keeping in mind that the weight will diminish by about two kilos per day (food and fuel consumed) is encouraging.

Throughout the crossing the Expedition encounters countless sastrugis: waves of frozen ice formed by the wind.

Saturday, 8 November (Day 5)

Good-bye to the Petrels

This morning, sunshine. Get up at 8.30; it is still blowing about 40 to 50 km/h.

I am beginning to understand just how terrible these Antarctic winds can be. A permanent racket; in the tent or in the hood of the jacket; the noise is infernal. Furthermore, it chills us right through as we go along. As it often blows from the side, we have to protect ourselves all the time. Of course, it gets in everywhere. When we don't have it head on, or we turn our backs to it to try to find a little lull, the wind, constantly changing, comes swirling in at our faces. And that's even worse. In fact, with these blizzards of the ends of the Earth, there is no possible respite. Just one example: the chore of cleaning the storm mask when it is steamed up from too much effort. To do this, you have, of course to put your back to the wind. But just as you turn around and struggle to remove the moisture from the plastic, the fine particles of snow that have been caught up along the hood or the jacket come swirling around in front of you and settle on the inside of the mask. Wasted effort, begin again. And so on…

The banks of drifting snow make the landscapes completely surrealistic. It is as if the ground is suddenly covered with white vapour and that this, swollen with grains of

Putting up a tent in strong winds is no mean feat.

When this picture was taken it was blowing at 90 km an hour.

To carry out repairs, out of the wind, Alain uses a plastic shelter.

snow, begins to move over the ice at great speed. The faraway forms of the mountains emerge above this floating mirage, at once heaven and earth, beautiful and pitiless, tangible yet unapproachable.

We have been gone only 5 days and already I am face to face with the inexpressibly beautiful. Ever since I began trudging to the ends of the Earth, this rapture transports me, pushes me onward and calls out to me. Simply the fact of having seen this astonishing phenomenon justifies my having come here.

We leave on foot, crampons fixed; the terrain rises. The sastrugis are increasingly in evidence. After two hours, the wind drops to 30 to 35 km/h. Immediately we get out the small 6 m² sails.

As with every morning, we are visited by two Antarctic petrels; this will be the last sign of life for a very long time. Soon we will be on our own, lost in the infinity of the biggest desert in the world. From now on, we will meet no living soul, not even an insect. With luck, we may see a few men working at the South Pole. We will live in a self-inflicted ostracism that will last three months...

In order to be able to keep up with Dixie, who is lighter than me, I decide to deploy the 12 m² sail. A few small adjustments and I now feel the wind pulling well in the sail. OK! Everything is all right.... However...

In the Antarctic, when things seem to be sorting themselves out, one must be particularly suspicious. For the barometer is never set to "fair" on this mysterious continent. The proof? The wind was drawing my sail well and I thought I could fairly soar along. However, suddenly, the devil take it, it strengthens... In all logic, I ought to see an increase in my speed. But, not at all... It becomes too violent for the size of the sail I am using. What should one do in moments like this? Stop and change the kite; pack up the 12 m² sail and take out the 6 m² one? This will take time, one of the problems that we will continue to encounter throughout the whole expedition. If I stop for just 5 minutes, that could be long enough for Dixie, who is travelling some 300 metres ahead, to surge forward and disappear completely. In cases like this, we planned to use walkie-talkies, but at this particular moment, we have not yet had time to try them out. There is no question of becoming separated in this immensity. Whence the decision to hang on at all costs. I try to raise the sail as high as possible into the wind to reduce its effective traction. At this speed, avoiding obstacles is a dangerous business. When I raise the kite the harness rises as well, and at the same time hitches up my jacket. Result: the wind gets into my clothes. It is only −20°C, but I am very cold. As misfortune never comes singly, on two occasions I lose a ski while crossing a sastrugi, and as I fall, one of the lateral reinforcement fittings of the tackle breaks.

Just our rotten luck – already.

16.40: I catch up with Dixie, but I am totally exhausted. I feel as though I am losing it. Frightened of cracking up.

Finally, we are getting close to an altitude of 500 m. The contours of the Sør Rondane on the horizon are clearer. I can make out, in the west, the entry to the Gunnesstadt Glacier that we will have to cross. Closer, the outline of Mt Romnaes is like a giant sphinx. Its granite face is black, which is why we can see it from so far away. A curious detail: one can also make out from here (even though we are at least 30 km away) the huge cirque of ice formed at its foot by the wind.

We stop and set up camp for the evening. The wind is blowing pleasantly at about 25 km/h. It takes time to repair the harness and to re-stitch the sails and it is already 9 p.m. It's time for soup. Despite being freeze-dried, the cream of broccoli is excellent…

These are the lessons of this first long day under sail. One, we will often have to wait for one another. Two, communication between the two of us will be a problem, despite the walkie-talkies which we will have to use sparingly, in order to conserve the batteries.

Sunday, 9 November (Day 6)

The Damage…

As yesterday, the wind wakes us up in the middle of the night. It is so strong that the rear wall of the tent, normally some 20 cm from my sleeping bag, is blown out of shape until it is actually touching my face. Moreover, as happened yesterday, we have to get out of our feather beds to go outside to see what is going on. A most unpleasant chore, but we have no choice; it has to be done. There are gusts of wind of nearly 60 km/h. *Bigre!* That does not prevent us from noticing the errors that have been made. The tent has not been shored up, and Dixie has still not managed to put enough weight on the flaps of the double roof. I am furious but we will settle this disagreement later. For the moment, we have to act or the whole thing will be blown away. After this interlude, we regain the tent and sleep until 8.30.

Breakfast in lee of the wind, we strike camp with care, and depart on foot… As we did yesterday, after two hours we get the sails out as the wind begins to drop.

At the last pause, I had to break into a sprint to catch my windbag – it is a large nylon bag that we keep ready at the front of the sledge to shelter in, if necessary, during the breaks. It flew off, but fortunately got caught a few hundred metres away in the jaws of a "shark".
For the rest of the day, we successively try out each of the different sails, one after the other. However, the terrain is difficult, very difficult. Between two sail changes, we are astonished to see some few hundred metres to the west, an automatic weather mini-station, part of the Japanese Asuka base. We feel a human presence that is not there. Clinging on to the tillers because of the head wind, we do not deviate from our path.

I advance better, regaining my confidence. On the plateau, with better snow, it's certain that we will be able to make proper use of these contraptions, that we have spent over a year trying to perfect. Then, of course, I fall. The ice is as hard as concrete. The suspension lines of my sail are tangled-up in the hollow of a sastrugi. I take out the spare, fall over again, then re-tie the lines. This time I'm dragged flat along on my stomach from obstacle to obstacle over several dozen metres before being able to pull sufficiently hard on the rear lines to come to a stop.

Here, some explanation is called for concerning the handling of these contraptions. The traction sails that we perfected with Patrick Nassogne are sails with a single surface. This is why they are called "sails" or "traction kites" rather than "parafoils" (box sails with dual partitions). Four lines, two in front and two at the rear, connect to two control tillers (simple bent tubes attached by a cord to the harness). The first two (those that are attached to the upper part of the kite) are used for putting the sail under pressure. The other two (those that are attached to the lower part) are for steering or reducing the pressure in the sail.

At the time when I fell over and over again, I only had to grab the rear lines and roll them round the tillers half a dozen times. It was one of the best ways we had found for stopping as quickly as possible. This manoeuvre, however, has its inconvenience. On most occasions, when the wind is blowing hard, the sail twists into a butterfly. Therefore, it is imperative, if you don't want to waste too much time, to change the sail and put off until evening the lengthy job of unravelling the lines and the fabric.

The phenomenon of drifting snow banks is unique to the Antarctic: it consists of a more or less thick layer of snow, which the wind drives along parallel to the surface of the ground.

Repairing Alain's sledge at the entry to the Gunnestadt Glacier leading to the polar plateau. A runner had been driven right into the bodywork.

We soon came to realise that it is preferable, during breaks, to keep the wind in the sails, subtly manoeuvring the tillers and the lines to lower the sail to the ground while keeping it inflated.

Two falls, one after the other. The sailing is not going to work any more today. We continue on foot.

I take up my sledge again and let Dixie go on ahead. He's had to wait for me a while and must be chilled to the bone. I retrieve one of my skis lost in the fracas and try to keep up close to him. But I have this curious impression that I'm not progressing as I usually do, whereas Dixie is pulling away at the usual rate. I cannot fathom it out. Am I that tired?

Worn out, sweating profusely from the strenuous effort, after twenty minutes I stop to have a closer look at the sledge. Perhaps it's split? I remember that the year before, in the Patriot Hills, a fuel-can that I had put into the sledge to simulate the weight had fractured the Kevlar.

I look, I lean even further forward. I lift the sledge on to its side, get closer... It is not true! I do not want to believe the sight that suddenly confronts me. The right-hand runner has embedded itself into the hull. Along its entire length! This is terrible! I can't believe my eyes...

We are scarcely 100 km from the start, and we are nearly 3750 km from the finish, we haven't even reached the polar plateau, and here is one of the sledges, about to give up the ghost. It's just not possible...

After more than a year spent testing the equipment – in Greenland and in the great Canadian north – I imagine the worst. A thousand times, day and night, I have run through the whole gamut of possible catastrophic scenarios. I didn't think, for an instant, that my sledge could forsake me in this way, and, worse, be so severely damaged!

This is one of the first times – on an expedition – that I do not immediately find a solution to the problem encountered. I surprise myself however by staying calm.

"Hello, Dixie, you must come and see what's happened, I need a hand..."

A few minutes later, in a silence that speaks volumes, my companion helps me to drag my sledge to his. We set up camp for the night. We naturally spend the evening trying to work out various solutions. Only one preoccupation for the moment: get a good night's sleep and to carry out the repairs in the morning.

We take advantage of the delay to send our first e-mail to Michel[6].

Later, half asleep, I try to understand. The damage has been caused by the unexpected torsion, which has weakened the rigid structure of the hull. For technical reasons, I had chosen a type of runner which had a reduced area of contact with the hull of the sledge. This inevitably placed a greater pressure on the layers of Kevlar, whose resistance had been calculated for a wider area of contact with the runners. If I had had the presence of mind to reinforce the composite material at that point – if only by two layers – the damage would never have happened.

Monday, 10 November (Day 7)

"A11–B4: Hole in Alain's Sledge"

I am lying on a four-poster bed under a mosquito net. I am deliciously awakened, in a neo-colonial pavilion of the Safari Park Hotel in Nairobi. With the concert of bird-song, the croaking of the frogs, the soft flurry of wing-beats of the pigeons, the African luxuriance, the breeze rustling softly in the branches of the royal poincianas. Johan, a somewhat eccentric fellow steward, has had the great idea of taping the sounds of everyday life from around the globe onto a mini-CD. Thanks to his inspiration, I am now taken on a whirlwind trip around the world. In this kaleidoscopic sound-fest, there are some Kenyan atmospherics, as well as a guitarist from Benin who has written a ballad in honour of our adventure, the bustle of the Chicago streets, the brouhaha of Wendy's fast food joint, that man from Conakry who speaks Swahili but who also has a go at Dutch, the bustle of the Lomé market, etc. I burst out laughing when I hear the African merchant cursing when he discovers Johan recording his words. This is followed in rapid succession by some Japanese phrases which I cannot make out at all, the commentary of a football match between Holland and Belgium, and the good wishes of the catering manager of Barnako. In short, this morning it is pure escapism…

After this, I let myself be tempted by a little music: Andreas Vollenweider and Dvorak, Dire Straits and Ingmwie Malmsteen. But back to reality. We unload all our equipment to assess the damage. Imagine our horror when we see that my sledge is showing the same signs of fatigue. It certainly won't last much longer.

We have worked four hours this morning trying first just to patch up the sledge. We get into the tent, which becomes a makeshift workshop. What bloody chaos! Luckily, I like that… Then the repairs proper; to prevent the runners embedding themselves again in the U supports of the hull to which they are riveted. We drill holes into their sides so that we can tie the runners back on again with rope (we have 100 metres of

6mm for the crevasses). As the runners tend to slip to the side when gliding, I put in a few vertical nuts and bolts to hold them against the Kevlar and then tie some cord to them which, when fixed to the inside of the sledge, should tighten the whole thing up. To complete the work, we have to find a way of propping up the two U's of the sledge so that they don't take too much punishment from the constant rubbing against the ice. My idea is to cram as much material as possible there and to stuff it as though packing a suitcase. My companion however has a brainwave: fill the two U's with snow and then pour boiling water on them so that when they are frozen they become like girders of ice.

We bind up Dixie's sledge as well to strengthen it as a precautionary measure. After which, the three small sails have to be re-stitched. It is 19.30 when we have finished reloading the sledges. Another day without…

Later, we send Michel the Argos message "A11–B4" (Hole in Alain's sledge): he will certainly wonder what has happened because the code is not very explicit.

As misfortune never comes alone, now it's the turn of the laptop computer to play up! As we were late with the preparation of the equipment, we have not had time to test it properly before we left. Not surprising that it breaks down. Remembering tips I've picked up here and there, I first test the strength of the batteries, but it's only when I tighten a regulator screw, designed specifically for coping with voltage irregularities, that everything falls into place.

This evening I open the letter my wife Catherine gave me as I left. "*Keep fighting*", she reminds me, "*you'll win in the end if you believe in it enough, and you know well that when you are short of energy, and at times you will be, all you have to do is to take the next plodding step… You leave, I stay. We share the roles about the children, each in his extraordinary way… That's my way of being completely by your side…*"

This adventure has indeed begun very badly. I ask myself what I'm doing here when at home, in the little hamlet of Harsin, winter is quietly beginning and in the house, the wood-fire cooking-range is gently purring. Why, good God, am I not capable of staying there, calm, by the fireside, drinking a cup of coffee? Why can I not be content with the countless challenges of everyday life? Why am I always driven by this imperative need to undertake out-of-the-ordinary projects, to confront such hostile environments and to find myself, as with this expedition, in the middle of nowhere…and in debt, moreover? Is this adventure going to bring me a little more of that "wisdom" that I hope will arrive one day, to allow me to accept life more easily?

Sending an email to HQ in
Brussels.

Tuesday, 11 November (Day 8)

Above the Conveyor-belt, the Sky is Dense and Blue

A very strong wind today; 70 km/h. We have to wait a little; the conveyor-belt effect of
the banks of drifting snow is impressive.

It is, of course, not easy to make progress in these conditions – the loss of balance,
the poor visibility, the discomfort of having snow unceasingly whipping the body and
the face, the tiring visual effect. In a crosswind, it's even worse. We stagger along thinking that with every step we are about to fall over. Never having known such banks of
drifting snow, I have been caught, more than once when losing my balance, finding
myself *in extremis* on my ski sticks. Sometimes this horizontal storm paints the sky with
supernatural colours – when, for example, the sun is low on the horizon. This morning, however, it is white and colourless. Consolation; above, the sky is blue, dense and
strong. An astonishing sight!

A pivoting carabiner links the
sail steering tiller to the
harness.

Storm, storm, storm!
No use taking risks outside with these violent assaults of nature. I get back into my sleeping bag and put on my earphones. It's amazing how music can awaken emotions and create intensely spiritual moods. Being a guitarist myself, I listen to the orchestra with an ear that analyses the composition, the purity of sound, the complexity of the musical phrases, the changing rhythms, and the dialogue with the public that one feels even though one doesn't always hear it. On the programme this morning, Stef Bos, Dutch singer-pianist-guitarist Uncomplicated minstrel, his melancholy is right in tune with my emotions.

Before leaving, Catherine gave me (apart from the letter) an envelope with a hundred words written on a hundred bits of paper. One word, one theme for each day. For the first time, I pull out the surprise gift; "Hold tight".

It comes at the right time, for I have to "hold tight" onto my sticks to proceed across the banks of drifting snow, but also of course I want to "hold tight" my wife and children in my arms. And then, after this profusion of bad luck, I have to summon up all my energies and "hold them tight" within me, "hold tight" on to the idea of this mad enterprise, "hold tight" to the lines of the sledge, "tighten" the harness so that I'm not cold. Suddenly it's such a sweet phrase, "hold tight". Catherine has, once again, found a very personal way of enriching my daily life.

Since we are not setting out straightaway, I make the most of the time by writing a few lines, and by listening to a little music (good old Neil Young). In a whole week of adventure, this is the first moment that I've been able to relax, to dream and to think of the world of men. To be conscious that here, I'm going around in an imaginary bubble, a fictional universe built entirely around this damned objective that I have to meet. What's more, I don't want to hear anything at all about what is happening anywhere else, or even with my family. I realise that this attitude may seem profoundly selfish but, like everybody else, I have fears that I recognise and want to eliminate.

Outside, the wind isn't dropping. We decide to make a start nevertheless.

The slope is steep. We are sweating, but we ought not to be, because the moisture we give off freezes and rapidly encrusts the fibres of our clothing. We then have fastidiously to brush off the ice crystals that form.
This morning I took 6 packs of food from Alain in order to lighten the load on his moribund sledge.
Question: are the sides of his sledge going to get worse? Is it the beginning of the end? Would it not be better to send for new sledges? We are not yet even 150 kilometres from the coast. Although replacing them now would destroy our ambition to be totally independent, there would still be an important consolation: if we succeed, our exploit will, in any event, be the longest ever crossing of the Antarctic by sail.

Six good hours marching across a more regular terrain: I'm in fine form and have no wish to stop, but Dixie's heels are hurting. Luckily, we are not yet at that stage of the expedition where we must "eat up" the distance at any price.

A halt at 18.30. It is the first time that we have put up the tent in such a violent wind. First we fix it to the ground with two ice-screws, and then we stretch out the tent hoops. While I hold them down, Dixie secures the two edges. We then put up the double roof, this time with sufficient snow on the flaps. We position the sledges about a metre from the tent in the form of a V. It's a way we have found to create a kind of depression between the tent and the pulkas which prevents our tent from becoming totally snowed in within a few hours.

Since morning, the sky has been covered with magnificent lenticular clouds, a sign that the wind will persist. Visibility is getting worse by the hour and the barometer is now falling fast. This does not augur well.

The repairs seem to be holding up. Nevertheless, I'm beginning to wonder whether we shouldn't take advantage of the fact that we are still relatively close to the departure point; to ask HQ to make two new sledges and have them sent out to us.

Wednesday, 12 November (Day 9)

A Question of Ballast

Damn wind... did I say wind? Goddamn blizzard, more like it! . Storm winds of 70 to 110 km/h. Antarctic hell knocking at the door.

Ninth day of the expedition, this is no time for anything stupid. It's better to stay put.

During the night, I had to get up to increase the ballast once more on one side of the tent. Upset at having been woken three times already, and for having to go outside to remedy a situation that would have been avoided if Dixie had done his job properly, I moan a little. OK, it's not too serious, but I want to talk about it. On expedition, confidence in the other's work is absolutely vital. Dixie's first reaction is to suggest that I do that particular job myself. For me it's not a case of avoiding the problem by shifting the goal posts, but rather of making sure that each is entirely confident of the other's work, a question of never having to worry about it.

This rotten weather reminds me of a storm that Didier Goetghebuer and I lived through on the Arctic ice field. It also occurred very early on in the expedition (after only a week's progress) and we were forced into a prolonged stop which, on that occasion, lasted 48 hours. At the same time, I think of the misadventure that befell a team of three Norwegian adventurers who had also set out for the North Pole and who were preceding us a little on the ice. They tried to avoid having to stop during a storm, with the result that two of them got severe frostbite to their hands and so they were all obliged to give up.

The storm has become our travelling companion. The earplugs are still our best allies; they bring me the rest at night that I so badly need. Except when Alain wakes me up in a bad mood and reproaches me for not having covered up the flaps of the tent sufficiently. It's true that the unspoken agreement is that this job is mine. But it's not so easy. There is no point in raising your voice in this deafening storm, which only serves to fuel the aggression being felt. So much better to go back to bed and wait for things to calm down. In the morning, nevertheless, we clarify the situation.

Outside, the wind is blowing at more than 100 km/h and the barometer is dropping: we have to stay in the tent. I open the little notebook that I circulated among my friends and relatives before leaving so that everyone could write a little something for me to read when alone on this frozen continent. A few words to help overcome without fuss the difficult moments of the expedition by keeping in touch with the outside world. This morning, I stumble across a few lines written by a female colleague:

> *Sunshine is delicious*
> *Rain is refreshing*
> *Wind is bracing*
> *Snow is exhilarating*
> *There's really no such thing as bad weather…*
> *Only different kinds of good weather*

Thursday, 13 November (Day 10)

Turned into a Snowman

A night of storms. The wind has been frighteningly violent. It's still blowing like crazy today. My God, what a spectacle this Antarctic blizzard makes.

When the wind exceeds 60–70 km/h, the racket is deafening. You literally have to shout to be heard. What's more, it seems as though it's never going to end. After a while it gets on your nerves and dissipates your energy. Which is why one must have the power of concentration at moments like this, as well as total confidence in the equipment, especially the tent. Imagine for a moment that it is blown away with everything that is usually inside it: a lovely death is guaranteed.

I have to admit that, at times like these, I'm close to feeling real fear. It was during one of my crossings of Greenland that an incredible storm struck the expedition. The French mountaineer, Laurence de la Ferrière, who was accompanying us, had wanted to stay fully clothed in her tent, her bags packed and organised, ready to face the worst should the canvas be ripped to shreds.

I risk putting my nose outside. The diagnosis brooks no second opinion; a complete white-out (everything is white, earth and sky, visibility near zero). The programme for the day is pre-ordained: stand-by.

Bad weather formation of a drifting snow bank.

Breakfast is followed by a sortie for shoring up the tent flaps, filming a little, and looking for one of Dixie's ski sticks buried in the snow.

It's not cold and the snow is sticky. A metre away from the flaps, the tent is surrounded by two walls of snow some 80 cm high, in the shape of a giant horseshoe whose extensions get lost on the other side, far away on the ice cap. The sledges have become little white hills. Without this device (putting the sledges in a V) the tent would long ago have been buried under two metres of snow.

The morning sortie lasted barely ten minutes; which is enough time for me to have been transformed into a snowman by the time I get back to the tent. Meticulously I brush the clothes and sweep the floor – one has to be organised.

It's already noon. The barometer keeps on falling, and there can be no doubt as to what will follow. Our first genuine Antarctic blizzard. What a charming welcome!

Although it arrives at a time when we don't yet need rest, the storm provides the opportunity for a little relaxation. We play a game of cards. After which, I take the daily measurements (temperature, atmospheric pressure, direction and strength of the wind, weather forecast), then I slip into the sleeping bag and draw out Catherine's word of the day; "Solitude". Solitude? No comment. For the moment…

These frightful weather conditions make me think that this time we really are cut off from the rest of the world. Suddenly, the task seems enormous. We are only at the beginning of the adventure and already problems are piling up.

Dixie brings me back to earth as he sets about lighting the stove. More particularly, the nice smell that comes from burning the thermo-retractable wrappings of the food rations (the evening meal) on which there are always some crumbs of food or spices. These aromas transport me to the slopes of Kanchenjunga, where in the evenings I used to grill delicious, freshly cut corn cobs on the log fire at the base camp… I feel life coming back; I'm getting warm once again.

This evening, for the first time, I open one of the two books I allowed myself to bring in my luggage; it is *"La Souveraineté du Vide"* by Christian Bobin, an anthology of texts given to me before I left, by a lady friend. I like this man and his outlook on life. *"Reading, not for knowing…no, nothing like that. Reading rather for forgetting, for drifting away, for losing oneself. To be alone again, infinitely alone. Alone enough to never be so again…"* Curious; isn't "Solitude" the word of the day?

A little further on: *"Drifting, endless drifting, these walks, these readings, these letters, work, an absence."* These few words make me think of Philippe Sohet, a friend and accomplice in my craziest projects who lives in Montreal. It was together, on my way back from the geographical North Pole in 1994, that we laid the groundwork for the Antarctica Exhibition in Brussels. We love to dream up our mad schemes during our long walks, our conversations and in our letters. How many times has he managed to get me to accept impossible challenges?

The only time you leave your tent during a blizzard is either to take photos, or to answer the call of nature.

Friday, 14 November (Day 11)

The Complete Works of Monod weigh 1,200 grams

No change in the weather: third day of the storm...

This forced halt at least has the advantage of letting us economise on our food consumption. For the time being, we are managing to save at least one daily ration every two days.

Before we left, the Reverend (this is the name Pierre Dillenbourg and I have given to Didier Goetghebuer because of his love of long words) gave me the complete works of Monod. I hesitated a long time before deciding whether or not to take it with me, because of the weight, of course. I should point out that I spent most of my time in the pre-expedition period weeding out superfluous weight. Managing to save even a few grams was a victory each time. However, I was also superstitious. On the one hand, Didier had given me the book. Didier, with whom I had shared some of my finest adventures. On the other hand, this particular book often talks about the desert. What is the Antarctic if not a huge desert? Did I need other omens? In the end, I took it with me; an extra 1.2 kilos.

This excess weight would have been less on my mind had it not been for the fact that Didier and I had a habit of making mad bets, for bottles of champagne. On this occasion, as it happens, we had bet on the 200 kilo limit per sledge. He believed that I would exceed it, whereas I stoutly maintained that I would not. At stake was a bottle of Mumm Cordon Rouge or a Veuve Cliquot (unless there was a special offer at the local supermarket) for each kilo above or below this weight. This morning, the thought occurs to me that the decision to take Monod to the Antarctic has cost me 1.2 bottles of champagne! I suspect that this thought might have occurred to Didier before it did to me.

If the work of this great naturalist reminds me that I've lost by 1.2 kilos, it also reminds me that by now I've been able to reduce the weight of the sledge to 181 kilos!

Monod opens the door for me to another desert, a sand desert, from Cap Blanc at St. Louis to the doors of Senegal. From the book "*The Meharies*":

"The polar world, oceans of ice and deserts of snow, completes the trilogy of spaces which demand perpetual motion, navigation, nomadism, eternal flight, daily, through circles that are continuously reborn but never crossed, of a horizon before you, which sometimes seems to wait for you so as to vex you but which never allows you to reach it...It is to advance without halting through an immutable yet changing landscape, always the same to the eye and distinguishable only by sextant, compass and watch.. To savour the bitterness of feeling oneself prisoner, while marching, in a space without bars, and yet more closely confined in this free immensity than in the narrowest of dungeons... Nothing is closed, nothing except this implacable horizon, immeasurable but sealed."

Here, for the time being, those are exactly my feelings...

White-out and storm. Nothing new. But morale is good and we are making the most of the respite.

Warmth, rest, shelter from the wind, oceans of time. We check and reorganise the equipment for the third time; each item is sacred. To be able to function properly in this confined space with as little frustration as possible requires everything to be meticulously in apple-pie order. Every little thing has its place. Even inside the bags.   After a while, sibylline links are made in this universe, even with inanimate objects.

After breakfast, we use the teabags for refreshing our faces. Alain taught me this excellent little trick the first time that we went to Greenland together: wiping the face with a just-used teabag for the morning ablutions. It avoids having to melt more ice and therefore saves stove fuel. After which, one usually throws them away. But this morning I found a third use for them: dry them out in a little muslin bag (either by having them on my person throughout the day, or by putting them in the sleeping bag) and then slipping them like a pot pourri into the clothes to get rid of the bad smells. Alain reckons that a collection of 400 wet teabags constitutes superfluous weight.

Saturday, 15 November (Day 12)

Between Two Question Marks

Fourth day of the storm.

Wind, and more wind, with hellish gusts of more than 100 km/h.

Going out to measure it with the anemometer and trying to take a few photographs of the blizzard – they are so rare and so beautiful.

Because no physical effort is being made today, breakfast is rationed. We'll only eat yesterday's left-overs: no coffee, no soup. Just a few snacks during the day and some tea.

Once the household chores are done, anxiety begins insidiously to surface. How many more days is this damned blizzard going to hold us up? Shouldn't we risk leaving anyway? What about the sledges? Will they last? Will they let us get to the South Pole? Shouldn't we decide to replace them before it's too late? How are they going to respond when we use the sails again? Are we going to make up for lost time? So many questions...

So I'm in a hurry to leave and to struggle on; that's what I'm here for, but at the moment it's more of a mental struggle against inactivity that I'm engaged in.

Card games, siestas, arranging our belongings for the fourth or fifth time, seeing if we can improve on the clothing (how many layers should I put on when in traction with the sails? What type of gloves shall I wear for the march? Where shall I put them

Digging out the sledge, after a storm which forced the Expedition to halt for five days between 12 and 17 November.

in my jacket? Where shall I keep my storm mask so that I can get to it immediately without taking off my mittens? Should I knock up a more efficient nose cover? A bit of writing, revising the notes, stretching exercises, yoga for Dixie, reading and lost thoughts, discussing all the questions that arise. Time passes...

Little by little we are getting used to the noise of the wind.

The barometer is still dropping but it can't go on forever.

It's 16.00 and I make some tea.

Sunday, 16 November (Day 13)

Philo, Snobbery & Co.

Tonight the tempest is stronger than ever: the barometer has lost 200 meters, which is a lot. So today, we are going to have to stay huddled in the tent.

Dixie has again raised the question of replacing the sledges. They certainly will not last until the South Pole; the notion of *re-supply* is taking root.

A decision such as this is far from simple. Apart from the considerable logistical and financial challenges that it entails, it cuts to the quick in other sensitive areas. Re-supply would shatter our dream of a completely unassisted crossing. A simple matter of pride? Loss of media interest? Who knows? But how can we get people to understand that the real stakes are elsewhere?

For me, the notion of autonomy is intricately linked to the philosophical underpinnings of the entire undertaking. It conditions the type of relationship that one wants to engage in with the natural environment. To be motorised or not, to be re-supplied mid-way for a lighter start or not. These are for me like clauses in a marriage contract. To set out independently is to choose a path where the only dialogue possible is the one with the surrounding natural world. It also means paying meticulous attention to the preparation of the equipment as, without re-supply, errors cannot be allowed. It is also a question of ethics, since the notion of taking everything with you naturally implies bringing everything back with you. The real challenge is to deal with this process of eliminating waste in a proper ecological manner. Thanks to modern technology, this process is now feasible.

Since my first adolescent readings, the dimension of intuition has always fascinated me, especially in the accounts of the great migrations of earlier times. To allow an aeroplane to bring additional victuals or equipment would mean an acceptance of the fact that technology, with all its aggressive presence, would come to interrupt the fragile dialogue with the environment that one was now engaged in. I have acquired, from my many expeditions, an instinctive, somewhat obscure or animist belief in the forces of nature. In a survival situation, I subconsciously relate to the cultures of native peoples, Red Indians, Eskimos, Aboriginals, for whom Mother Nature is the ultimate nurse, and who devote all their energy to revering her, come what may.

Morning ritual; filling the flasks with tea.

I strive then to put as few artificial obstacles as possible between the environment and my adventures. For me, this choice is nothing other than a general calling into question of man's place in his environment.

I have accepted the fate, which has come to mock the autonomy of the venture, with the greatest of serenity. To my great astonishment, actually. As I am one of those given over to perpetual self examination, it is probable that the damage to the sledges has brought me face to face with myself again.

God, how one's fate depends on so little, especially when it comes to calling into question the precious ideas that we fight for! It is true to say that having to replace the sledges has also hurt my pride. But on the other hand it strengthens my appreciation of the irony with which fate brings man back to his station of man. We decide to contact Michel at HQ to discuss the matter; two new sledges are, apparently, already being built. Well done, old chap! It's a good job we have you to count on.

What does the rest of this adventure have in store for us? Plunged as we are, into this hallucinating landscape, I have the growing impression that there's nothing I can do about all this, that I'm being ignored, merely tolerated no doubt with the greatest of indifference. Is the wind taking care to blow around our fragile shelter rather than quite simply burying it? What a question! The world here most definitely does not revolve around us.

I cannot even explain the contradictions that I impose upon myself in the course of such an adventure. In some respects, there is that certain taste for freedom, for the challenge, the fascination for limitless horizons, for the ascetic nomadic existence. On the other hand, each time I'm in the field I ask myself if there is not some other way, less tortuous and less ambitious, of achieving the same state and experiencing the same sensations.

Dixie is asleep. It's 15.20, I stretch out on my sleeping bag and dive into the Brahms Requiem that Catherine gave me before I left. Magnificent!

At the end of the day, the wind appears to be calming down a little. It is still blustering about us, but with less menacing gusts. The clouds are beginning to break up and the light is blinding. Is the storm finally abating?

I leave the tent. What a relief! The Romnaes are still there! It's reassuring to realise that we haven't been carried off to another planet. The intemperate weather has completely remodelled the countryside around the property.

Far away to the east, the sky is still black, but in front of us the Antarctic plateau is cloudless. It is almost as if it's calling to us...

It's time to begin to dig out the sledges. Hang on a second, there go the pair of petrels that have just effected a fly-past. Tomorrow, I know it, I feel it, we will be on our way again.

I switch the beacons on and transmit the message A0–B13 ("bad start to the day, good end"). So Michel will know that we are heading off again.

Monday, 17 November (Day 14)

The Hard and the Soft

I have decided to think of this expedition as a form of personal expression, a work of art. Something requiring a great deal of dedication and investment, but also a large dose of love.
It's not so much the distance that matters as the way in which we cover it. To place each foot as it should be placed, to pull the sledge rhythmically and smoothly, to keep the body in line. Like the pas de deux of two dancers, the undulation and perfect movement of a wave or the recitation of a poem instead of a long speech.
This morning we can leave! Quickly get everything together, and we're off.
In the distance, we can make out traces of the storm in the sky, like a tornado of snow, spectacular but of no immediate danger. And suddenly, silence. After 14 days of uninterrupted wind, it drops completely! It's as though we were suddenly in another world.

A big, beautiful bank of drifting snow, as is often the case after bad weather. We have to work for an hour and a half to free the sledges and strike camp. More uneven than ever, the terrain consists of intermittent areas of soft and frozen snow. It's hard, very hard, but morale is high. Especially after six days and nights spent in the tent. I have never been forced to spend so long sheltering during an expedition.

After a four and a half hour march, we can get out the sails to cross the huge expanse of blue ice which is to be found under the prevailing winds to the west of the Romnaes. We shan't, however, be seeing the Japanese Asuka base, which is on the other side.

18.30. We are obliged to proceed on foot again, but not for long as my sledge reminds us of the sad reality: these four hours of sailing on the hard ice have again dislodged the runners and, once again, I find myself toiling on the ice as if I was dragging 300 kilos. Dixie comes to my aid.

Alain's sledge cashes in it's chips.
I unhitch myself to go and help him to drag the resisting contraption as far as the bivouac. There, quite without embarrassment, a large brown bird – an Antarctic skua – perches on my sledge and shamelessly pecks at Kevin, my bear mascot! Not allowed: I chase it off. Okay, It's a beautiful bird, but a mascot has to be respected. The end of the day brings me an unexpected burst of energy, and I feel on top form.

In one week, the sun has climbed a few degrees over the horizon – it's at about 20°. In around ten day's time, it will be high enough in the sky to begin to bring us a semblance of warmth in the tent. One finds ones comfort where one can.

Tuesday, 18 November (Day 15)

March, Fall, Break Loose, Go On...

The wind picks up at about 8 o'clock in the morning while we are mending the sledge for the second time; a check on the sails and 11 o'clock sounds the off.

A 50–60 km/h wind finds us on foot again.

It's not too cold, -12°C. But the terrain is difficult and the snow unceasingly whips into our faces. At around 2 o'clock the wind drops back to 35–40 km/h, which encourages us to try the small 6 sq.m. kite. A lot of fine-tuning is still required to the sail handling technique. They have been researched and developed in Greenland and Canada, but it's only here that the final touches can be polished up. Starting, for example, is not always straightforward when the wind is blowing and tangling up the fabric. We discovered the trick of helping each other but the technique is not yet refined. In a few weeks time it will be better.

We have been marching at a good pace for four hours. Later, we get out our secret weapon to try to make up for lost time. We fly from one bump to another, flying over hundreds of snowdrifts, but without letting ourselves go for fear of falling.

Tuesday, 18 November, the blizzard finally subsides. It took two hours to dig out the equipment.

The problems begin again. This time it's Dixie's turn to have trouble. Once, twice, take off the skis, start off again, fall down again, lose a binding strap from a boot, a heel grip, break the two buckle fasteners on the belt of the sledge's traction harness belt. Despite everything, he still wants to go on.

"That's enough now, Dixie, or you're going to break everything. We'll stop as soon as we find a flat surface for making camp…"

My impatience has been punished by my falling into a hole, resulting in severe pain to the right knee and quadriceps.

At the end of the day, we march to warm ourselves up, but after half an hour of limping behind my companion, we have to face the facts; it's quite ridiculous to try to go on trudging along in this way expending enormous amounts of energy, when tomorrow, perhaps, each kilometre that is taking us half an hour today might be swallowed up in a few minutes under sail. Hence the wise decision to make camp.

I try to go to sleep despite a splitting headache.

Happy birthday, dear Evelien! Four candles on your cake and have a good time with your pals. I think of you every day when I eat with your Donald Duck spoon that I also brought back from Greenland. Soon, we will drop from exhaustion after a day's games. I will tell you all about this wonderful continent, the depth that it gives and the desire to shout out loud that life is beautiful.

Wednesday, 19 November (Day 16)

Blood on the Hips

What warmth this morning, the weather is superb and the wind is zero!

I really could do with a wash, so I slip off my clothes to take a "snow-bath". Considering the ambient temperature, I have to move quickly. This is how it's done.

First take some balls of snow and rub them on to your arms and legs to allow the body to enjoy the cold. The rubbing of the crystals is an excellent abrasive and the skin reacts immediately: natural protection by shrinkage. Sometimes, when the snow isn't so hard, one can roll in it. You must pay attention to the feet when they are in contact with the cold; move them about all the time while taking care of the rest of the body. The cold is so invigorating! What a delicious start to the day!

Ablutions over, we repair the sledges for the umpteenth time and notice that Alain's is on the verge of breaking up. I lighten it once more by taking some more packets of food and stashing them at the back of my gear, where the Kevlar is at its strongest.

Finally, the wind tires and passes over the baton to the sun, which means we have to keep our goggles on and cover our faces with a thick layer of total sunblock.

Repairs to the sledge and an 11 o'clock departure.

A leaden sun; it's warm, and very soon, too warm. We are almost at the level of the last nunatak, the Vesthaugen, which lies just before the entry of the Gunnesstadt Glacier. The slope is getting steeper by the day and the sastrugis are again criss-crossing our path. They are however not too high, but just sufficiently ill-placed to impede our progress. Even zigzagging is no use; it's the same type of terrain everywhere. Sastrugi here, sastrugi there...

God knows that I've done my share of pulling in my life, but the work here is inhuman. It defies the imagination. I'm in a continuous state of "resistance", sweating profusely, my heart beating at a rate of more than 160. For most of the time I'm on the tips of my crampons and the straps of my harness are cutting into my shoulders. On top of that, my hips are bleeding. When we were advancing towards the geographical North Pole in 1994, I don't recall having had to make such a huge physical effort. I repeat all the time; "it's hell, it's hell!" Why this lunatic effort? What's the point of this frenetic activity?. Perhaps I'll find the answer in the Divine Comedy. For didn't Dante Alighieri imagine hell as being filled with people condemned for eternity to pointless acts?

Luckily, I've no problem with my feet; no blisters, no cuts. But we have to be careful because we are at the mercy of the slightest error; a torn ligament or muscle could lead to disaster.

Seven hours of progress under torture, eight kilometres covered at an average of 1.2 km/h; we're not proceeding very quickly, to say the least! However, we have already reached an altitude of some 1,100 metres.

The effort is so extremely strenuous that I haven't been able to digest my daytime victuals. It's without a doubt complete madness to go on with this dying sledge. But I don't have any choice. I know that better days are ahead when the new sledges arrive. But when will that be?

The Sør Rondane mountain chain is stretching out before us. Naked and unspoilt; beauty in its purest form! In the evening we study the map; 2000 km left to the South Pole. 2000 km, not to mention what comes after!

Thursday, 20 November (Day 17)

Crevasses in Sight

Perhaps due to the light we have no trouble getting up this morning. Our mood lifts with the return of good weather. It seems to me that we both have the capacity to see the positive side of things. The usual repairs, and then we're on the road again, but not for long. My sledge soon falls apart again. I repair it on the spot, empty the hull, saw off bits, and try to re-attach the runner… Three quarters of an hour of work.

Further on, we are on less chaotic terrain. We are at last making good progress, and now the sledge is gliding sweetly behind me. I even surprise myself dreaming a little, reflecting on the word of the day, "Lose". Learn to lose, lose you, lose me, lose ourselves. Lose time because of a stupid sledge…

Looks like I'm on form.

At the end of the day, the sky is covered over with long cirrus clouds. The light seems unreal, wan, giving a translucent colour to the crevasses that we can now see more distinctly in the distance. The mountains are closer. I stand stupefied before the grandeur of the spectacle, with its extraordinary exaggeration. Am I not in the process of witnessing the creation of the world? To the east, grey bluish masses, interlaced with giant ferns, vertical like walls, seem to be lost in this infinity of ice. To the west, one can see a rosary of nunataks poised on the ice like black islands, as if showing the way to the mountains leading up towards the Polar Plateau. With their sharp ridges and their sculpted peaks, the contours seem brutal and crude. Here and there one can see a few granite and gneiss peaks which stand up like towers. Here we are at the gates of heaven – or of hell.

I'm struck by the majesty of the surrounding mountains. I realise just how savage, beautiful, pure, magical, immense and inhospitable everything is. I have hours, days, weeks and months to immerse myself in it!
What a privilege! To have discovered the ends of the earth.

Yesterday it was too warm. Today it is bitterly cold…

In the tent, I don't want to talk. I light the stove. Sip the soup in silence. "Lose" myself a little in my solitude, listen to a few notes of music before falling asleep, huddled up in the arms of the Antarctic.

Friday, 21 November (Day 18)

"Long live Belgian Chocolates!"

"Straight ahead": today's word from Catherine brings me down to earth. To look straight ahead also means that one must go fast and see far. Since we haven't until now had the chance of getting out the biggest of the three kites, why not make the most of this coincidence, and of the favourable conditions, to do a stretch being hauled along by the 21 sq.m. sail? But after a few minutes of fiddling around, I realise that the time has still not arrived. Not enough wind, and what's more, not the *right* wind!

A word of explanation. Unlike the two other sails that we had had time to perfect before leaving, this giant 21 sq.m. sail had never really been subjected to practical tests, because the winds that can raise such a surface area of sail are rare throughout the

During the first twenty days of advance, the two men went up to 2,500 m. To the right, the nunatak, Vesthaugen.

world. It has to be said that the 21 sq.m. is a very special sail. Weighing only 651 grams, with such a large surface area, and being designed using a single rather than double membrane surface (as with classical box-kites), it is twice as efficient as anything that has been produced to date.

When I went on a reconnaissance mission to the Antarctic in December 1996, I quickly realised that if we couldn't harness the little laminar winds, the venture was impracticable. We therefore needed a sail which could help us proceed during fine weather. Back in Belgium, I brought together the "sail trio" that I formed with Nassogne[7] and Dansercoer. The three of us cover every possible form of wind utilisation: Patrick is a traction-kite specialist (ground winds), Dixie is a windsurfing champion (sea winds), and I'm a paraglider (air winds). This brainstorming had only one objective: to invent a revolutionary new big sail.

It was a complex problem. We were not certain that we would be equal to the task ahead if we based ourselves on the model adopted for the other two sails[8]. We couldn't simply take the 6 sq.m., for example, and multiply its surface by 3.5. We still had to combine its shape and size, modify its harness, find its correct angle of deployment in the air, and optimise the length of its lines.

So, such a sail was born that nobody would have believed, but on which all my hopes were riding. The future was to prove me right, even though this morning we were a bit clumsy in trying to raise it and find its best settings. The 21 sq.m., "The Integral" as we later called it, became *the* sail of the expedition. We would never have reached the other side of the continent without it.

Because of a lack of practical experience, we were still unable to keep it under pressure, due to a question of wind and of setting. So we had to find the time for tackling this problem.

At 11 o'clock, at the end of the second halt, I take up my ski sticks for a 9 hour march covering 100 m of elevation and 14.8 km.

Nothing like it for recovering the morale, and for a little distraction. I find myself back in this little café in Rochefort, close to where I live, where, one evening in February 1997, an old friend, Philippe Lecomte, was teasing me, between bottles of Guinness, about the amount of pemmican that I had eaten on my previous expeditions.

"Alain, why don't you study the food for your expeditions in the way that I do for my cattle?", he suddenly suggested.

Philippe is a research agronomist and has at his disposal a "digestibility" laboratory, which enables him, to apportion the nutritional input according to the energy output of each animal. Both of us being engineers we set to wondering whether it wouldn't be possible to adapt this principle to the expedition.

It was during that evening that the idea was born of a food supplement to be taken to coincide with moments of great effort. The increased energy yield would lead to a

Approach to the Gunnestadt Glacier, chosen as the route for the ascent onto the Antarctic ice cap, situated 1,000 metres above the point from which the picture is taken.

The rock outcrops flanking the Gunnestadt Glacier on the left are the last mountainous terrain that the Expedition will encounter before the Trans–Antarctic Mountains 2800 km away.

reduction in the weight of the foodstuffs carried. After several attempts at mixtures based principally on butter, we came up with something not only edible but with a definite plus factor. This plus factor was to become what the Americans at McMurdo were to call "Belgian pralines", consisting of a healthy dose of ground cereals and anhydrous milk fats, almost as delicious as our famous chocolates[9].

Alone on my skis, this flashback made me laugh out loud as I remembered Philippe by my side weighing me several times a day in his stables. Here I am, once again, in this imaginary world; talking to myself and laughing aloud with tears in my eyes, (me on the scales next to a cow!)…

For a few moments only. For the cold and the ice bring me back quickly to the harsh reality. In this reality, one has to concentrate on the next step to be taken, which, due to the repetitious quality of the actions, I think of sometimes as a kind of medita-tion – a mantra – which helps me to keep going.

We spent 9 hours advancing today and climb 100 m. Result: 15 km covered.

Saturday, 22 November (Day 19)

A Beautiful Day

A beautiful day today. A tentative go at using the sails only to resume marching after a very short while. The terrain was easier and the snow less hard… A pleasure for me with my plough…

The end of the glacier that we have to take is now visible: it must be nearly 20 km away. I can even make out a path that seems to be winding its way along the left bank of the glacier, as Van Autenboer had indicated; but it seems to be carpeted with crevasses. What thrills to come!

Along the way, we pass by a chain of old eroded mountains, with some beautiful granite peaks. I can't get out of my head the idea that I'll be back here some day, for climbing. That's for sure.

Point C4 (one of the azimuth points taken to guide our progress), earlier marked on the map and to the right of the glacier, has a terrible power of attraction for us.
We take the 12 sq.m. sails but soon fall victim to the wind as it begins to rise. It makes me fall to my knees; at which point my wind compass must have come undone. I discover its loss later. These are the beginnings of the glacier. We set up the best camp of the journey in a very moun-tainous arena. All around us the mountains are shimmering from the combined effect of the high level of humidity, and the particular angle of incidence of the light. Bands of light lie across the countryside, a bit like a mirage…

9 hours of progress and a total of 14.6 km swallowed up today.

This evening, we halt at 18.30: we are at 72°S. The second degree has been crossed. We set up the tent on a pass not far from a ridge marked out by three small rocks placed there like guard dogs. We decide to name the camp "Three Dogs".

The following days are all different from one another; yesterday I was fed up; today I'm so happy to be here. The stress of making progress and the tension of putting together this huge venture are at last beginning to fade away. That said, my feet hurt; it is so hard that at each step I have to draw myself together, tense the muscles of the legs and stretch the tendons, over and over again.

Sunday, 23 November (Day 20)

A Bath of Ice

Superb weather, no wind, want to sleep… Normal, it's Sunday.

A good handful of snow on the face to wake me up, and a small coffee. Yes, life on this frozen continent can be wonderful!

I start out alone in front, while Dixie takes a side trip to go and visit the "Three Dogs". These shapes intrigue him, and he takes the opportunity to film them. I continue peacefully into the glacier, it's warm and for the first time I leave off my jacket. After two and three-quarter hours, I stop for a siesta and to wait. After Dixie has caught up with me, we continue along the left bank of the glacier, the crevasses for the most part are narrow and well filled. The hard ice begins to invade the terrain. We will soon have to put the crampons on again. At 17.30, the sun disappears behind the mountains, the wind rises from the south, and the temperature falls: -30°C.

We should certainly reach the upper part of the glacier tomorrow without too much trouble. Is our luck changing? Will we be able to make up for lost time?

As we get near the Polar Plateau, other questions begin to bother me. Once on the plateau, will we be able to use the katabatic winds[10] on which we have based so many of our hopes? What will the landscape be like up there? When shall we be re-supplied? Has Michel been able to organise everything? Won't there be too many crevasses when the plane arrives? We are right up in the mountains and we can't reach Blue One on the radio: how are we going to advise them of our position? Are the pilots going to throw out the sledges or land with them? If they don't land, what shall we do with the old sledges? There's no question of becoming the polluters of the Antarctic. Will the sledges be properly reinforced this time? Have they understood everything in Brussels? Will we arrive soon enough at the South Pole to be able to go on to McMurdo? And if we pass the January 30 date, how shall I be able to pay the $7,000 a day surcharge which ANI will demand for maintaining their infrastructure (pilots, plane and doctor) in place beyond the dates envisaged for tourism? Will I able to handle this tension? How have I managed to put such a load on my shoulders?

Daily food rations for two, including the Belgian pralines, the morning meal and the evening meal. (See Appendix 3, The Polar Diet.)

It's time to remind myself that, in my wish to commemorate the centenary of the *Belgica* and to re-awaken the Antarctic in the imagination through "The Last Continent" exhibition, there was also a force projecting me into the future. It was time to make use of it…

Yesterday evening, we saw three strange shapes in the distance.

Armed with my video camera, I hurried towards the "Three Dogs", as we named them. Little by little, things became clearer: the three identical shapes were in fact three BP oil drums! My surprise is even greater when I discover there some bamboo sticks, some slippers, some cardboard and an unopened tin of "Marie Thumas" with the label still legible, as if it were from a super-market shelf or an old cupboard. A little further on, a box of matches "Union Match Brussels Belgium" and a bottle of blood serum from the Belgian Red Cross. Back in Belgium, Professor Tony Van Autenboer was to confide in me that it was probably not a real bottle of serum but a pee-bottle (for use in the tent).

What is certain in any case is that some of our compatriots were carrying out research here at the end of the fifties. This particular spot was probably their stockpile.

My first reaction to these leftovers is: what a mess! But then I quickly realised that those scientists were of another generation and that, in their time, ecology was not such a burning issue. That said, one could deduce from the preserved state of the items that they present no immediate threat to the Antarctic environment.

I can't stop myself from climbing up a small crest to survey the site from higher up. I start dreaming there and get into the time machine. From this perch the view is superb.

Moved, I go down by the other side: take care not to fall, especially when alone. Alain, indeed, is now only a dot on the horizon. Perked up again, I collect a few trophies and set out on the climb to catch him up and tell him about my discoveries.

He is truly surprised when I show him my evidence of the earlier Belgian presence in Antarctica.

Monday, 24 November (Day 21)

The Wisdom of the Stones

Quite extraordinary what Dixie found yesterday. What a feeling to be suddenly in touch with the Belgian researchers who were walking around this area 40 years ago. Without doubt, Marie Thumas has given us a taste of eternity.

Today we are changing roles. Dixie will be going on ahead, while I stay behind and have the luxury of a small excursion. I want to go and look for the body of one of the Van Autenboer dogs that died on expedition (he had told me that it would almost certainly still be visible at a precise spot on the glacier). I also want to get as close as possible to these rockfaces and to touch them. I have need of physical contact with Earth

Advancing along the left side of the Gunnestadt Glacier.

before going further into the infinity of ice. Long years of mountaineering have instilled in me a special relationship with the mineral world. If I love climbing so much it's because I need to let myself be imbued with the power of the stones, to learn to live in their intimacy. I can divine a genuine soul in them. They exist on a different kind of timescale, and appear to have a kind of wisdom and self knowledge.

I collect a few pieces of granite as souvenirs, and put them in my pocket. And then I hang around a little as this is one of the most beautiful sights I've seen in the world. One could be on the moon! But taking your time isn't in the Antarctic vocabulary; I'm busy dreaming and Dixie has already disappeared from my field of vision. I must hurry because the visibility is deteriorating. Farewell to the stones.

I catch up with him after two hours. Here the slope is even steeper; we are permanently on the tips of our crampons. There is no question of a halt to relax the effort because the weight of the sledges would immediately drag us down again.

Tomorrow we will have the stiffest part of the climb up the glacier; the pain in the heels is sharp. "Give it everything, no brakes" is the cry of encouragement of one of my best friends. It suits this situation very well. We are pulling as hard as we can; these last hours, our grunts reveal the beasts of burden within us.

This evening I'm on my knees, finished, done for, hungry, thirsty. We put the tent up, I can at last stretch out and regain my breath. I close my eyes.

Yesterday, we saw a sea of ice.

Today, our camp is surrounded by mountains. Talk about contrasts.

Tuesday, 25 November (Day 22)

The Queen on a Plateau

This morning, I cover my helping of cereal with a solid dose of olive oil, and that sticks in my stomach. I almost have to throw up, I have to march slowly so as not to waste my breakfast. I feel terrible.

Five hours march and at last we arrive on the Queen Maud Land plateau. That at least is some achievement. It's sumptuous. What a privilege to be here… especially as we are now entering a new phase of the expedition. Very few men have ventured as far as this. Perhaps some Japanese researchers, it would seem, looking for meteorites. When I was preparing the itinerary, the eye witness accounts of the Belgian scientists always stopped short of the Sør Rondane mountains. What happened beyond them was always a mystery. Crevasses? Who knows? The nature of the ice? Ditto. The climate? Even less. And here we are about to lift the veil on all these unknowns. It is difficult to describe my inner feelings at this time. But it's something enormous. As if we had been charged with an important mission, and that the discoveries we were about to make would make a real contribution to man's knowledge of this part of the world.

The sky is suffused with stratus clouds, the sun (at about 40°) is encircled by a halo, the light is wan and diffused. Far away to the north, Mt Romnaes and some nunataks look like icebergs in a sea gripped by the icefloe. This landscape reminds me of our arrival at the charming little village of Isertoq, when, after we had crossed Greenland, we descended onto the ice cap towards the east coast. As we are arriving in a crevasse-free area, we decide to stop because it's a perfect place for a landing. We could do well to wait here for the arrival of the aeroplane and the sledges. No luck: in touch once more with Blue One, we learn that the weather is bad and that we cannot expect anything for the next few days.

We decide to change our itinerary and attempt to get in touch with Blue One. Between the crackles, we understand that the Hercules C130 hasn't yet arrived. Nothing to be done about it, no point in crying into your soup; a spot of yoga and everything is fine again. The tent is certainly a very restricted space for devoting myself to this exercise. But it's done. Alain is getting used to seeing me in all kinds of positions and for me, I realise that the tent, when all is said and done, is sufficiently spacious to enable me to string together the slow-motion performance of the movements which bring me much needed release after a long day's march. Never before have I been so supple. Perhaps that's normal after the series of flexions and contortions that I've been subjecting my body to throughout the day. In normal times, yoga is for me an exercise in concentration; here I practise it more for tearing myself away from everything and making my mind a blank. The void is silent, infinity is beautiful.

Wednesday, 26 November (Day 23)

Sexy Shorts and Blue Ice

A bad night; I'm not on form this morning.

I dip my hand into the envelope; the word "Emilie" comes to my aid. She is the youngest of my three children. She is 15 years old. Always ready for a laugh, she can restore my morale. I can see her already coming to massage the nape of my neck a little when she can see that something's troubling me and letting drop one of her cheeky remarks: *"Don't worry, we like you with your curly hair and your sexy little shorts…"*

The weather is getting quickly worse and a white-out occurs. It's snowing. With the wind blowing, I repeatedly lose my balance. The terrain seems to me to contain crevasses; for reasons of prudence we put on our skis. But the sledges are too heavy, the slope is too steep and the skins don't grip properly. We take them off again… A few minutes later, my foot suddenly plunges through the snow, and I'm thrown backwards.

On 25 November the two men arrive at Queen Maud Land on the polar plateau. They have a further 1950 km ahead of them before they reach the Pole.

I have just narrowly missed a snow-covered crevasse that must be 30 m deep but which is luckily only 30cm wide. What a relief!

Leading the way, I put my skis back on. We soon arrive at one of those immense areas of blue ice that are so characteristic of the Antarctic continent. It's the Nansenisen region (between 72.5° and 73°S), which was visited by the Japanese in their search for meteorites.

A word of explanation. Blue ice, is so called because it is due to the ultimate transformation of snow, at which stage it assumes that typical colour. It can be explained by two phenomena. The Antarctic glaciers move (the precise term is "flow") slowly towards the ocean. So, a snowflake that falls in central Antarctica will take between 500,000 and 1,000,000 years to cover the distance separating it from the coast. When a natural object gets in the way of this slow progress – in this case, for example, a change in the relief of the underlying rock formations – the ice surges around in an attempt to find a way through, and in so doing loses its depth. When it reaches the surface it experiences the phenomenon of evaporation, which keeps it bare. It's on this type of terrain that one can hope to find meteorites that fell to the ground perhaps several million years ago.

Is this, then, a region for meteorites? This morning, I have the impression of finding myself in another world: the Antarctic spectacle is majestic. A confused landscape made up of three colours: milky white, pale grey, and translucent blue. The white is the white-out and the areas of fresh snow which streak across the surface of the ground. The blue is the background of the picture, the fathomless ice that hails from the furthest time. The grey is those strips of lenticular cloud that are disintegrating in the wind. Am I on earth or in the sky? That's without mentioning the lunar atmosphere and the banks of driven snow, which cause me to lose the last of my landmarks. Am I going to dissolve or evaporate in this immensity?

Enough of this morning's *Son et Lumière* spectacle. As far as the conditions for progress are concerned, things are very different. In order not to lose balance and get swept away, we are obliged to keep the sail close to the ground. On this icy billiard table, the skis slip sideways all the time and brake savagely when they hit a patch of snow: the body, which is leaning forward, doesn't always have time to react properly. Furthermore, we've made the mistake of using lines instead of shafts, which means that the sledges, whenever they leave the less slippery areas and find themselves once again on sheer ice, keep on going and thump us violently in the back.

This torture has lasted for hours. I was surprised on several occasions to fall and to crash against the ice, panting, out of breath from trying all kinds of tricks to avoid losing my balance. At 16.30 I fall flat on my face definitively in a mound of snow that I hadn't seen coming.

It's about a month now since we left. I'm trying to feel close to all those who are asking where we are and what we're doing. Breakfast in the tent, which is flapping noisily as it's buffeted by the powdery snow.

After the meal, I feel very weak. Alain is groggy. We've both got a headache. Could these be the first symptoms of altitude sickness? We are only at 3000 m, however. It's true that we climbed very quickly these last few days, and that in the Antarctic the partial oxygen pressure is about 20% lower than elsewhere, which means the effect of altitude is felt more keenly. But we are too well acclimatised and too fit to feel it. Is it then that the light is too intense? Or fatigue? Or the smell of the stove?

A small crevasse.

I devote myself to the household chores (I organise the first-aid kit, tidy up the tent, check the contents of the bags, and so on); it helps to pass the time. Eat when one should eat, write when one should write, sleep when one should sleep. On the outside, a marvellous world is opening up. The omnipotence of nature dominates everything, and opposite her, two little men of no significance, dream sweet dreams.

In the evening we both feel pretty unwell, as though oversatiated. We are both suffering from splitting headaches and unusual irritation around the eyes. It's inexplicable.

I try to get to sleep but my heart is pounding, and I can't relax.

I try to write in my diary but my writing is terrible. Too shaky.

Thursday, 27 November (Day 24)

Regional Information

The storm has raged all night and the barometer has dropped sharply..........

We're trapped in the tent again, for yet another day. We tidy up, we mend the gear. Darn the mittens and the gloves that have been holed from gripping the ski sticks and hanging on to the tillers of the kites. Re-sew the wolf skin trimming of the hood. Knock up from a plaster and some polar fur a nose-piece to attach to the goggles. Fix the sheath of the harness that has come undone. We also spend a ridiculous amount of time untangling the suspension lines, which, no matter what we do, always get twisted up. At this very moment, the threads are dangling everywhere like in a rope-maker's workshop. We check their points of attachment. When they are on the point of giving up, we reinforce them. We unroll the 15 metres of line of each assembly to inspect their hubs. We make the most of the sails' being unfurled to inspect them. The slightest hole or beginning of a tear is repaired with a special tape. As the headaches don't let up, I carefully disassemble the stove, and examine the pump, the jet and the washers to try to see from where the leak might originate. Everything is in order. I should also repair the sledge one more time, but the blizzard makes me not want to put my nose outside.

Friday, 28 November (Day 25)

Sweating at −58°C

Strong wind. Cirro-stratus clouds. Impressive snow banks. Visibility: 8 metres. The picture isn't very encouraging but we set off nevertheless.

The terrain is still hard. Very hard. As yesterday, we have to pick our way through a succession of blue ice and soft snow patches.

I'm angry. We have had to proceed with crampons for a month already; we're never going to cross the continent like this. If only the skiing was good!

I'm fed up. I take a kick at the sledge and shake it from side to side. It's a new technique of mine to try to get the runners into line.

I suddenly remember, after 30 minutes, that I've left my ice screws at the camp. What would I do without them if I were to fall into a crevasse? I have to go and fetch them because I don't have any others. No choice. I leave my sledge where it is, tell Dixie about this unexpected development and retrace my steps. I had thought it would only take me about ten minutes, but, already, I can't make out our footsteps any longer. No matter, I go on. We were marching in a crosswind so I can't go wrong (in the Antarctic, one often uses the angle of incidence of the wind on the skin to keep one's bearing). What's more, the wall of snow around the tent was so high that I can't possibly miss it. But then, after ten minutes, I don't know where I am any more. I have the impression after every 20 metres that I'm going to come upon the spot where we pitched our tent. I go off to the left, to the right, retrace my steps towards the north, thinking that this time I can recognise this morning's wall of snow. But with this wind and the tons of snow that it displaces, the sastrugis create and recreate waves of every kind. Brusquely, a little frisson of panic grips me: I want to retrace my steps. But which steps? Turning round, I can see that there are no marks at all in the snow around me. The raging wind, now twice as strong as it was, has smoothed everything over. I take a fierce grip on my ski sticks, as if to reassure myself in some new way. It doesn't last, because I now realise that I have neither radio nor GPS with me. If I'm lost, I'm done for, completely and utterly done for. When one says that in the Antarctic death is loitering around the corner all the time, it's no joke and certainly no exaggeration. I imagine someone here in my situation going crazy: even though his companion is only a few hundred metres away, heading straight for disaster.

What mindlessness, in any case! Blunder, blunder, blunder! I set off 90° to the east, and then 90° to the west. The direction of the wind, luckily constant, is my only guide. Now it's real panic: my throat is dry, my breathing turns into panting. Then, just when I'm beginning not to believe it anymore, there are my screws right in front of me. I now know that all I have to do is march due south to find Dixie. Poor guy – he was scared stiff…

Alain has disappeared into the void to go and pick up his gear left at the last camp site. It's always a real trial to watch one's travelling companion being swallowed up in a few minutes by the driving Antarctic snow. And as a result I have to wait, freezing my derrière.

I have to keep moving, keep the circulation going, or else…. I try little short sprints, forwards, backwards, to the left, to the right, always making sure that I don't lose sight of the sledge. It's at times like these that all those stories about polar explorers who got lost and died a few hundred metres from their shelter come back to you. Scott and his companions, having survived their epic journey, died of hunger and cold on the Ross Ice Shelf, only 18 km from their last stockpile.

This time, Alain is taking an eternity to come back!

I'm cold, so very cold, just too cold.

The weather is so rotten that I can hardly make out the end of my sledge. My anxiety increases. Where on earth has he got to?

Suddenly, as if seized by some unknown demon, I can't wait any longer and I decide to go and look for him. I know that following ones steps is dangerous. Because of the dual risk of not being able to find him and then not being able to find my sledge again. I set off. I can't see a bloody thing. Hell and damnation!

It's only after a quarter of an hour's cautiously feeling my way that I see him emerging from the fog like a reincarnation, or may be a ghost...

We have set off again for a 9-hour march.

Nine long hours, during which we have to fight against the powerfully driven snow, hauling the sledges along step by agonising step, on the very tips of our crampons, gripping on to the ski sticks with all our force. I can't feel my fingers any more. I even have to stop several times to slip them under my clothes to prevent them from getting a fatal frostbite.

Seeing the state of my sledge, which every day gets a little more twisted, the slightest mound becomes a veritable mountain. On each occasion I have to gear myself up, accelerate, fill my lungs with air, stretching my muscles as far as they will go, and then catch my breath before going on again.

Although I'm wearing only two layers of clothing, I'm sweating, despite the ambient temperature (−58°C taking into account wind chill factor). What's more, I have to keep my outer mittens on because of the strength of the wind. They are covered with ice and accelerate the freezing of my fingers. It's sheer hell: there's no other word for it.

Under such conditions, you would expect that we would retreat into the self, become introspective, and totally focussed with wrestling with the physical suffering that we are undergoing. Not a bit of it. When at the halt, our eyes meet, we smile, we laugh...

That's what I call morale!

In the evening, it's −26°C. Blue One informs us that the Hercules C130 has still not arrived from South Africa.

Saturday, 29 November (Day 26)

I Didn't Even Feel Myself Go...

The same scenario as yesterday. But even more terrifying, if that's possible. We didn't manage more than two hours of progress before putting up the tent. We have to do this with the utmost care, because the wind is in excess of 100 kmh.

I was certain that the weather would have improved today... Not at all. The blizzard is back and the storm is raging again, when, in fact, we ought to be enjoying a more "continental" and drier climate as we get progressively further away from the ocean.

In the tent, the stove is again releasing bad smells. I can't understand what's happening. I've already replaced two washers, but it hasn't made the slightest difference… It's all very odd!

It was while I was drinking my bowl of soup that I, suddenly, began to have the same feeling coming over me as I had had two days previously. My head began to ache violently, and then nothing more.

I didn't even feel myself go…

The wind is blowing in gusts of up to 90 km/h. It's −25°C outside. With what the English refer to as the wind chill factor, the effective temperature is about −70°C. In other words, the frozen hell continues.

We are well and truly set for the same saga as yesterday.

I have always wondered how a stalked animal can sense the presence of its enemy, or how a peasant will know when it's time to bring in the hay. We, too, allow ourselves to be guided by our instincts and intuition. We feel in an uncomplicated way that we must act. We stay a little longer in the tent, because there is no point in trying to make any progress in this storm, but as we must also avoid becoming lethargic, we decide to leave at around noon. A titan's task, an activity quickly impossible to justify. I constantly flap my arms to prevent frostbite; for the first time, my feet are cold in the middle of the day. It's crazy. We march without stopping for two hours and then look at each other, and decide without exchanging words to stop and to put up the tent before it's too late.

The GPS displays today's average: 1.5 km. It's a really revolutionary device this miniature receiver –transmitter. You hold it in your hand. No more need for a sextant, or a wheel tied to the back of the sledge to measure the distance covered. All it needs is to locate one of the 24 satellites circling the globe in order to instantly calculate and display the latitude and longitude of your position, within an accuracy of a few metres.

Alain quickly sets to lighting the stove, to melt some snow. I suddenly hear a cry of distress. Alain is moaning and panting. He suddenly topples over, unconscious.

Bloody hell, what is going on?

I have to do something. I rush to put out the stove. I open the roof of the tent to let in some fresh air. Because the wind is blowing, the snow comes in as well.

Above all, stay calm.

I attend to Alain. Because he has already been sick once, I'm frightened that he might choke. I sit him up, I see his eyes open again, and then roll back into oblivion. I grab one of the two saucepans to put under his mouth to protect the floor; I have trouble keeping him upright because of his bulk. His body is limp and then contracts again. He's sick once more.

Bloody hell! For God's sake, Alain, wake up, old man!

Meanwhile, the tent is full of snow and I have to close it.

I feel so ill myself that I repeatedly have to slap my face and hit myself so as not to pass out. I straighten him out again and put whatever I can find beneath his back.

The two men place the sledges in a V up-wind from the tent, forming an aerodynamic barrier which prevents it from being buried during a snow storm.

I shout into his ears; his eyes open a little, at last a sign of life.

Confused words tumble from his mouth. In Dutch! He's trembling violently and I understand that he's getting hot (or is it cold?) so I try to cover him with his sleeping bag. Hell, why is the tent so small? What a mess! I keep on talking to him to stay in touch, and little by little I begin to make out a few Dutch words among his babbling. With great difficulty I manoeuvre his limp form into his sleeping bag.

I take him in my arms; try to stop him trembling, speak gently to him, wipe his brow, and cradle him. Emotions spill out with the tears. I think I understand that his head is spinning. I wipe his face with a cloth, I stroke him like a baby, I massage his whole body with a regular rhythm and try to cajole him: "Everything will be all right. Don't think about the cold, relax." His whole body is rigid, stressed, which is a normal reaction to a lack of oxygen in the cells. "Breathe in and breathe out calmly, Alain, you're warming up again".

As soon as he can talk again, he wants to know whether his crystal talisman is still on his chest – a rhodocrosite (a stone known to influence the pericardium and help overcome fear), which a friend practising energetics had given to him before he left.

Things seem a bit better now. He appears to be emerging from the depths, and thinking more clearly. I continue to massage him, and we talk for a while until he tells me that he is terribly tired. At this juncture, I feel the calm returning , and I look around. There is total disorder in the small tent, clothes and equipment are all jumbled together and the whole is covered with snow.

I pass my hand over my forehead, and close my eyes. I try to regain my lucidity, and to recover from the maelstrom of emotions which I have just been through.

I philosophise a little on the theme that an expedition such as this is only possible with several people. I'm glad to be in Alain's company. The day may well come when I have to rely on him. This evening the Argos beacon will relay the code : "A9 B11", namely, "stove malfunction". What a euphemism!

When I come round, everything is moving, I feel far away from the world. Dixie is trying to get me into my sleeping bag, he seems to be talking to me. I can vaguely feel his hands on my body. But where, exactly? I'm shaking; all my muscles are fully contracted, almost paralysed. The only sensation I have is that of my heart beating. In fact I feel that the cardiac muscle is the only one still functioning, the rest is a vacuum, nothing…

Hang on to this shred of life. Try as hard as I can to relax this tetanised body of mine. Get my senses back, one by one; breathe, touch, smell, speech. Get back on the road to consciousness; tell myself that just I cannot go on like this. Not now.

Little by little, warmth begins to return. The convulsions get weaker. The cramps begin to fade away. I have no idea how long I was unwell for, but I do know that the banging inside my head goes on for several hours. It's strange to think that this little drama is being played out with the wind raging outside at more than 100 km/h!

The episode reminds me of Richard Byrd, the legendary American figure of Antarctic exploration, who nearly died of CO poisoning, in 1934. The ventilation chimney of his shelter became blocked with ice while he was wintering alone, some 200 km from his base, in a minuscule shelter which he had dug out two metres under the snow.

Slowly but surely I regain my senses, but without believing that the worst is over.

Why should I die today to be re-born in this way? I who never had any real problems, either on expedition, or in my everyday life. What happened to me? And to think that the theme of the day, the word from Catherine that I drew this morning, was "Energy"! What a troubling coincidence…

Sunday, 30 November (Day 27)

The Final Circle

6.50: I feel a bit better but I've still got a murderous head, and to put it mildly, I don't feel up to putting out to sea today.

Outside, the storm is still raging and the wind is blowing at more than 80 km/h. The light is dull and visibility is hardly more than 4 metres.

Stand-by: this is the eighth day without advancing, out of the 27 days of the expedition. That's not a very good statistic. Too bad for the expedition. All the better for me.

It's Sunday today. My daughter Gaëlle is probably working at the bakery. And tomorrow it's already December: exam month for the children. This fleeting escape to Harsin does me good…just enough time for coffee, and a game of cards – it's always the same game, *rikiki*, but we like it – and then I venture a preliminary analysis of what happened to me yesterday, to see things (no pun intended) in cold blood.

Firstly, we can be certain that what came over me yesterday is in no way connected to altitude sickness. So if it's not altitude, what is it?

I can only imagine one possible answer – poisoning! Unbelievable, really, to have suffered from carbon monoxide poisoning in the middle of the largest and purest desert in the world!

It would have to be the MSR stove which is malfunctioning. I don't understand it, because I've been using it for years. I take it on all my expeditions and I know it by heart. Between it and me there is, dare I say, a long-running love story. Its gentle hiss reassures me. Its mechanism as well. Its output is worthy of the finest tool that ever was. It is simplicity itself. For eight years I've put it through the worst conditions and it has never let me down. That's how I know that on some days it's on form, and on others not. Throughout the years I have learnt not to resent it for that, and I'm always prepared to accept its moods. What do you want? Animism isn't dead. I would even go so far as to say that every expedition needs some. If I didn't experience a genuine sensuality as well as a feeling of absolute safety every morning when I touch its still cold container of naphtha for the first time in the day, perhaps I would never succeed in these crazy ventures.

Despite all that, that no good so-and-so has almost cost me my life! Due to the smells floating around the tent in the last few days, I had already replaced more than a couple of washers since we started, which is a routine job, seeing as I can easily dismantle the whole thing.

If it's not a leak, what could it be?

Thinking it over with Dixie, and examining the MSR from all sides, I think to myself that it's perhaps a problem of combustion. In all my expeditions, I put the stove in a Kevlar box with a hole cut in the side to let the air through so as to ensure the best possible combustion from the gas/air mixture. On this occasion I had not cut the hole (so that the box wouldn't lose its rigidity). Moving around this vast Antarctic environment, I was subconsciously persuaded that the air here could easily enter the box from above.

It can only be that. Good! Brandishing the small pair of pliers that I always keep in a corner of my pocket, I set about cutting out the customary orifice in the Kevlar. A few moments go by, and then once again we have the reassuring purr of the MSR with its beautifully coloured flame. So it appears that everything is in order again, and this article that I have always considered to be one of the principal tools of the expedition will cause no more trouble.

Outside, the wind is a little calmer: 50km/h. Dixie is engrossed in his yoga. I start with some sewing. It's always the mittens. Later we will send an e-mail to Michel to tell him about all these incidents.

We must at all costs reach the South Pole before the 15 January or run the risk of not being able to continue nor arrive in time to take advantage of one of the last ice-breakers[11] leaving the continent.

As there are still 1,941 km between us and the American base, and we have to do it in less than 45 days, it means covering an average of 45 km per day.

But calculations such as these are entirely dependent on the wind, the absolute master in the Antarctic. There's nothing for it but to submit, even though at every moment of every day in this adventure we try our utmost to force its hand. A dynamic paradox between submission and determination, confrontation and humility. An unpredictable succession of moments of exaltation and of total impotence.

How can I explain that other paradox that drives me to seek serenity by undergoing such a gruelling ordeal? What is this inner need that forces me to weigh anchor and head off for other horizons? Is it for the simple fact of going far away so as to experience the things that everyday life cannot express, to get one step ahead of this mocking destiny? That's certainly a part of the answer. But how can I ignore these heartrending experiences along the way, which urge me towards a quieter life? Can one really make ones own destiny be like Dante's man on his journey, and reach the other side of oneself beyond the last circle, the hell of ice, to be born again – to oneself and to the world?

I departed convinced that this immensity would furnish me with at least part of the answer.

I'm beginning quite seriously to believe that here we are nothing more than actors in a play that is part froth and part tragedy at one and the same time; even though at moments like this it seems to be panning out more in the way of a comedy. A title? "Two yaks in the hell of ice".

While lingering on the last words of a poem called "Vespers", written by Monod, riding on the back of a camel somewhere in Mauritania one evening in March 1949, I try to find a few crumbs of sleep.

"On waking from a long dream, will one suddenly be able,
To, finally, enter reality, alive?…"

Monday, 1 December (Day 28)

When the Antarctic gives you your Entry Permit

It's a stressful day because of the uncertainties over the re-supply. For a few days already, we are ceaselessly preoccupied with when the sledges will arrive. HQ has no idea. Nor has Blue One. We're fed up.

I had Michel on the line this morning and he asked me to ring him back at around one o'clock. You can hardly imagine how much energy is required to ring HQ. This is what it entails: put up the tent to deploy the Inmarsat – just think what would happen to such a hi-tech instrument if it were suddenly to be covered in snow. This means stopping, disconnecting the sledge, taking off the harness, opening up the sledge, taking out the tent, putting on the double roof, brace it as though it were evening, pile snow on the flaps, take out the transmitter. A hideous waste of time. And then, one has a furious desire to go on again. I was doing the sums yesterday. Making progress must become an obsession. If not…

So we weigh anchor, even though it means stopping again after a few hours to call Michel. It could well seem banal, even incomprehensible, to curse in this way about something that will only be happening in five hours time. Deep down, even with all the extra work involved, the real problem in fact lies in the rhythm. The rhythm that progressively enters your legs and muscles, and then your mind, as you supply the effort. The same rhythm that enters you gently, and makes you suffer, but which in the end develops into a sort of reflex, which is vital for executing the repetitive actions needed to advance. Despite the huge weight I'm dragging behind me, I'm physically becoming part of my sledge. Eventually, a part of myself instinctively forgets it. I remember the hard moments on the Arctic ice with Didier where, after several weeks, we were clearing ice crest after ice crest without caring any more about the pain that was wracking our bodies.

From now on, we're ready. Physically and psychologically. It has taken 28 days for us to pass the examination of the Antarctic, with honours.

Tuesday, 2 December (Day 29)

Blue One isn't Answering

Seven in the morning. No way of establishing the satellite link with HQ.

Breakfast. Dixie breaks a tooth. He gets out his cavity filling kit and turns himself into a makeshift dentist. We strike camp. Damn…

82, 87, 94 km/h: the wind totally mad. Same terrain as yesterday, we will have to fight. Cannot complain, after all that's what we're here for.

The diversity of the ice formations, covered in snow brought by the squalling wind, makes me think of the Belgian coast.
Nostalgia for that intense period of surf, wind, sea, waves, sand, dunes and sun. In fact, our means of progressing here is very similar to that of a wind-surf board: the same driving force (the

Tuesday, 2 December, after 269 miles into the crossing, a Twin Otter from Blue One joins the Expedition camp at 2700 m, bringing with it the new sledges.

wind), the same means (the sail), the same jumping over obstacles, the same feeling of melting into infinity…

So I dream a little of one day making my own sea-sledge that I'd pull along behind me on the water with my sail so that I could achieve huge distances along the coastlines, without assistance, of course. And then, why not apply this technology to the great deserts? An ingenious system of putting wheels beneath the skis and the pulk and Bob's your uncle… For me the great African expanses. For me the Gobi desert. For me, dreams…

In the evening I mend the crampons because they came off six times today. A quick nip with the pliers and everything's in place. They're a bit worn, I know, but I like them because they're strong, reliable and light. And I took them with me each time I set foot on the slopes of Everest.

It's astonishing how warm it is in this tent. As the Antarctic summer approaches (21 December), the height of the sun describing a circle around us remains almost constant above the horizon. From now on there will be a difference of 10 to 15°C between the inside and the outside, which makes for exceptional comfort: one recovers better, there's less brushing, the clothes dry more quickly, less naphtha is required for melting the snow, one can write without wearing gloves, the condensation is less, there is less frost on the sides of the tent…

It's one of the essential differences between Antarctic and Arctic expeditions. The former benefits from the fact that adventurers can choose the best season for going there, whereas for the latter to be successful, they must always start earlier in the year, or else the water released from the continuous melting of the ice-pack will make it almost impossible for them to proceed.

In touch with Brussels, at last, we learn that the plane has left with the sledges, and that right now it's at the site of our last camp. It's trying to locate us, and it should arrive at any moment.

Wednesday, 3 December (Day 30)

Beer and Fresh Bread

Ten past midnight: the sound of an engine in the sky, a quick flight over our tent and then the wing of the plane comes to a halt above our heads.

Greg Stein, the pilot, and Al Gilbert, his co-pilot, offer us a beer and some fresh bread baked by Mike, the man in charge at Blue One. How can one refuse such a gift? There are also letters from our loved ones, some press cuttings about the expedition sent by Sigrid, head of public relations at Compaq, a pack of cards for Christmas from Anne Kershaw and finally this word of encouragement from Remy: "Go right on to the very end, for you, for us, and for all those who dream standing up", with a few lines taken from *"The Seven Pillars of Wisdom"* by T. E. Lawrence ("We were bound together in affection by the immensity of the open spaces, by the savour of the limitless winds…").

We hurry to load the new sledges and to stow the old ones into the hold of the Twin. A quick visit to the tent, a few quick jokes and congratulations on the exemplary maintenance of our camps – which is definitely not an everyday affair in the Antarctic.

I discover a small wound on my right knee that seems to be infected so I decide to open it to put some disinfectant in it. Is the day ever going to come when everything will be all right? We have used up one third of our time and covered one 20th of the distance.

"Focus, focus". These words, inscribed by Julie on the toes of my boots before I left, fill me with encouragement.

I feel her close by me. Decidedly, she's pushing me on. When necessary, giving me a kick up the backside.

Thursday, 4 December (Day 31)

Is he Flying, or What?

Rise at 8.30. I've finally managed to have a good night's sleep.

Mend the two sails that were damaged yesterday, readjust one of Dixie's boots to his ski binding, strengthen the shaft where the strut has broken again.

We get under way at 1 p.m. After a march of three hours, Dixie suggests hoisting the sails. There's the usual moment of confusion in carrying out a manoeuvre that is still not quite mastered. But something is wrong.

I can see Dixie drawing away and slipping sideways. The wind is strong. He seems to be incapable of controlling his tackle. And suddenly I see him up in the air, lifted two to three metres off the ground. What on earth is he doing? Is he flying away, or what? Has he decided to show me a new acrobatic turn taken straight out of his beloved Zen? Or even… I can't believe my eyes. A second or two later, and he falls heavily back to the ice. His sledge overturns. He's not moving… His sail changes tack and goes off in a different direction, stretched to breaking-point. It's no longer a joke. As he has kept hold of his lines, the time it takes for them to tauten and off again, a few seconds after the sail, he's literally plucked up from the ground, and propelled into the air a second time. He is torn apart between the 150 kilos of sledge stuck in the ice and the incredible power generated by the traction kite. He falls again. More violently this time. The ice is as hard as concrete. I hold my breath…

"No, Dixie, no… Not that". I clench my teeth, impotent in the face of this drama. I can see that he has lost a ski and that for a third time he's lifted up in the air, some two metres from the ground, then his sail rips and collapses.

It's awful! He's bound to have been knocked out. The whole thing took no more than twenty or thirty seconds, and I instinctively folded my sail. I rush towards him. From a distance he appears to be inert, but as I get closer I can see that he's moving a little.

What relief, it's less serious than I was beginning to fear…

For me to be able to look after him, I first have to put the tent up. Then help him to get inside. I can hear him mumbling, talking of stars, visions, his mother… He's completely stiff. He's moaning. As far as I can see, he has no open wounds.

I hope he hasn't broken anything. The best thing for him to do is to try to sleep to recuperate.

He drags himself with difficulty on to his sleeping bag, and I cover him with mine. A few moments later and he's asleep, while I try to finish putting up the tent and recovering our gear. Thankfully, he doesn't seem to be in too much pain.

I fear the worst and I can already see myself having to continue the expedition without him. While fussing about, I mechanically draw up a list of all the things I would need to take in my sledge for going on alone. But I quickly expel this image from my mind; things are certainly not that bad. Dixie is extremely fit; perhaps after all he's only in a state of shock.

I calm down. I go back into the tent and spend the next three hours sewing up his sail.

Outside, the wind has lessened; 20 to 30 km/h, and in a perfect direction for our sails. The weather is superb. If we hadn't been so impatient this afternoon, if we had waited for just one hour, we would probably have been able to cover more than 50 km. This type of accident is quite ridiculous. And above all preventable. If we had taken the precaution of harnessing ourselves with shafts rather than lines, it would never have happened, because man and sledge together are too heavy to be lifted into the air.

Dixie pulls me out of these thoughts. I hear him moan. He wants to get into his sleeping bag, so I help him to undress. He thinks that nothing is broken, but he hurts all over. Especially his back and his ribs. He's worried. I reassure him by saying that we'll see to all that tomorrow.

"It's time for you to sleep now, Dixie. Keep cool, kid, everything will be OK…" But is this what I'm really thinking? We have been beset with problems. The sails have been ripped, the sledges have been damaged, I have been asphyxiated, Dixie probably has some broken ribs… We are suffering cruelly. More than ever, it's pure hell. The image of a prison without bars comes to me: The *Malebolges*! These are Dante's *Malebolges*, those horrible accursed pits of a thousand indescribable tortures that are rampant in the ninth circle of hell.

In the evening, I set the beacon on "A4–B8; Serious accident Dixie". What's Michel going to think?

It's not until 9.30 that I can begin to prepare the evening meal. A few notes of music to calm me down… And a little turn outside to get some air.

No more mountains on the horizon. We are alone here in this virgin immensity, after such a crucial day. And what if we had needed help?

I'm labouring behind Alain. The only way of making progress today, I told myself, was with power-kites. The wind is strong, my knee is suffering badly from the unevenness of the terrain. I help Alain get ready, and then limp back to get the sledges. I give him my sail, I unfold it as far as I can, and then comes that delicate moment when Alain has to let go. The sail climbs up rapidly, until I pull it back to the ground in the right direction. This new sail doesn't feel right, but once everything is under control, I'm less worried. I let go of the tillers to look behind me to see if Alain is still ready to leave; then I see nothing but stars. The sail goes straight up with incredible force; I feel myself losing touch with the ice. I try to catch my breath, as I'm lifted several metres off the ground, and then suddenly this dull shock.

The rest for me is a mystery, as I lose all consciousness.

For the first time in my life, I see visions. I'm suddenly very calm, in another world, where my mother is speaking to me about something trivial. An unknown woman joins the conversation; we are in an empty room.

I like this peace and quiet; where is this ambience coming from? The earth's force of gravity – yes, even in the Antarctic – smashes me against the hard ice; I regain consciousness. In a flash, I understand the danger. The out-of-control sail is still pulling me, which is dangerous for the sledge.

A stupid mistake on my part; I should have used the shaft instead of the lines. Luckily I manage to pull one of the rear lines of the power-kite towards me; the sail loses all its power and crumples up like a dishcloth. Panting and shaking, I wait on the ice for a moment. I close my eyes: the first sensation is one of frustration. Yet again, we have not succeeded in getting under way.

I'm fine here, time no longer exists.

Then suddenly… the pain. The whole of my right side is sending out distress signals. Meanwhile, Alain has arrived and is running towards my sail to fold it up.

"That wasn't much fun to watch…" I want to help him roll up the lines, but when I try to stand up, my body doesn't obey. It is bruised and swollen in many places. I can't hold back my tears…

I let myself go.

For the rest, words are useless; Alain gets the gear together and puts up the tent. I go inside with difficulty, like an old man crippled with rheumatism.

The cold takes hold of me and the shock makes me shake uncontrollably. Lying on my back, I have pain in my knee, in my quadriceps, in my back and in my chest. My hands feel frozen, my tears as well. Alain undresses me and tells me what he saw. "Well, old man, I was really afraid for you". I hurt all over.

Luckily I've got a good nursemaid, although perhaps not all that sexy. Still, one mustn't ask for too much!

Friday, 5 December (Day 32)

"We've Seen our Black Snow"

A touch of humour on discovering Catherine's word of the day: "Champagne". A question perhaps of celebrating the end of our troubles. "We have eaten our black bread". The similar expression in Dutch suits the context better: "We hebben al onze zwarte sneeuw gezien", "We've seen our black snow…"

I'm champing at the bit because the weather outside is glorious and we could have really made some progress. But the main thing is that Dixie is feeling better. His morale is unbroken. What a man! While he's going through different exercises to get his feeling back, I check the state of the sails and re-stitch the traction belt. Then I go outside to mend the cover of his sledge that was ripped in the escapade, and I reorganise its load.

73° latitude south.

As we are now on the Polar Plateau, I mustn't forget to collect the snow samples for the Laboratory for Environmental Glaciology and Geophysics at Grenoble[12]. I get the titanium tube out of the sledge; 3 metres long, it's not easy to handle. I plunge the core borer into the snow, withdraw it and empty its contents into one of the jerrycans of naphtha with a division in the middle. I mix the snow and fill two little pots with it whose numbers are to be written down in a special notebook showing the exact place where the samples were taken – as scientific rigour demands. This exercise is to be repeated every 50km throughout the entire crossing, except when there are mountainous passages.

One interesting aspect of this experiment is to collect snow samples at places where man has practically never been. The only expedition to have ventured this far was the

Queen Maud Land Traverse, a huge American reconnaissance operation which took place over three years from 1965 to 1967. A poignant detail: command of the third phase of this project had been entrusted to an Italian geochemist living in Belgium, Edgard Picciotto[13]. The general public is hardly aware of this eminent scientist, a pioneer in the field of Antarctic science. It is interesting to know that he was the first person to bring back three tons of ice, for the Geology and Nuclear Geochemistry Department of the Free University of Brussels in order to determine the incidence of extraterrestrial particles falling to Earth. An experiment that has never been repeated and whose findings have never since been contested.

Dixie goes out for a little walk. It's a good sign, and I now know that we'll leave tomorrow.

This evening, and it's not always the case, the atmosphere is relaxed. We throw ourselves into a great social debate, which, for the umpteenth time, puts the world to rights.

Saturday, 6 December (Day 33)

Marching in Front, I Love it…

It's Saint Nicholas' Day!

All worked up, I get up first because it was agreed that I would ring home. I imagine that everyone there is waiting for the sound of the bell and that the atmosphere in the home around the woman I love and my children is calm. I put the remaining bar of chocolate under my belt; every movement today is much easier. I'm fully confident that we can leave.

At 8 o'clock precisely, little Jasper picks up the phone at Huldenberg; I can hear the excitement behind him. The rest of the family follows suit. The first thing to do is to reassure them because they already know about the accident. I tell Julie what happened; her apparent calm does not conceal her anxiety. The weakness of the battery makes us cut the conversation short. Words can never say enough.

A superb start to the day which will give me wings. With my handicapped status, I have to prove to myself that I can gallantly bear all the pain. The most annoying thing is that I can't find enough oxygen to breathe, which makes every pull on the sledge an anaerobic effort.

When we take a break, I realise that I have not closed the thermos properly; everything has spilled into the sledge, and has of course frozen.

This time I have the impression of being in the middle of the ocean. The play of light and shade undulating between the sastrugis reminds me of the swell of the high tide on a windless day.

It's warm and I have time. Time to be in front, time to see to which side I am going to go…

The scientific part of the Expedition consists, in part, of taking snow samples by means of a column, a procedure known as "carrotage". The sampling was carried out for the ITASE (International Trans Antarctic Scientific Expedition) Project, run by Dr Majewski of the University of New Hampshire.

I cross new snow as I proceed at my own pace. Marching in front, I love it... Whether it's picking ones path across these undulating fields of ice, or crossing the remote valleys of the Himalayas, or finding a way up a rock face, or choosing the itinerary to get to the top, or clearing a way through the maze of compression crests on the ice-field, in short, to have the feeling of being in a universe where I can endlessly draw, feel, decide, force or invent my path.

Dixie is following me as best he can. What courage. This little lad from Huldenberg impresses me greatly.

Our adventure is coming back to life, since in 7 hours we have covered 15.7 km. As if to give a boost to our morale, the Antarctic has allowed us to reach 3000 m in altitude.

In the evening, I make the most of the fine weather to continue the scientific experiment that I started yesterday. The difference being that today the work is entirely different. It's no longer a question of plunging the borer into the snow for collecting samples, but of digging an actual well in the icecap (1.2m by 1.2m by 1.5m deep) so as to achieve a series of measurements and observations about the snow – stratigraphy, temperature, density, size and shape of the crystals. The fundamental difference between the two halves of this scientific mission indicates just how multi-faceted

The scientific mission entrusted to the Expedition by the Laboratory of Glaciology and Environmental Geophysics (LGGE) in Grenoble required a 1.5 m deep pit to be dug in the ice before sampling.

The analysis of the shape and form of the snow crystals collected in the Antarctic was carried out for the European Project on the observation of the snow fields on the polar ice cap, Polar Snow

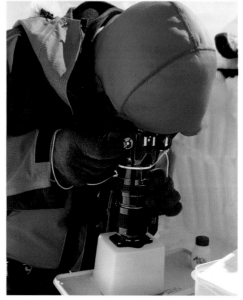

Macro-photography of snow crystal.

glaciology on the continent now is: the samples collected yesterday will help to plot the "climate / isotopic content" relationship, whereas this evening's work (as well as all the other wells that I am going to have to dig as we cross the plateau) will allow the researchers to add these measurements and observations to the data they already have (mainly satellite information) on the subject of the Antarctic snow cover[14].

Towards 23.00h, work finishes with a photo session. Macro photos of snow crystals at 4 different depths (with 7 or 8 different samples at each depth). Once digitised, these slides will serve to show their exact size, shape and characteristics. What is more eloquent, in fact, than a good illustration? But there's a problem, because the macro field always requires an extremely sharp focus – the precision of the observations depends on the precision of the slides. However, the conditions of Antarctic life don't always fit easily with the accomplishment of such meticulous work. Having tackled this problem by trying to find a focal point that wouldn't be disturbed by uncontrolled movements, Denis Dupont and I dreamt up a little technical ruse. Take a Tupperware box, attach it to the macro lens, fix a box to the inside of the lid the height of which corresponds to the required range of focus. All that then has to be done is to place the crystals on the box and to close the Tupperware; the final adjustment is soon made, the camera doesn't move, nor do the crystals of snow, and in this manner one can achieve not only a degree of comfort during the work, but also extremely reliable results in terms of picture sharpness.

All day long I've been promising myself to smoke the cigar that my friend Daniel gave me. So this evening, I indulge. Even Alain, who doesn't smoke, seems to be appreciating the puffs of blue smoke from this sacred weed.

Sunday, 7 December (Day 34)

Where it's a Question of the "Inner Continent"

Sun and a slight breeze this morning, but far away to the north-west the stratocumuli are visible; it's going to become overcast.

Leave at 9.30; the light, three-quarter tail wind encourages Dixie to try the large sail that we still haven't been able to control properly. Without success. To be looked at later, then.

We set off over a fairly regular terrain while the visibility deteriorates; the sky is grey and it's beginning to snow; real December weather back home.

With nothing to look at, I march along for several hours, just paying attention to the tip of my ski stick so as to keep in the right direction.

I love walking. This method of getting about often leads me to the very heart of the universe which I otherwise wouldn't have reached. Here, everything takes its time, the repetitive succession of horizons, the awareness of another dimension of time. The Antarctic is indeed as Jean-Louis Etienne wrote: "*This land of self-discovery through the conquest of the inner continent…*"

It's now nearly ten hours since we left and I still can't see anything because of this damned white-out. My head is spinning, so I stop and put up the tent, while waiting for my pal to arrive, exhausted; the pain in his ribs prevents him from breathing deeply, and that must be really hard when one has to make an effort.

"*At every bump*", he tells me, "*my body asks me what on earth I'm doing to it. It's a bit like having someone sticking a knife into my lungs all the time…*"

Assessment of the day: 18.5 km in 10 hours. So where are the katabatic winds that everybody was talking about?

It's cold this evening and I feel tired. I need to down arms, to feel the stiffness gently invade my body, the weight and the heaviness of my aches and pains, the fatigue; quite simply… I want to be at home, to read, to daydream while looking out of the window, reassured by the purring of the wood burning stove.

Monday, 8 December (Day 35)

We'd be Having a Great Time, if…

The wind changes and brings back the good weather.

Dixie sails off sweetly. I am a little behind, on foot, before following his rhythm.

Aeolus blows all day long; it's the first time we can take advantage of a good katabatic wind. Not too many technical hitches on this 35th day of the expedition, and 38.7 km on the clock in the evening. Our record until now. But because prudence reigns, we don't cry victory too soon.

The 21 sq m sail was the largest traction sail ever made. Without this innovation it is doubtful that an unsupported crossing of the Antarctic could have been possible.

On several occasions the two were obliged to travel at relatively large distances apart. The possibility of losing sight of the other added to the stress of the crossing.

The more so as progress is no longer easy. Firstly, because there are still these sastrugis, higher and lower in different places. Then, we stumble more and more against little walls of fresh snow, (they too formed by the wind, but by the winds of the summer storms and not by the katabatic winds) which cut across the paths of the sastrugis. Imagine how hard it is: each time is as though you were sliding over a water-ski ramp; first it slows you down a bit; then you go up; then jump. At that moment it is as though you're lifted by the power-kite – to come down again a metre further down on the corrugated iron of the sastrugi, which is as hard as concrete. We'd be having a great time, if it weren't for the sledges. But with these loads at our back, what could have been a game is anything but. As you jump, you are first held back by the 180 kilos which are still on the slope behind, then thrust brusquely forward when the sledge resumes its speed as it comes down again. These thumps in the back are not too pleasant, I can assure you… And everything is repeated hundreds, even thousands, of times every day.

Tuesday, 9 December (Day 36)

Oh, Solitude

Suffered from violent pain during the night, so Alain helps me bandage up my ribs. I hear a little cracking sound, a sort of internal rubbing between the bones that I feel when I try to get up and get out of my sleeping bag. I now know that I've got a broken rib. What's more, my back and my lungs hurt as well. There's no point in describing the one thousand and one contortions that I have to go through to be able to resume the position of Homo Erectus.

A few hours of maintenance are required before striking camp. Reinforce the sails because their seams are continuously under pressure. The wind is strong (47 km/h); we have to leave on foot and do an hour on skis before we can again be pulled along by our little pieces of canvas.

A very sticky layer of snow is slowing us down; when faced with a steep slope, we have to pump the sail to make figures of eight with it so as to as to maintain sufficient traction.
For the first time, a wide horizon opens up to the south; this means that we will no longer have to climb up these slopes that are worthy of their name. All the more so as we are about to step foot in Antarctic regions that have been visited only once by man. [15]

What is also frustrating with this mode of progression (after the unpleasantness of negotiating the sastrugis) is that the type of terrain we encounter often means that we have to navigate far apart. This in turn means that we have to deal with problems on our own. We can't communicate by walkie-talkie (the constant need to save energy prevents their being kept on permanent stand-by). Sometimes, these short spells of solitude weigh heavily on us, and it's frustrating not knowing what's happening to the other person. We have to learn to stop getting worked up about it: "Why won't he wait for me?" "Why is he stopping without taking the walkie-talkie?" "Is it serious?" "Should I retrace my steps?" Questions like these no longer get asked.

We join up at 17.30 and finish the day on foot.

A note this evening on our reaction to the high fat diet. We are beginning to realise that we are making a few small mistakes. Either we eat too quickly (rush, stress, cold), or we eat too much (three chocolates instead of one, for example). That said, the concept of polar nutrition as developed for the expedition with the help of the dietician Arnaud Tortel, seems to me to be almost perfect. There are two possible improvements. One: to reduce the morning ration by 150 grams (to eat so much fat early in the morning is not such a good idea). Two: to replace the olive oil (the only oil that freezes at the correct temperature) of the morning ration with sesame oil or a mixture of sesame and rape-seed oils.

Wednesday, 10 December (Day 37)

Even Though I End up in a Cardboard Box…

Yesterday, we only advanced 19 km; there's no doubt about it, we're progressing at a snail's pace. It annoys me a little more each day.

As today there's not much wind, Dixie, who's lighter than I am, is in front again; he has to wait for me at each break. Since I want to go faster, it's now or never for taking the big sail and trying to get it right once and for all. I spend a good half-hour trying different settings. Finally I realise that the front lines have to be shortened by about 30 cm. In other words, change its angle of deployment.

This time it works! I am making good even rapid progress in this light, variable and three-quarter tail wind of between 8 and 12 km/h. It's extraordinary, quite fantastic! My morale shoots sky high. So I was right to have concentrated on this size: perhaps we have here the secret of our success.

In the evening, however, comes the cold shower. Michel, to whom I had announced the good news about the big sail, informs me that we can on no account arrive after 30 January. Nobody is prepared to lend the money for the unavoidable insurance surcharge beyond that date.

The last thing we need right now are money worries? What you don't know, dear co-ordinator, is that, if we make up for lost time before the Pole, we will go on, no matter what the cost. Even if it means selling the little that I own, and ending up in a cardboard box. Today, nobody must get in my way because I'm beginning to feel dangerous.

To hell with HQ! We have enough problems to solve right now, without worrying about what will happen after 30 January. The only way to avoid being distracted from our daily focus of concentration is not to ring Brussels anymore. And from now on to communicate only by e-mail with the laptop. Neither Michel nor the others should be in any doubt as to the hell we're going through.

I nearly forgot: Happy Birthday, Gaëlle!

Thursday, 11 December (Day 38)

Biblical Apparitions

This morning, thanks to a nice little wind, I finally achieve once again the gliding sensation that I had in training. Furthermore, as far as the surface of the ice is concerned, the terrain isn't too bad, and eventually one gets used to the sastrugis. We can pick our

In order to increase the range of wind speeds that could be harnessed, Alain Hubert developed three sizes of sail for the Expedition: 6, 12 and 21 sq. m. This allowed the two to use winds ranging from 7 to 60 km/h for sailing.

way through them better, we more quickly learn how to cross them, we can make out more accurately if they are dangerous or not. In short, practice makes perfect.

However, it's far from nirvana. Even though we're going faster and the body movements are improving all the time, we still keep coming up against those inevitable technical hitches which lead either to halts or to falls. For example, at around noon, when I unstrapped to go to Dixie's aid, we were left standing by impotently before the spectacle of my sledge heading off on the ice by itself. I had made the mistake – to save time and to avoid folding the sail – of attaching it to the shaft. In the early days of the expedition such a mistake would have panicked us. Just imagine if the wind got up suddenly and the pulk disappeared into the distance without our being able to do anything about it; it would have been a disaster. Now, we prefer to have a good laugh at the mishap before deciding to run after the flying sledge. Proof that after 5 weeks spent on this continent, one particular sort of danger has been definitively tamed.

Acquiring a certain kind of ease with our situation also means that we are more relaxed and better able to enjoy the magnificent scenery all about us. Every day I marvel at the thousand and one light forms with which this continent at the end of the earth is inundated. There is, first, the subtle interplay of light and shadow that changes according to the sun's position on its daily circuit. To see the heavenly body follow a radically different course from the one we are used to at our latitude creates a strange impression of closeness to the cosmic elements. It's positioned fairly high in the sky and turns around us following a gigantic circular path which remains at almost the same height above the horizon. Then come the various phenomena of refraction and reflection of the sun's rays by the ice crystals suspended in the atmosphere. The effect is quite simply magnificent. The best known is the "parhelion ring", a white halo around the sun on which streaks of light appear from time to time. Sublime! When you have had the good fortune of observing two aspects of it, one on either side of the heavenly body, you can boast about having seen what is known as the "three suns" – a rare and marvellous manifestation. Other effects come in all shapes and sizes. There are little and large halos, crowns and luminous shafts strangely like the biblical apparitions of popular belief. It's a pity that it's the wrong season for me to be able to witness the always astonishing spectacle of the *aurora australis*. Even though I have more than twenty years' experience in exploring the ends of the earth, I have never seen anything quite like it. Even at high altitude. Here, the sensations provoked by these extra-terrestrial spectacles are not the same as those which rain down on you in the mountains and, most especially, in the Himalayas. At 8,000 m, I am above the clouds, with just a few peaks breaking through, and, even though the air is rarefied and the mind is slow, I often have the feeling of evolving beyond the world of men. Here it is radically different; in the heart of this frozen infinity, I feel myself become insignificant and submerged by the flow of the wind, by the power of these indefinable and changing flashes of light. I lose my bearings. I feel fragile, I begin to doubt myself…

Friday, 12 December (Day 39)

Offering Ones Body to the Snow

The euphoria continues; we have the impression that we are "speed-sailing" on the Belgian coast. Absolutely splendid. Without worries or knocks of any kind, we are advancing on a terrain that is so flat that the speeds achieved make the adrenaline flow; we cover 55.6 km in six hours. You might not think so, but we're making good progress.

I am wondering whether what we saw a little while ago (a gigantic curtain of cloud in the sky around the sun) was in fact a katabatic shelf[16]. Hubert Gallée had described this rare phenomenon to me during a conversation about katabatic wind circulation; perhaps we should have gone there to check whether the atmospheric pressure had dropped sharply (it's one way of measuring a shelf of this kind). That would have been of great interest to him, as he observes and computes phenomena such as this via his mathematical model. But we didn't dare. It should also be said, that as it is always difficult to estimate distance here, we couldn't say if this curious screen was 5 or 20 km off our route. That will just have to remain a mystery.

Among the various refraction and reflection phenomena caused by ice crystals suspended in the atmosphere, the most well-known is the Parahelic Circle, a white halo which surrounds the sun and from which sometimes emanates a strong luminescence.

We have already covered 170 km since the first well; it's time to dig a second for the study of the dynamics of the polar ice-cap[17].

A pleasant routine is setting in: I dig the hole for science, and then take a little walk. I then start making dinner while Alain carries out his observations in the well.

As I often save my cheese ration during the day, I usually let my companion have the benefit of it at aperitif time. A little touch of surrealism; today I present him with the precious cube, with a grain of pili-pili on it, outside where he is working at -30°C, if you please.

The cold is intense, but as I want to celebrate in style our 40th day on the ice (tomorrow), I decide this evening to offer my naked body to the snow.

Saturday, 13 December (Day 40)

Gliding in Wonderland

The azimuth obliges us to head straight into the wind. All the time I have the impression that the horizon is leaning over, but it's obviously an illusion. Materially impossible, but when the body stays bent like this for several hours, the brain tries to create its own logic and the eyes see a false picture. A solid white-out has set in: we can now see hardly anything at all.

Today we reach an altitude of 3,920 m.

60.3 km accounted for in seven hours of travelling. It's the 4th consecutive day that we are *riding* well. From now on this word is part of the jargon of the expedition. "Ride" is not the only word that we have written into the dictionary of the expedition. It now includes "*sharks*" (for the sastrugis) "*ride*" (for making good progress), "*surfing*" (a reference to Dixie's past), "*steer or luff*" (nautical terms for describing manoeuvres

Of the 3924 km comprising the total crossing, 3340 km were covered under sail.

with the sails), "*embark*" for start, "*Jeannine*" (the imaginary owner of the bistro where we take an aperitif when morale is low). This language is not entirely playful: it adds variety to the daily monotony, brings us closer together, creates an intimacy about the adventure by personalising it, making the impossible more accessible.

However, I'm still not satisfied. We are still not advancing quickly enough and the problems with the sails recur too frequently. Dixie doesn't agree with me: he doesn't

Because of their, at times, peculiar shapes which bring to mind terrible predatory creatures, the sastrugis were nicknamed 'The Sharks' by Dixie.

like it when I react in this way. But he of all people ought to appreciate that I have sacrificed one whole year of my life (my professional and my family life) for finalising this project, with all the risks involved. I've dropped practically everything to mount this adventure. What's more, I'm up to my ears in debt. For me this expedition is a mission that has to succeed.

Would I be capable of accepting defeat if we aren't able to make up for lost time?

All these questions clutter up my mind, and it helps to be able to write them down. But the best that could happen to us now is to advance.

ADVANCE! ADVANCE! ADVANCE!

Sunday, 14 December (Day 41)

Little Eaten, Nothing Drunk...

Sunday morning. "Would you go and get the croissants, Alain?"
Just my luck, there are no croissants in Antarctica! Back to reality.
Just a few moments of lazing in bed, but at the first sign of the wind, we're up and ready.
Leave at 9 o'clock with the 21 sq.m. sail. Our initial speed is good despite the snow being a little too soft. We can now control the trajectory of the traction-sails very accurately.
For the first time, I start to "mind-surf"[18] *while proceeding with the sail; it's a kind of day-dreaming that is only possible on a relatively easy terrain.*
With the relaxation of pent-up tensions, playful tendencies are quick to re-exert themselves. We try to cut a few stylish figures and attempt to hand across a piece of chocolate while we ski. Another amusing pastime is to try to get as close as possible without the other realising (not forgetting of course that the sail is always ten metres in front of you) and then playing a dastardly trick on him (suddenly unbalancing his sledge or latching on to him so that he suddenly feels that his brakes are on, or rubbing a lump of snow full in his face). Kids' games...

Seven hours of gliding, and, above all, seven hours without stopping. Our daily average is consistently rising: 70 km. Since the wind is stable and we now seem to be more proficient with the sails, it's best to make the most of it. Too bad then for the regular stops we imposed on ourselves from the beginning of the adventure. For food, we emptied the leftovers that we found in the jacket pockets; a few "pralines" and a piece of chocolate. We drank nothing. We are far too frightened of the technical problems that occur with the kites when we stop. A pity that we can't glide like this for days on end...

It's because we are beginning to tame this confounded big sail. We even allow ourselves the luxury of a few acrobatics; you've got to enjoy yourself, even though it's dangerous. The daily routine is demanding enough as it is.

Some time ago, I talked about the rhythm that transforms the monotony of forward progression into a sort of mantra. Now I add to this threnody of noises that surround us all the time. There's the monotonous crunching of the skis which precedes by just a little the creaking of the joints of the shaft in the connecting coupling of the sledge, which is joined by the constant hammering of the runners on the uneven surface of the sastrugis. A bit like the bogies of a high speed train…

I need very little sleep. In fact; of the 6 to 7 hours that we allow ourselves for rest, I sleep for only 3 or 4 of them. That's enough, however, for a really restorative sleep.

Monday, 15 December (Day 42)

The Mathematical Model was Almost Perfect

From now on, we are employing the technique of starting the power-kites on our own. Being out in front, I have to wait a long time for Alain who must have some kind of problem.

An intense cold starts to pierce me. I turn round again and through the fur-lined collar of my hood I can see that Alain has again mounted the inner tent. Via the walkie-talkie I learn that his frozen fingers are preventing him from solving the problem of the sail and that another half an hour's work is needed.

There's nothing for it, but to try to fight this paralysing cold, I visualise the jottings in my ideas notebook, I chat to myself. A little later, I pull the sail on the ice a bit without paying attention and wham, it's my turn to get it into a tangle. This time it's my companion who has to wait for me.

The day started badly. First I broke one of my lines in trying to fill the sail for the departure, which caused a confusion of knots, which then got tangled up with the suspension lines.

Assessment: an hour and a half of work for undoing all that. If only today the spare sail had been in proper working order! But the problems were soon solved and we were able to weigh anchor, for the second time, at 10.30.

This time we have it; we are off for three hours at great speed: 90 km – incredible. The wind drops a little, and we end up with 101 km for the day. What joy! A new speed record: 33 km/h. We are advancing well! Fantastic! What a performance! What speed! Has anyone ever been so fast on this continent?

The direction of the wind is conforming perfectly to Hubert Gallée's mathematical model[19]. If we continue to match his forecasts, we can begin to believe that we have a very real chance of success. It's encouraging. It opens up whole new perspectives for us.

This evening, we dig the third well. An hour for repairs, and then we can sleep with a feeling of satisfaction from a job well done.

Tuesday, 16 December (Day 43)

According to the Time Clock

A big leap and a false start: the clips joining the shafts of Dixie's sledge to his harness break once again.

Departure at about 9.30 with a more severe wind than yesterday. We often waste time in the morning because we have to repair the attachments which hold the shaft to Dixie's harness. When we were preparing the equipment before the expedition, I opted to use an attachment that easily snaps shut. One of those male / female clips that you often find on sporting gear nowadays. This clip broke, initially, at the time of Dixie's accident. Since then, we do our best to replace it with ropes and snap hooks, as we are doing this morning. If I had thought to bring along some spares, we would have saved a great deal of time. Details, details. Each item, each element can put the whole venture at risk.

> *We are now managing to control every movement of the para-wing. We are as if at one with it. It's still fairly stressful, however, because you have to continuously watch the skis, the sledge and the sail.*
>
> *The enormous attraction that the Pole has over us is extremely motivating. It's a real magnet that makes us completely forget our tiredness. It's as though it's speaking to us: "Come quickly, it's magical here…" In any event, I realise that it's the Pole that will be the deciding factor in the continuation of our adventure.*
>
> *Meanwhile, we're labouring. Little by little, the body weakens, the cold bites a little more deeply, it becomes harder to concentrate. We cheer each other up so that we can do a few more kilometres.*

Unfolding and weighting down the sail before departure.

Only one pause, at about 14.30, brought about by a spectacular fall from our wind-surfing champion. We were a few hundred metres apart when I suddenly noticed that he wasn't moving any more. I was expecting the worst when a phlegmatic voice calmly reassured me: *"Don't worry, man, I only need 15 minutes and we're away."*

We tell ourselves that today we'll advance for ten hours, no matter what the conditions. Almost like civil servants. Sometimes we need to feel like that: subjected to the banality of the time clock. To break up the monotony, I start humming an old country and western tune sung by trekking companions. *"Country road, take me home…"*

We finish the day at about 19.30 and, surprise, when Dixie switches on the GPS he announces 202 km, exactly twice yesterday's distance.

202 km today: 303 km in two days! These figures could give the impression that the going was easy. This would be utterly false. We have had to painstakingly wrench each wretched kilometre away from the Antarctic, keeping an ever a watchful eye on the sail, on the terrain, on the skis, on the sledge (so as not to lose anything), and on the distance between us.

303 km, an average of 78 km a day for a week. Once this hits the Web, (or the press), I can just imagine the speculation that will be raging from Peter to Philip, via Denis, Baldwin, Didier and the others. There will be a lot of talk at the watering holes of the "Commander's" peregrinations around the frozen wastes of the Pole. But wait on, lads, *you ain't seen nothing yet!*

Alain Hubert jots down scientific observations in minute detail.

Wednesday, 17 December (Day 44)

Not Enough Strength for Cleaning the Teeth

We are like two little old men who can only allow themselves, one after the other, to do the same slow things at the beginning of the new day. Then, as soon as it's time to leave, we become like two workers off to start their days' work.

The whole morning goes by as though we were balancing on a billiard table; the terrain is really extremely flat and I'm making the most of it – with relish. Everything here is harmony, and I let myself be overwhelmed by the immensity of it all.

In the afternoon, on the other hand, chaos is back, with snowdrifts in every direction; on this ocean of ice, we are like sailors at the mercy of sharks who keep breaking surface to snap at our sails.

In order to go more quickly, we have decided to pile on the canvas. Make room for the 21 sq.m. monster. We didn't count on the terrain becoming like corrugated iron sheeting, undulating in every direction, with sastrugis from 5 to 30 cm high. They are everywhere. Everywhere. EVERYWHERE!

As our sails are not at full stretch (the wind is more or less behind) and our feet are unable to put lateral pressure on the skis, we have to do a balancing act all the time. Without mentioning that the skis have a tendency to go off sideways, nor the lack of visibility caused by the mask misting up, nor the strain on the legs toiling all the time without enough oxygen. To give them some relief, I switch to using skating steps. This rhythm carries me off to the Jura with Pierre and Fofo for our ritual winter get-togethers, those long walks where sometimes we surprised ourselves by executing some real balletic moves.

The day ended prematurely because I tried to get too close to our Flemish friend from Huldenberg to tease him a little. Result: a nice collection of knots, and extra work in the evening.

At 23.30, after an interminable session of polar sewing, I don't even have enough energy left for cleaning my teeth. A short day with 91 km on the clock.

Friday, 19 December (Day 46)

Heading East

The wind is strong. As yesterday, we set off with the smallest sail. Are we set for an incident-free day?

My team-mate, who is clearly still in considerable pain, doesn't seem to be confident in his actions. He's not able to get his sail completely above his head so that it doesn't pull too hard; the manoeuvre hurts his ribs too much. On several occasions I can hear him talking to his sail. Is the monk becoming a pagan?

When we make a sail-change, I have to take the 6 sq.m. sail again, despite my fear, and for the first time since the day it had the wild idea of making me fly through the air. I talk to it now. Whenever I detect the slightest hint of anger, I calm it down with encouraging words as if I was coaxing a team of horses.

That doesn't prevent it from bringing me to my knees today. I fall heavily, my head hitting the ice. The brain is shaken up and I become distracted. Hard, too hard!

And then the wind turns to a storm; the only way of proceeding with the kites is to let them fly high above our heads. But when I do that, the belt of the harness squashes my lower ribs, exactly where it still hurts a great deal.

At times such as these I think of the little note-book with the jottings of my family and friends, and I conjure up some of their words. That does me a power of good. With the feeling of being loved, of having a home and everything I need to be happy, the effort and the suffering become easier to bear. An expedition such as this intensifies these feelings, makes you want, makes you achieve.

Suddenly, we decide to let ourselves drift eastwards to avoid having to stop to change the sails. Steering is difficult, scant visibility because of the huge snowfields, difficult terrain… Routine stuff. But technical hitches are also, inevitably, routine. A moment's inattention sends my suspension lines into the jaws of a shark, obliging me to take the spare sail. Dixie, for his part, puts a 40-cm tear in his sail on another sastrugi. But luck still seems to be smiling on us; we have in fact swallowed up 76 km in ten hours.

Fifth well dug this evening.

It's 23.15 when we go to sleep on our sails, totally exhausted. My God, the days are long!

Saturday, 20 December (Day 47)

It's It or Me

I notice that for some days now we've been in a part of the world where no man has ever set foot. What a privilege. I feel here a strange connection with the forces of nature. Where does such perfection come from? The Yin and the Yang: life has need of death…

We don't sleep much but I'm on form. The weather is fine and the tail wind is promising; now I hope I can get out the large sail.

Leave at 11.30. Or rather attempt to leave. Dixie has already gone on, slowly, so as not to put too much distance between us. I put some snow on the large sail before finishing my harnessing and offering it up to the wind. I fill it up. It climbs, revealing what we are always afraid of at this moment – a knot. The lines are crossed just before the suspension cone. The sail is "steerable", certainly, but I'm not prepared to leave like that. The rubbing of the ropes would soon have broken a line.

A hitch, due to some bad folding the evening before or to the mood of the sail? In any event, this is now the third day running that I haven't been able to set off correctly. It's difficult to imagine how frustrating it is to be held up in this way each morning.

It's too much. Furious, I open the safety hook that holds the sail. Released from its tension, it dies a death a few metres further on, inevitably increasing the collection of knots. I should have realised. But at times like this one doesn't think. In the heat of the moment, I forget to warn Dixie by radio, convinced that things will be all right in a few minutes. Outside, with the temperature at −50°C, I get it into my head to untangle it all as rapidly as possible.

Obstinate as I can be at times, remorselessly pitting myself against the nylon, cursing against the rest of the universe, fuming for not being able to set off sooner, furious for having let go of this stupid son of Icarus, disheartened by seeing Dixie already so far in front, I fulminate. How can I explain why this morning it should be completely tangled up when yesterday evening I had folded it away so carefully? I rail against this sea of snow, with its infuriating drifts, and revile the accursed katabatic winds. For more than ninety minutes I struggle to remedy the situation. Normally, you have to protect yourself from the cold, first, with a thin pair of gloves, one or two pairs of mittens (one for walking, two for sailing), and a pair of outer wind-proof mittens in the event of storms or when steering the kites. You almost always keep the first pair on. But when you have to work with bare hands, as is the case this morning for undoing these recalcitrant knots in lines which are barely one millimetre in diameter, it all depends on the conditions in which you have to work. If you are hot, as you would be after several hours of walking, you can easily stand working without gloves for a few minutes because the circulation is intense in the extremities of the limbs. When you have to face up to unforeseen situations of survival, the body seems to forget the cold and adrenaline kicks in to help prevent frostbite. But starting off cold in the morning, your fingers are guaranteed to be numb with cold, and as hard as concrete. You are forced to stop everything you're doing and warm them up again until you feel powerful pins and needles, a sure sign that circulation is returning.

That's of course what's happening to me this morning, even having to put on gloves when it wasn't a question of untangling in the true sense of the word, making sure to keep my back to the wind and frequently warming my fingers. A hell that lasts 50 minutes before getting this confounded contraption back to rights and, hitched up once again, ready to leave. Just as the sail begins to take the wind, the security hook fails … and the sail is tangled up again.

No! No! This is unacceptable!

It's now become personal; it's me or it. IT OR ME.

I at last think to notify my companion who suspects that I must be fighting with the sail. He tries vainly to reassure me and urges me to join up with him and to take the spare from his sledge. "That's what it's there for, for God's sake!".

Too late, it's become a matter of self-esteem. I will fight to the death to bring this piece of fabric into line, I'm the boss here, for heaven's sake! The fate of the expedition is hanging on this sail. It's the only one that can get us through. Suddenly, the enormous pressure of this madness wells up, the thousands of hours of preparation, the debts, and the doubts... The combat is rejoined, more earnestly this time. But right now I'm too cold, and I sense that I'm going to lose the battle. I finally have to face the facts, and I collapse on to the sledge with hot tears springing from my eyes.

Dixie is frozen stiff when I rejoin him. He must be furious...

The wind having increased in the meantime, I take his big sail; he, the medium. Leave at 13.30! What a waste of time. It takes me more than two hours of concentration on my breathing and on sliding before I regain my calm.

Later: on a becalmed sea, two sails drift in silence...

Assessment: one fit of rage, 44 km, the thirteenth core boring, a double ration of "Gras du Valais" at aperitif time. And, as always, the knots.

This morning, the Walloon seems to be having a problem with his sail. Technical hitch, nothing new, these things happen all the time. Even from afar I can see that he's getting upset. It's clearly not possible for me to go back, so the radio is the only means of contact. He'll switch it on soon.

But no, nothing but silence. For a whole hour I try to keep a grip on myself. I'm cold. The uncertainty is unbearable. "Call, Alain, call!".

Suddenly I see his sail climb, jump and then quickly subside: his quick-release must have opened.

Damn! I gesture with my walkie-talkie. When at last we are in contact, I suggest that he takes the spare sail, but he won't hear of it.

I can guess at his rage and powerlessness from the sound of his voice. He is angry with the sail, is personifying it, he wants his tenacity to win the day. But in the end a sail is only an inanimate object, it's a thing, it's we who animate it with the wind. It is only matter, it has no soul, and we surely aren't going to let it aspire to our level.

That's really stupid, we really can't allow ourselves to give way to such fits of temper. That's not at all the way to succeed...

It's hard to stop myself from telling him off. I understand that today we are going to need lashings of tolerance and understanding for each other.

After twenty or so minutes, he gives up and rejoins me.

Monday, 22 December (Day 49)

Magic? Yes and No...

In the Antarctic, everything has to be foreseen. In the Antarctic, nothing can be foreseen. Can you understand that? I can't. Or rather, only a little. But even so, I try to explain it. The master of the place, the wind, is completely unpredictable, as we have long since come to understand. Raging at 2 o'clock, it can fade away to nothing a couple of minutes later. Within half an hour, the horizon, which can be seen to be clearing, can be drowned by a white-out. While being incapable of accomplishing the slightest project, one must nevertheless be ready for anything, to have in one's head a packet of solutions taking all the uncertainties of the terrain, the equipment and the weather into consideration.

This morning, we hurried to make the most of the wind that appeared to be good. As we got up, the forward horizon formed a gradation between the sky and the ice. An indistinct area which indicates that a few banks of driven snow were on their way, perfect for feeding a good katabatic: stable, laminar and not too strong. It's truly the only Antarctic wind that can be called gentle and even pleasant. When it's around in the morning, it obliges the naïve to believe that an excellent day lies ahead. It's a pleasure to fill your lungs. It's something that caresses, invigorates and puts you into a good mood. With it, the world opens up little by little, is recreated, becomes marvellous... A hell of a magician... Ah, this seven-week experience of the ice that makes one puff out ones chest and believe that one can foretell the weather. No way!

Without our knowing why, towards noon, the haze on the horizon has disappeared, in less than thirty minutes. No word of warning, and no clues to explain this change in the weather. At once, almost no more wind, just a patch of cirrus that appears in the sky. Inexplicable.

Six hours of sail and four on foot; 22.5 km plus 8.7 km equals 31.2 km.

The day before yesterday, as I was re-stitching my sail in the evening, I fell asleep. A sign of tiredness? That's why I wasn't embarrassed at having slept a little longer than usual. The bow can't be kept at full stretch all the time...

I think about the circles of Zen that try to reach the strength of the void. On a flight to Japan, I was attracted by Zen Buddhism. In Tokyo, a Japanese family welcomed me into their home, and I used to spend the day with them in the Sonjiji temple at Yokahama. A veritable haven of peace, silence, serenity and meditation. Conversation with the Zen Master in a bare room with creaking floorboards, peaceful colours bringing together the four quarters of the temple, sobriety in these spaces of water, stone and wood, serenity of the students with their long, black robes... The magic of these happy moments!

The South Pole is coming slowly nearer. I'm curious to know how man has managed to install a permanent base in such a hostile land. Summer begins here today. At home, it's deepest winter.

Tuesday, 23 December (Day 50)

From high in his Isba, *Lenin looks towards Moscow*

Let's not mince words: we are not a little proud this morning. Proud of belonging from now on to the distinguished group of people who have come near to the Pole of Inaccessibility – just twenty or so men at the most. We are now only 400 km away from this mythical place, the furthermost point from the Antarctic coasts, where there is still a miniature Russian station established on the occasion of the International Geophysics Year of 1957–58 and abandoned donkeys' years ago[20]. It seems to be a sort of *isba*, flanked with an arthritic derrick and topped by a bust of Lenin, looking towards Moscow. If we had deviated from our route, we would have had the privilege of adding our signatures to the golden book that is still there to this day.

This is also an important stage in the expedition. For several days now we have been losing altitude. So we are certain that the highest point of the itinerary is behind us. Even though we can't feel it in our daily progress, we know that from now on we will be beginning a gentle descent towards the South Pole. We will no longer be having to drag these confounded sledges upwards, but rather downwards.

Psychologically, that's a fabulous touch of the whip!

What's more, we've now reached the 50th day of the adventure. Half the time envisaged: 100 days to commemorate the 100 years since *The Belgica*, the schooner on board which the Belgian explorer Adrien de Gerlache and a team of scientists were the first to successfully confront the terrible austral winter. 100 days of food, as well. If we have already consumed 50 days of rations, that means that the sledges are 60 kg lighter! Simply saying that they are lighter makes them even lighter still… It's an inescapable fact, less effort will be required from now on.

We have consumed half the provisions without having covered half the distance. There is no further communication except via Argos beacon messages that Michel must decipher as best he can. In any event, we calculate that we are still 870 km from the Pole.

For Alain, this expedition is very psychologically demanding. For he has to bear all the weight of uncertainty about the outcome of the project on his own. What will happen if we cannot go further than the Pole? Exactly what are the financial extras demanded by the insurance company if we go beyond 30 January? To have organised an adventure such as this on his own, as he has, is a task of superhuman proportion, which merits the respect that I feel for him.

On 23 December Alain and Dixie approached within 400 km of the Pole of Inaccessibility (see note 20). The bust of Lenin faces towards Moscow.

Wednesday, 24 December (Day 51)

The Angels' Share

We are getting up earlier and earlier; today, it's only 4.30 when we leave the sleeping bags. Less than two hours later, we're on our skis and under the great spread of canvas. As the wind is pretty poor, we have to work to increase the effective traction with our arms (in effect, to make large "eights") so as to advance a little. By manoeuvring the sail in its window of flight, one increases the effective wind. Very quickly, Dixie is nothing more than a speck on the horizon. The "featherweight" makes better progress than the "heavyweight", of course.

In getting up so early, I had hoped to make a good day for celebrating Christmas beyond 83°S. However, there is, effectively, no longer a puff of wind. The sun is over-powering and the immobility frightening. Dixie is waiting for me. I've had enough. I stow the sail and walk.

But I want to make progress. In the Polar Regions, one tries to march in one's shadow to follow the right direction according to the heading given by the position of the sun at a given time of day. But it's impossible, or at least too difficult, because we are going in a southerly direction and our shadow gets longer behind us throughout the day. So I seek out landmarks to help me tame this milky infinity. From far off, I fix my eye on a chosen point. A mound, a group of sastrugis more prominent than the others, a different undulation in the ice, a particular shimmering, a black line… It's an arduous task, because just a split second of inattention and you can lose your bearings. So I have to concentrate and forget everything which could come to disturb the ritual.

Alain, during a pause.

Forget the pain, forget the weight of the sledge, forget the equipment, the effort, the cold. Even forget the wind. Then another cosmos opens up within me. Little by little the landmark gets closer. I begin to recognise it; I even give it a name, I humanise it, I sing it, I transcend it. Not for long, however. Because one has to pick a new target, preferably in line with the first. And so on for hours. Ceaselessly abandoning the objective without having reached it. This is coming close to meditation.

During the stop I like to turn round and contemplate the work that I've just achieved: my tracks. When they are perfectly straight and melt away into infinity, (proof that I've performed well), the feeling that comes over me is something close to ecstasy. Is that over the top? It must seem ridiculous to philosophise in this way about simple impressions left in the snow. But it's my way of reminding myself what I am: a few specks of dust on this earth. The ephemeral beauty of the tracks. To make tracks to become tracks, nothing more than tracks. That's one answer, among many, to those who ask why I throw myself into such mad escapades.

Dixie and his improvised storm mask.

That's three hours of forced march. I must have reached the 20 km that I swore I would cover today. The most astonishing thing is that at the end of the day I stop, from instinct, without having taken the slightest GPS reading. Dixie, arriving a little later, says: *"Alain, we've done 20.6 km!"*

The boss has already mounted the tent and welcomes me warmly when I arrive more than an hour later. He's already had a nap. All that remains for us to do is to dig the well, take the measurements and the samples to bring the work aspect of the day to an end.

I take a quick shower in the snow, slip into the tent with frozen hair and start to prepare the Christmas dinner. On the menu: Gras de Valais *with pili-pili for the apero,* consommé de pois de Périgord avec jambon de Strasbourg, *mashed potatoes with olive oil and essence of mustard-flavoured pemmican suffused with diced peppers. It being a feast day, we allow ourselves a sumptuous dessert: cream of black chocolate and nuts, Julie's biscuits and a surprise for Alain (which I had kept hidden until now) – a small bottle of Cognac accompanied by a delicious Havana. The whole is served on the box of the stove, draped with a tiny Belgian flag. Afterwards, some animated games of cards until midnight: the moment I'd been waiting for to open, at last, the Christmas card from Julie. "Focus, Dixie".*

Thursday, 25 December (Day 52)

A Christmas Gift

"Everything comes to those who wait". I was waiting yesterday for a Christmas Eve gift from heaven: it arrives today.

"Dixie, do you think there is any wind?"; it's the ritual question early each morning. Affirmative. Good! That's good news indeed. Which leads us to decide to make up for yesterday's poor average.

In more favourable conditions the sail is more stable and can therefore pull more strongly and more quickly without going out of shape. On this flat terrain, we have reached 45 km/h, which gives us a very strange feeling. But at regular intervals the sastrugis reappear, which of course slow us down again. No matter. After 10.5 hours of sailing we have covered 128 km across some of the worst terrain yet encountered. A pause for self-congratulation!

If the physical effort has been hard throughout this day, it was, above all, the cold that was difficult to bear. The difference between the two? Physical effort can be controlled, rationed, even transcended. The cold, no. Here it's as omnipresent as the air we breathe. At any moment it can summon its allies (the wind, the dryness of the air, the disappearing sun, the night) to complete its work of undermining us. The Antarctic cold stings like nowhere else; it gnaws, pinches, stretches and tears the skin. It burns naturally, blackening the ends of the limbs like the plague; it has the power to put one to sleep like a slow hypnosis. Moreover, nothing gets in its way; it infiltrates everywhere. One only needs a zip to be left open and it's there surging through the forgotten breach. Even the skin around the nail and the cuticles is often torn, and bleeding, which hurts enormously at the slightest touch, which obliges one to put some grease and bandages on every day. Another illustration? The tip of the nose slowly whitens, becoming nearly transparent, as though on the point of decomposing. Sometimes, the cheeks freeze and then peel. But as far as we're concerned, it's the hands that suffer most of all. Despite five pairs of gloves, one has to wiggle ones fingers all the time when they are fixed either on the sail tillers or on the ski sticks. In short, even though one obeys all the rules, there's no way of avoiding it. For, on top of everything else, the intense cold stops one thinking clearly, it increases tenfold the effort required, it dilates time. All this is clearly not so easy to live with. The daily round of the Antarctic forces one to remain in a constant state of alert. A quarter of an hour of inattention could be fatal.

This evening, there are 727 more kilometres to the Pole; I'm almost certain that we'll reach it in early January.

Friday, 26 December (Day 53)

Martin

The atmospheric conditions in Antarctica change rapidly. As we get up, the wind is promising an excellent day (22 km/h). Two hours later, when we weigh anchor, it changes completely, clouds invade the sky and visibility drops to 100 metres. A pale light gives the waves of ice an eerie look and the suspension lines of the kites are covered by millions of snow crystals, like dewdrops. A superb yet fleeting moment of happiness: then the forced labour to which we are sentenced calls us to order. I don't know why, but when I experience a few seconds of pure ecstasy like this, I feel terribly alone and incapable of sharing – or describing – the anxiety that comes over me. As if all the barriers are closed, the signals become mute, the senses turn in on themselves…

We find ourselves suddenly surrounded by a bank of wet fog creating a fairylike atmosphere. Spectral vision. Turning round, I can't see Alain. Alone. All alone.
What should I do if I get lost? Do I have all I need in the sledge to go on alone? Clearly not: Alain has the tent and other indispensable items. And for survival? Perhaps… I catch a glimpse of imaginary black points that disappear when I try to get a fix on them. This blasted fog is dangerous.
I watch out for Alain's arrival. The wait seems to last forever. At last his silhouette emerges from the white-out. We tell each other that we must be completely mad to allow ourselves to get so far apart.

Luckily this morning I draw the word "Martin". He has been accompanying me like a fleeting shadow in the bosom of this isolation. *"How's life, son? One day, when I'm back, we could discuss your sastrugis and mine. You're progressing, you too, with a resolute step towards your horizons. The terrain doesn't matter provided the energy is there. Have a good journey, my boy, I'll get on with mine. I entrust these few words for you to the wind…"*.

8 hours on the road, 84 km, another well dug. We have just crossed 84°S.

Saturday, 27 December (Day 54)

Huldenberg – Ostend and Back

93.8 km a little further south.

For the first time, Dixie appears to be convinced of the successful outcome of the project when he announces enthusiastically: *"There is now only twice the journey from my little village to the Belgian coast and back between the Pole and us, that's a good point of reference. That particular trip I know by heart as I've had to make it so many times during my wind-surfing competitions."* What I find reassuring today is that I can feel him letting go, dropping his scepticism and joining his confidence in our success with mine. Even though we each have our own individual apprehensions about Polar life, it's essential to join up now and again to experience that sense of connivance that strengthens team spirit.

We immediately attack the slope next to yesterday's camp. The sastrugis are more numerous. Without respite, we have to cross them at an angle of 30°: so there's no question of letting oneself go. We have to pick the best path, surf the waves and traverse these long rounded bands of softer snow that criss-cross between the snowdrifts all the time.

Measuring the density of the snow in the sampling pits.

A sort of game develops between the ice and me as I'm absorbed in the action; I can feel it invade me, speak to me, guide me. Instinctively, I trust it.

When I lift my head, I get a feeling of intoxication from the elusive light suffusing the horizon, a fleeting impression of having access to renewed consciousness. How many times today, as I lay the sail down in the wind, have I seen it snapped up by a sastrugi, entangled, *entrammelled,* as we call it? How many times has my sledge gone off with the sail as though wanting to go on without me, telling me perhaps that we weren't going fast enough?

How we've laughed out loud in these slapstick situations. I've even been turned upside today, held by my titanium harness, with my legs caught under the sledge. These minor mishaps are now part of everyday life. They intersperse the days, punctuate our progress and help pass the time, which seems long, very long, often too long…

Sunday, 28 December (Day 55)

One Hell of an Average

It's not until 23.00 that I can finally open my logbook; in the appropriate columns I write 89.9 km, 8 hours and 15 minutes. That makes nearly three weeks now that we are proceeding at an average of 80 km per day; is our expedition about to become a story of trains arriving on time? And to think that Michel had predicted this improvement during a recent contact some two weeks ago. I had thought it was just wishful thinking on his part.

Outside, the wind's quietened down a bit, but it was still blowing at 55 km/h. I would never have thought it possible to use the sails in such conditions and over such a difficult terrain. Now we are beginning to feel certain that we will reach McMurdo. We are convinced, in effect, that from now on nothing can stop us.

Monday, 29 December (Day 56)

Crash!

We got off to a bad start this morning. To avoid lagging behind and seeing Dixie always in front, I wanted to take the intermediate sail, the 12 sq.m. But very soon a suspension line got caught up with a shark and I found myself having to undo a large number of knots. As I had attached the sail to the sledge, the latter once again went off without me. After recovering it by running after it as though it were a tram, I yawed twice. At once, four suspension lines were cut clean through by the edges of one of my skis. So I got out the spare sail. Only to find that it was badly rigged. I don't know why. To avoid wasting too much time, I borrowed Dixie's and we set off again.

But after an hour's gliding, the wind got up again. With too much canvass up, I no longer felt comfortable. Stress from the gusts of wind, fear of falling, a ski binding that was in danger coming off. I often found myself panting, having great difficulty in breathing without ever being able to stop.

At 3 o'clock, I was caught out twice, in quick succession, by two unusually treacherous snowdrifts. Another collection of knots. We decided to stop; and we had to dig another well.

I really don't know why but as I unstrapped myself, I was fuming. I kicked my sledge up its backside and yelled at it soundly, and threw away one of my skis where the binding had been causing a lot of trouble today.

Once again, Dixie didn't appreciate this. I knew that he found reactions such as these destabilising, and he was less and less prepared to tolerate my fits of temper. But I made amends with him by explaining that I needed to exteriorise my anger. From now on we had better try to keep a tight rein on Old Man Hubert.

Tuesday, 30 December (Day 57)

Happiness has no History

Slow start, slight breeze, big sail, we head east to harness a better wind.

Ten hours on the boards with just one stop to have a drink. The terrain seems to be getting easier, as we had been told. How seldom do you find flat calm days like this. But how lovely they are also. For we proceed at much the same speed as the wind. At a constant speed. Without breakdown, without falling over, without bumping into snowdrifts and without much physical pain. I start to imagine an uneventful crossing, a long glide over a smooth flat terrain, laminar winds arriving on time, according to the mathematical model… But I don't think that we have come this far in search of an easy life…

Assessment of the day; a few laconic words to say that we have covered a trifling 124 km! Decidedly, happiness is a thing of the moment.

Wednesday, 31 December (Day 58)

The Dead Polar Explorers Society…

It's New Year's Eve and we are 188 km from the Pole. We have crossed the 88th degree latitude south.

For me, it's a frontier, a mythical circle. That goes for the North as well as the South, moreover.

Here in the south we have the memory of the Irishman, Ernest Shackleton, who organised the first expedition to the Pole in January 1909, but who had to turn back (for lack of victuals) just 180 km from his goal. At the other end of the globe, in the North, the 88th degree sees a good many expeditions having to turn back. As happened on three occasions to the British explorer Ranulph Fiennes.

As for me, this circle reminds me, above all, of one of the most surprising sights that I have ever witnessed, which occurred during my expedition with Didier Goetghebuer to the North Pole. We were proceeding along a huge inland sea that was barely frozen. The dark ice was sparkling with thousands of snow crystals. In the distance, black plumes of smoke were sitting majestically above a polynya, and the sun in the background gave these mists a totally surrealistic appearance.

Here and now, is the 88th degree once again going to seem like a critical threshold, a change of fortune? I hope so. For the summary of what we have been able to achieve in the previous weeks is not brilliant; one month ago I almost died, Dixie cracked his ribs on the ice, we experienced serious problems with the sledges and we were hardly making any progress. Long periods of doubt had gnawed at the entrails of the expedition. But we would love that to change. Crossing over into this circle could act as a trigger for the definitive extraction of this adventure from the infernal downward spiral that it had got sucked into. *"Dante, friend Dante, is this the last circle of hell? Are you at last promising us purgatory?"* For my part, I believe so. For a few hours, I have had the impression of emerging from the darkness, of at last being carried along by this continent that until now has been so hostile. In any event, there are a few clues pointing in that direction.

Firstly, the snow: for a few days now, it is less hard. Then the terrain; oh miracle, is getting flatter, smoother, easier, less terrifying. The frightening areas of snowdrifts seem to have disappeared. No more waves, the sea is calm. Lastly, the technique; we no longer have any problem getting started with the sails. In short, crossing this frontier strengthens my belief that the most painful hours of this adventure are, from now on, part of what I would dare to call ancient history. Naturally, such a climate of confidence and optimism encourages a degree of unwinding. A moment ago, between 2 and 3 o'clock I think, I was surprised to find myself skiing with my eyes shut.

A few seconds later, without any communication between us, Dixie and I simultaneously unfurl the big sails. As though to say: *"Here we are at the pivotal point of our crossing, we must ward off fate and show the 88th degree that we recognise it, and that by raising sail we pay homage to its existence."* Stationary, we each take separate bearings on a black cloud sitting above the horizon. I am certain that Dixie, just as I do, believes that it's an indication of the route to follow. Our senses alert, we listen to the crushing silence that is hardly troubled by the soft trembling of the sails. A few days ago we would have again cursed the white-out that suddenly covers this part of the icecap. Today, our good humour gets us intoxicated on this white fog that comes to welcome us, as if we are

When the wind was not strong enough or was too violent, progress was by ski: 500 km were covered in this fashion.

about to enter one helluva no man's land, and that on the inside, we will find the planet in a state of lethargy, which I would like to call the sleep of the earth.

> *The little morning breeze was barely enough to pull us forward. At a certain moment I decide that it doesn't matter any more, and stretch out on the sledge in a pique. I think of Julie, whom I miss terribly. Ah, love… A few sweet moments of lassitude.*
>
> *But I quickly stand up again reminding myself of our mantra, the "kick in the butt". With the firm will to awaken Aeolus. Slowly I begin to resume my dialogue with the sail, the sledge, the wind, the snow and the ice. I forget my frozen feet. Being continuously chafed by the strap of the harness, my buttocks have become totally numb; I can no longer feel the contact between my fingers and the steering tillers.*
>
> *At the end of the day, I take a crazy delight in slaloming between the sastrugis, from now on less frequent. I string together a series of gibes to remind myself of the pleasure of sail-boarding. Pure sensuality of gliding. I feel on top form, and I let myself drift off into daydreaming in the encroaching white-out. Who are we in this hostile universe? Nomads? Migrating animals? Or just clouds driven by the wind?!*

Celebrating New Year's Eve in their own inimitable style – the iceman cometh.

As they approached the South Pole the surface of the ice cap became even more even.

On this New Year's Eve I want to do something futile; so I cut a pile of blocks of ice to build a snowman, an old project concocted before I left.

Thursday, 1 January (Day 59)

Home Sweet Home…

You're not aware of it, daughter of mine, but, at dawn on this New Year's Day, I'm taking you with me on this adventure to the Pole. It's fate that has decided it, because I don't know if she has told you, but your Mother has given me a pleasant surprise by writing down one hundred words for me, one for each day.

Today it was your turn; I drew "Gaëlle". So here we are together for this frugal breakfast. Like at home. Rather than helping yourself from your own plate, you naturally prefer to pick at mine, and of course, Dixie's, maintaining all the while that you're not hungry. To imagine you in my company for this first meal of the year gives this moment a particular flavour, with its mixture of generous and tender laughter and ironic or angry outbursts. And, I want to tell you that today really was "the super gas". We comfortably exceeded 45 km/h on several occasions. Do you realise? To go so rapidly in the Antarctic? We've covered nearly 125 km in all, but only 100 in a straight line for the Pole. Add to that the traction exercises with the sails, made necessary by the katabatic wind being so weak, and you'll know that your old man has had a spell of serious training for his next climbing season.

During breaks, wind conditions permitting, they had only to lower the sails onto the ice.

Friday, 2 January (Day 60)

The Pole is the Goal

We are 91 km from the Pole! Fantastic!

At this rate of progress we should reach our goal today. At least if the Antarctic allows us to. But that's thinking like an earthling, which of course is not appropriate; firstly, because this 2 January is one of the coldest days that we have experienced (the temperature fell to minus 40°C!) and secondly, because a fog that you could cut with a knife has settled on today's route. It is so thick that during the last ten hours of gliding I had the impression of moving around on the inside of a thick white wall. Like the prisoner of a shroud that was mysteriously travelling at the same speed as us.

Result: we have had to set up camp 19 km from the Pole. In fact, it's perhaps not such a bad thing to be held up in our impatience and obliged to make a halt just a stone's throw from the place that I've dreamt so much about. In any event it allows us to cool our heels for a few more hours, to maintain the suspense. How is the huge dome that I've seen in all the photos of the Pole going to look? Is a second camera waiting for us there (ours isn't working any more and I had asked Michel to send us a new one)? How are we going to be received? Will we have a guided tour of the place? Or will we be politely requested to continue on our way?

Relations between the private expeditions that come to the continent for adventure and the personnel of the scientific bases who are stationed there throughout the year are not always cordial. The Antarctic researchers' community has been obliged, on several occasions, to go to the aid of people in distress. Now, forewarned, the scientific community regards with a jaundiced eye the fact that their logistics (so expensive to maintain at these latitudes) should be compromised by the imprudence of a few rash tourists. Since then, thanks to the professionalism of polar tourism and the introduction of mandatory insurance cover, their intervention has become increasingly rare. But, for the researchers and especially for the authorities in charge of managing the international Antarctic agreements, polar explorers are still partly considered as tourists.

This evening, it's not so much the reception that's concerning me (because we could always decide to go on without stopping), but the wild desire (Dixie too, I think) to send an e-mail to HQ (I suppose it's possible from the Pole) to announce that nothing can stop us now. And that McMurdo is well and truly the final port of call for the expedition. The most dangerous part of the itinerary is now behind us, and of the 4,000 km of the crossing only 1800 remain. And despite the breakages and the obligatory daily maintenance sessions, the equipment hasn't suffered too much. At least, it's now well run in (to put it mildly) and in good condition. Moreover, information to hand on the route ahead (since it has already been followed on several occasions, initially by the famous Amundsen) leads us to believe that the risks that we still have to run down there are far less than those to which we have already been exposed on the first part of the expedition. In fact, this last part of the itinerary is made up of three parts. The first, from the Pole to the Trans-Antarctics, the chain of mountains that cuts the continent in two; it's the polar icecap, and, as far as the terrain is concerned, we cannot possibly find anything worse than we have found already. The second, the Axel Heiberg Glacier, which of course has to be negotiated with care; no problem either, I have experience of this kind of terrain. The last section is the Ross Ice Shelf – a floating platform of ice as big as France; a course reputed to be "easy" because this type of terrain, we're told, is less subject to surface formations – I should say deformations – caused by the katabatic winds. When I visited Børge Ousland in Norway before setting out, we talked about this. According to him, the Ross Ice Shelf doesn't present too much of a problem. In 1997, at the time of his solo venture, he took about 15 days to cross it (he had chosen the Amundsen route) of which two days were stationary because of a white-out. So these last 960 km shouldn't be too much of a problem for us either.

We're getting through the hours, but after today's first 40 km the going has been very slow, too slow. At the moment when we're calculating whether it's still worth while trying to reach the station this evening at any cost – it must be about 18.30 and the mercury is showing −27°C – I make out a black speck on the horizon. It's the Pole! Or at least the buildings of the Amundsen Scott station. There can't be more than 25 km to go! Softly, I say to myself: "The South Pole at last! The lowest point on Earth, the myths, the history…". I smile at the idea of a little Dansercoer walking upside down on the globe, like the lamppost lighter of the Little Prince.

Rejoicing at the sudden feeling that there are other human beings around, just a few kilometres away, my tiredness melts like snow in the sun. I beseech the heavens for a little wind. Just enough for us to fly to that little black speck.

Saturday and Sunday, 3–4 January (Days 61 and 62)

Hi Guys!

We get up early. With the South Pole as the focal point, we are evidently impatient to set off. The weather isn't too bad this morning; it's overcast with a light fog that sifts the light. As for the wind, it's blowing at about 15 km/h; just enough to clear away from our harnesses the thin covering of fresh snow that fell in the night. As soon as the sails are hoisted 15 metres from us in the sky, we ski in silence towards the black speck positioned like a pebble on the horizon.

A quarter of an hour after we strike camp, a first dark mass breaks through the fog; this rudimentary group of huts must surely be an experimental seismic station or something of the kind. Outside there remains an old arthritic snow-cat, straight out of

Alain and Dixie reached the South Pole on 3 January 1998 at 4.00 pm after 61 days on the ice.

the 50's. Could this place be inhabited? And if someone were suddenly to come out? He could think he was hallucinating in front of these two winged phantoms that have arrived from nowhere.

The second sight that we have of the South Pole is of wooden stakes embedded in the ice a few dozen metres apart from each other. Attached to them are pennants that seem from afar to show the way to go; they're probably beacons; we're on the road to the Pole! Some follow the main road, while others leave the track, rather like motorway exits, to lead either to an old bulldozer abandoned there, heaven knows why, or towards an isolated hut or research site. We can see all around, here and there, wooden sledges, aerials, skiddoos, measuring instruments and so on, on what must be the Royal Route towards the dome.

It's reassuring, all that. I put the GPS into my pocket – don't need it any more. Follow the pennants, we only have to let ourselves glide, slaloming between the beacons.
A few minutes later, we suddenly see a Hercules C130. It's cutting across our path going to the

The Belgians put up their tent, a stone's throw from the American Amundsen Scott Base, at the South Pole.

left. Since we are sure that we are going the right way, we tell ourselves that it's about to take off; but not at all, the monster's about to land!

It's scarcely believable, a real Belgian story in any event; for more than an hour we've been going the wrong way and we have passed by the Pole! Having covered more than 2000 km with just the compass, the sun and the GPS as navigation tools and then to miss the South Pole takes some doing. How could such a blunder have happened? Quite simply because we thought that the buildings that we passed on the left, two to three kilometres before on the "main road" were only the short edge of the perimeter. Additionally, we didn't take the time to turn round, being too preoccupied with wanting to see the outline of the dome before our very eyes at last. That's why we took the base to be a few outlying stations of no importance.

So about turn, then, and goodbye to the nice little wind. Pity, we would have loved to have greeted the Pole with the sails in full flow. One consolation; the milky sun is dissipating the last wreaths of mist remaining in the sky. About seven hours after striking camp, we see the guard of honour formed by the semi-circle of flags of the twelve founder nations of the Antarctic Treaty[21].

This time, no doubt about it, we've arrived. After having seen this symbol dozens, no hundreds of times, in books, films, articles, files, (on the Net too), we are at last going to be able to get into the photograph ourselves, goose-bumps and all. The twelve flagpoles are standing on the ice, just a few metres away. With their flags fluttering in the wind, like musicians around their conductor, they encircle the no less famous post with a little ball on top representing the terrestrial globe. It's no longer a

The Belgian flag flying alongside the other nation signatories of the Antarctic Treaty of 1959.

dream: the South Pole is here, stuck in the ice in front of me. I count my steps, I even accelerate a little, overwhelmed.

A few more metres and we fall into each other's arms

We made it!

The emotion is even stronger because on one of the twelve flags being flown there are the colours black, yellow and red. Although patriotism isn't at the very top of our values, particularly in Belgium, I think that any Belgian who came here would be unable to prevent a little flutter stirring in the heart. For me, there are in addition the hundred years of great polar adventures that are being celebrated by these flags flying in the wind.

A moment of intense excitement but one hell of a surprise as well. A few dozen metres away we spot three people – apparently adventurers like us – busy taking photographs. We go up to them, because after all this time without seeing anybody, we want to talk to, touch, look at some other human beings. It's unbelievable. It's Haraldur Olafsson, an old acquaintance of mine.! Somebody we met in Iceland when Dixie and I were returning from Greenland; I had used the stop-over for setting up the initial contacts for organising the press conference to announce the departure of South Through the Pole. At the time he had told us that he too intended to set up an expedition to the Antarctic. But I didn't know when he was leaving and of course I would never have dreamt that we would meet up here, just a few minutes after reaching the Pole. Adventures always contain coincidences! In fact, he has come here with his father, who is an Icelandic politician, and his brother. Setting out on foot a little more than a month ago from Patriot Hills, they arrived yesterday. Without sails, that's a great achievement.

At that moment, the Amundsen Scott station comes to life. Since the beginning of the expedition, Dixie and I are operating on Greenwich Mean Time. But here we have just aged twelve hours in a few seconds. And if our day is just ending, for the people here at the station it's just beginning. Doors open, people are getting up and putting their noses outside. Thanks to the Net, they know who we are and come to shake our hands. A young woman arrives in the middle of this commotion with a bottle of Champagne in her hand. Her story is an unusual one: This Frenchwoman applied for the position of taxi driver at the South Pole, after consulting the classified advertisements !

A little later, the Director of the base in person comes to welcome us on behalf of the NSF (National Science Foundation)[22]. Without palaver, David Fisher invites us to follow him to the interior of the installation to try to establish radio contact with HQ, a case of telling them that we've arrived and that we are transiting at the Pole. What a shock! After 2000 km on the Polar ice-cap, we find ourselves in a room crammed with communication devices of all kinds. But the line is bad and I can barely hear Michel's voice, which is coming to me via the Patriot Hills infrastructure. No matter; the message gets through and I'm relieved to hear that everyone in Belgium was convinced that we would not continue with the adventure.

Here at last is the huge metal dome. In fact it's nothing but a huge fridge of 2,000 sq.m. within which are the various huts of the base (looking like containers) like so many work stations, offices, scientific laboratories, radio, post office, library, kitchen, cafeteria, dormitories and so on. Among them there is even one sheltering a greenhouse with real earth and real vegetables. As for the living quarters, they are outside. As the dome isn't heated, conserving the provisions is no problem at all, nor is conserving the domestic waste either.

Since the birth of the ecologist movements at the beginning of the 70's, the international press and organisations such as Greenpeace have drawn attention to the protection of this last virgin universe. Several journalists have claimed that the bases do not all handle their waste with equal rigour, nor in accordance with the recommendations prescribed by the clauses in the various agreements contained in the Treaty. In any event, I can bear witness to the fact that I have seen in this dome at the South Pole some twenty or so crates carefully labelled for the sorting of household and other waste. They regularly make the two-way Pole – McMurdo trip to be emptied. Since we have taken the decision not to leave anything on our way, we don't deposit even the smallest bin bag here; they'll stay in Dixie's sledge as far as McMurdo.

Communication with Brussels over, we hand over the snow core borings collected since our departure to David Fisher, as had been agreed with the laboratory at Grenoble. After which the boss suggests a cup of tea. He also invites us to join them for the evening meal and asks if we would be prepared to hold a small conference afterwards. No problem! It's an opportunity to meet the people who are here, to chat a little, and who knows, perhaps to find a replacement camera.

As a result, we all pile into the cafeteria, which is where things take place here. Open 24 hours a day, Formica tables, self-service in the style of the 80's cafeteria, a constant coming and going (carpenters in working gear, workmen in overalls, technicians; in all there are 120 people here to build the new base), kitchen and grease smells, meals at any time of the day and night (after all, we're in the States), a suffocating heat; the place is fairly pleasant, but for Dixie and me, considering where we are coming from, I have to say that the surrealism of the situation is difficult to take. In normal times I like this building-site atmosphere. But here I feel a little lost, as if the two months spent on the ice-cap have seriously recalibrated some of my bearings. And even though the Americans who have just got to know these two cranks are more than welcoming, I don't feel at home here. I think once more of the Belgian flag flying close by, and can't help being struck by the thought that a country as small as ours should be so intricately involved in the fate of the Antarctic, and in consequence, of the world...

Furthermore, having now crossed half of this continent, I suddenly realise how big it is, how unified. A continent for peace, has one not often heard it said? I believe that I'm in the process of touching this vibrant reality with my fingers. A continent which, through its position, its configuration, its characteristics, its originality, its isolation, its ice and its virginity, controls the fate of the world. The simple fact of boring into the

ice to a depth of some 2,000 to 3,000 metres, as some Europeans and others are currently doing, allows one to go back in time to study the evolution of the planet's climate. Analysing the carbon cycle in the food chain of the southern ocean helps
mankind to know if, one day, this huge expanse of water will be able to absorb the
tens of thousands of tons of carbon dioxide produced every year. Discovering new
species on the ocean beds, each austral summer is also fundamental to the future of
mankind. And then, are we not on the vertical point of the most beautiful window in
existence on to the cosmos?

Automatically, I ask myself questions as to whether Belgium will continue to carry
out research in the context of international Antarctic co-operation. How to make
people understand that even though Antarctica is a faraway land, it is of great importance to each and every one of us. It's certain that during my conferences I'll tackle this
problem, which I find – and especially here I feel – to be of the utmost importance.

Everybody should one day have the possibility of coming into contact in a concrete
way with the grandeur of this continent; they would then without doubt feel a greater
responsibility for their environment and for the environment of future generations.
Indeed, this very conviction is what drove me to set up this project in the first place.

*Time passes quickly and it's already late at night when we visit the various installations on the
base. The head of the computer room, Drew Logan, even suggests that we send some news and
photos of the two little Belgians by satellite, if he can manage it. What's more, it's with his
video camera that we will be leaving. What luck!*
*While committing a few lines to paper for my people, what we are doing finally dawns on me,
and I feel – and say – that we are going to succeed. What an unforgettable day!*

Monday, 5 January (Day 63)

The Myth Lives on

In the tent. Because of the time change (the time at the South Pole, like McMurdo, is
the same as New Zealand), we hardly got any sleep. Just a few hours at most. When we
went to bed at the end of the evening of Sunday 04 January (base time), it was for us
the beginning of Sunday afternoon. And, now it's Monday 05 January, and as we have
to adjust to the local time, which is GMT[*] +12, we are in fact getting up on Sunday
evening, to leave the station at dead of night, at about two in the morning. You could
say that our stay here hasn't been entirely restful.

*Time to leave, 14.50 local time has struck. Brimming with confidence, we say farewell to our new
friends who have come to see our traction sails. From a mixture of tiredness, confusion and con-
tentment, we proceed for just four hours before hurriedly making camp and falling soundly asleep.*

Between 23 November and 21 January the sun does not set in the Antarctic. At the South Pole it disappears below the horizon on 21 March, and does not reappear again until 23 September.

This evening we are tired but happy. Happy to have experienced a few good moments, to have been able to communicate our intentions to HQ, to have been able to borrow a camera. But happier still no doubt to be able to admire the parhelion surrounding the sun. Ah, what a privilege to be able to witness such marvels; we're truly on another planet... Far away, high in the sky, I can make out a procession of clouds; they must be above the Trans-Antarctic chain, some 800 km from here. It's odd; when I look at them, it's not the distance in kilometres that first comes to my head, but rather the calculation that my sight and my senses are instinctively making. Dixie is already asleep. I leave the tent for a few moments because I want to be alone to savour the moment. The last few hours already seem to constitute an amazing parenthesis.

It's often said that a dream disintegrates as soon as it is fulfilled. But that's not the impression I have. Rather I still feel that the myth of the South Pole has well and truly survived. Looming up suddenly in this vast desert, the Pole was almost missed as we moved from our primitive life to a high-tech universe in just a few hours. And today, less than twenty minutes after our departure, all signs of the stopover have already been wiped away.

I have already experienced this impression of a myth living on once before – when I reached the North Pole. That geographical position is in fact purely abstract, because the permanent drift of the ice floe means that, just a second after you've reached it, you're no longer there. The Poles are fabulous symbolic attractions; they abolish time in straddling all the meridians and undermine space because from them all directions lead either north or south. Beyond time and space, they are places of ephemera, places of passage, places for perceiving the great relativity of existence.

Wednesday, 7 January (Day 65)

Which Way is North?

The surprise of the day: where have all the sastrugis gone?

For nearly 1,500 km; these confounded sastrugis have made our lives hell: continual falls, losing ones balance, rips in the sails, fear, bruises, senses on the alert… And suddenly they've disappeared! Since we left the Amundsen Scott base, the surface of the ice is very much flatter; it's also less hard, because it's covered by a thin film of snow. Not to mince words, it's very comfortable.

Immediate reaction; my brain is working overtime. We will certainly reach the Trans-Antarctics relatively quickly. As crossing them won't be anything of a problem, and as it's pretty certain that we'll have some wind once we're on the other side of the shelf, I can see myself reaching McMurdo on time and without incident.

A bit of bad luck; we've got the longitude wrong. Before coming to the why's and wherefore's of this, I should explain the rudiments of finding ones way in the Polar Regions.

In fact, it changes according to the weather.

Firstly, when it's fine. Since we know the magnetic declination[23], it's the compass that sets the course. From the moment that the course is known, one fixes ones bearings so as to avoid having to take the compass out all the time: in relation to the sun (angle of shadow of the ski stick with the course) or in relation to the sastrugis (angle of the ice with the course). One can also find ones bearings with a watch, which at certain hours of the day can indicate north or south.

When it's overcast, there are two other possibilities: either one is on foot (on skis) or beneath the sails. In the first instance, the easiest orientation is the angle between the course and the wind (its direction is shown by a little piece of cloth fixed to the ski stick). But when Aeolus is pulling us (the second possibility), the little piece of cloth is of course no longer of any use (because of the relative wind); when, further, there are few or no sastrugis (remember that snowdrifts always indicate the direction of the prevailing wind), things get a little complicated. There's one final method of finding ones way in the polar environment: feeling the direction of the wind on the skin of the face. But we are rigged out with so much protection against the cold (hoods, furs, goggles, storm masks) that the surface area of any skin left open to the air is reduced to rough leather. So there remains one last recourse: the GPS and it's little digital arrow that permanently indicates the course. Evidently, it's the perfect tool. But it's not a great deal of use in an unassisted expedition because, generally speaking, not enough batteries can be taken for it to be allowed to act as a permanent navigational aid.

Since today the weather is lousy, we are obliged to make regular use of the GPS nevertheless. Dixie is taking care of it.

From the different positions he has been telling me as time went by, I realised that the longitude was decreasing instead of increasing. This meant that the expedition was travelling in the same hemisphere, whereas the route I had picked out for reaching the Axel Heiberg Glacier was entirely to the west. It's a little as though one was heading for Lyon when leaving Paris when one had to go to Bordeaux. Bizarre! Are we off course? Should I stop to check? The problem is that we are really going strong. So fine, we'll look into it in the tent this evening.

It can't be helped, I'm worried. This morning, thinking that we were on the right course, we allowed ourselves to drift eastwards with the intention of avoiding what we knew would be a difficult stretch. The region is well known for it has been described by Amundsen, who christened it "the devil's ballroom" (djevellensdansseal); it's an extremely dangerous area of crevasses in which the explorer Amundsen got himself trapped during his famous thrust for the Pole. *"Suddenly one of Wisting's runners broke in a bottomless crevasse"*, he wrote in his logbook of 4 December 1911. *"We managed to put it back on without too much trouble. After extricating ourselves from that safe and sound, we climbed up a hillock. It was still ice but we discovered that it was full of invisible crevasses and that it was impossible to set foot anywhere without going through…"* At 5 o'clock in the morning, after eight and a half hours on the road, we bring down the sails and take refuge in our little canvas shelter. After the ritual of making camp, I come back to the problem of orientation of a while ago and ask Dixie to check the longitude; I have the impression that we are not following the agreed itinerary.

After a thirty-four stop over at the South Pole, the two promptly take to the road; their final des-tionation, McMurdo, 1500 km away.

A few minutes later, the verdict of the GPS is without right of appeal: 166.278° east…

But that's not possible. Why didn't he check whether we were east or west? For two whole days? What a waste of time. We are now heading for the Beardmore Glacier instead of the Heiberg. Bloody hell… The Beardmore! Incredible! Scott, Messner, Fiennes, they all came to grief in there. What's worse is that we don't even have a map of the area. And because it's so huge, we can't make out with the naked eye which side we should go through on.

– Listen, Alain, here's the GPS, take care of it yourself from now on.

– That's not the point, old man. I just don't understand how you could have over-looked something so important.

As Dixie can't stand confrontation or aggression, differences of opinion are quickly settled with him. We discuss, we compromise, we explain ourselves.

No matter what, one thing is for certain: the expedition is currently 50 km off track to the east. There are some 300 km left for correcting our aim.

Let's pray to all the gods of the polar ice-cap that Aeolus is not too contrary…

We haven't made many mistakes so far on this expedition. So why not explain this one? Yesterday evening, when we were dead tired, when I checked our position on the GPS I didn't think to say to myself: OK, now that the first part of the crossing is over (which was entirely in the eastern hemisphere so without east/west distinction to be made when checking our position in the evenings), I must from now on pay attention to this distinction.

I knew as well that if we made a slight error of direction in the first dozen or so kilometres after the Pole (where all the longitudes meet) it wouldn't be so bad as it would later on in the itinerary. What clearly caused the mistake is that when yesterday and today I gave Alain our position, the azimuth was right – but we were simply on the wrong side of the globe. Errare humanum est!

I have to say as well that I was still feeling euphoric after our visit to the Pole (where we had no time at all to discuss the tactics of the onward journey) and the last moments we spent down there: especially when we left under sail, taking to the airport runway for several hundred metres (before returning to the powdery snow as a C130 was approaching) – and, oh what snow! – with Drew Logan (who lent us his camera) following on a skiddoo to film our departure. A great souvenir!

Thursday, 8 January (Day 66)

To the East, Nothing New…

Once again, we've been taken in by the Antarctic.

We said as we left that we would be able to re-orientate the route and re-establish the course to the west. But the wind had got up and the snow had hardened. So the edges of the skis weren't biting well into the snow and we continued to drift to the east.

Result: although we had covered some 110 km we were still on the same meridian. Or almost. For we had at least managed to gain one degree towards the west.

What will our friends at HQ think? They are probably saying that we've changed itinerary and have chosen the Beardmore instead of the Axel Heiberg. There's nothing in the pre-established Argos codes that would enable us to tell them that we're sticking to the same route.

I don't think that I have as yet made the point that, for most of the time throughout the endless hours of maximum stress, we are proceeding at 10, 15, 20 km/h, perhaps even faster. The mental gymnastics that have to be employed all the time to achieve the best progress — for example, a weather eye open for all signs of danger or reminding oneself constantly of the parameters of the glide — is incomparably more demanding than when one has to be satisfied with proceeding on foot.

The constraints are not very different from those faced by skippers in a regatta; just like them, we have to go as fast as we can and adjust our sails all the time.

One difference: on the water, one tries to shake the other off, whereas here, one follows exactly the same course.

Friday, 9 January (Day 67)

Hand Games...

Wind, nothing but wind, always wind.

This morning, it's blowing from the right direction (we're fully unfurled) but irregularly: which makes steering hard work. The edges aren't biting, we're sliding all over the place and we have to hang on for dear life to the kite tillers to keep our balance.

What I failed to explain the other day when I was comparing the second part of the crossing (South Pole to McMurdo) with the first (King Baudouin Base to the South Pole) is that from now on we can no longer make compromises. For the clock is ticking… no matter the weather conditions, no matter the physical or mental state of the troops, no matter the nature of the terrain, no matter how cold it is, we must at all costs make progress. We have just lost precious time because of the longitude mistake, which means that this section of the itinerary will not be as *easy* as we expected after all.

Accidents are more likely to occur in at times like this. Dixie and I are both exhausted, worn out, weakened, and the skiing conditions are more difficult than ever; and as we have to luff all the time, we catch the gusts right in the face, the cold burns

Whenever the wind is not strong enough, the sails have to be packed up, starting with the lines which have to be rolled up carefully to avoid knots.

the skin on the face, and the eyes hurt… Worst of all are the hands. For the most part they have to be held tight, either on the ski sticks or on the tillers; as a result, the blood circulation slows right down. In normal times, it's a most unpleasant feeling. But here it's much more serious; after a while this permanent pressure causes terrible pain. So, fine, we can bear it. But the resulting numbness delays the detection of frostbite. And *that* is where the real danger lies.

We have a thousand ruses for preventing that from happening. The simplest method is to stop, take the gloves off and put the hands somewhere warm. But the smallest of stops means time lost. So we have developed little tricks for warming our mitts as we go along. Most often, I take off the first under-glove so that I can close the fist and flush out the small amount of warmth that is always circulating in the palm of the hand. (A detail: during these brief gymnastics, the gloves, which are wet through from perspiration, have time to get covered with a thin film of ice and to prepare a wonderful welcome for the fingers, which, scarcely warmed up, have to wriggle their way back into them again. Sometimes, I shake my hands furiously, while making quite sure that I don't touch anything, for the slightest knock could damage the ends of the blood vessels and make matters worse. When I'm using the ski sticks, rubbing the hands on the knob is also a good way of finding a little warmth.

What hurts most doesn't occur during the day, but in the evening in the tent. I would say just as you are slipping into the sleeping bag. You get the impression that the skin on your hands is on fire. So you instinctively try to press them against some part of the body where it's warm. But you can't do that because that would block the circulation again. So you have to ensure that you have your hands stretched out alongside your body before you go to sleep. And too bad if you're one of those people who like sleeping huddled up. Despite all these precautions, I need at least four to five minutes each morning before I can stretch the muscles. Carrying out simple tasks such as opening the zip of the sleeping bag, or lighting the stove, or holding a cup of coffee, can take time, a great deal of time.

For me, my trick against the cold is to swing my arms round and round, then to bend down, leaning forward, to leave time for the blood to get to the lowest point. I inflict this exercise on myself ten or twenty times a day. I also place my hands, without gloves, on the nape of my neck, with the thumbs directly on the throat, as if to strangle someone. That gets you warm! Nothing alters the fact that the only way of getting warm during the day is to move. Try to stretch the fingers as often as possible, to run, to feel the flow of blood increasing, because I often have the impression that circulation is bad, that it's blocked somewhere, that it's flowing less quickly...

Despite all that, it's the mental tolerance of the cold that's so hard, so very, very hard...

Saturday, 10 January (Day 68)

Has he Gone Mad?

Dixie must be wondering if I haven't gone completely mad. Proceeding a dozen or so metres away from him, he sees me talking to myself and laughing out loud. What he doesn't know is that I've just had a vision. The shape the sail takes on reminds me of genies from the 1001 Nights. Each time that the kite moves with the wind, I can make out the forehead, the nose and the mouth of Aladdin's genie. I'm surfing in another world. And to think that it took me 2,200 km to realise that we were being accompanied by a phantom.

The wind is weak and we set off quietly. As it gets weaker, we are obliged to pump. It's usually when the sail is rising that it pulls best. A flat calm (the genuine doldrums, in sailing parlance) sets in at about 2 o'clock.

For the first time we say to ourselves : "there's no wind, let's stop". For the first time we put up

A field of sastrugis

the tent during the day, just for the infernal wait for the wind. It's the first time that the big guy has taken such a decision.

Because of this, we are not heeding the philosophy of the expedition, which is to go on at all costs. Alain even suggests a siesta. To have a siesta in the Antarctic? Ok, after all, why not? One has to decompress now and again. OK; so I decompress…

Stretched out on my sledge, my senses benefit enormously from an hour and a half of beautiful thoughts before I wake up in the confined space of the tent. We spend the rest of the day doing nothing.

Today I'm taking lots of photos. And doing quite a bit of filming. I still have the little Contax camera in the right hand pocket of my jacket. I like it to be always available. It gives me a feeling of security, of being organised. One is ready for anything. The GPS in the left-hand inside pocket of the jacket. The tubes of sunblock (which freeze solid) in the bottom left-hand pocket. Everything is arranged like in a wardrobe; the storm mask; the spare gloves. In fact, with all these additional layers, I must look like Michelin's Bibbendum.

This evening, we still find time for the 11ᵗʰ well and the 34ᵗʰ core boring.

Sunday, 11 January (Day 69)

The Origin of the Four Winds

This time the wind is too weak and we're unable to luff. So it's time for the skis and the sticks. Proceeding like this means that we go more slowly and lose time. I have to admit that I actually look forward to these moments so that I can rediscover the sensations of being a skier.

Two hours later, it's time for sailing and for stress. Buffeted by a wind that is becoming increasingly violent, we are repeatedly forced to change the sails. After a while, the muscles seize up because of the continual sideways sliding that luffing demands.

I am reminded of the lines written by Shackleton during his attempt to reach the South Pole, when he evoked his approach to the Trans-Antarctics as if he was arriving *"at the ends of the world, at the source of the clouds and at the origin of the four winds…"*

The great explorer had forgotten to add that here one arrives at the gates of hell also.

This day, following the example of so many others but worse, is an uninterrupted succession of minor disasters, of inconvenient stops, of waiting around, of false hopes, of getting underway again, of disillusionment, of perpetual and unequal jousts with the wind… We wonder for just how long we can stand this little game.

Uncertainties…

A strange feeling – at a time when everything is becoming more laborious – that a force from beyond is busy pushing Old Man Hubert and the gentle Dixie further and further, towards horizons and frontiers of which they are not even aware.

I feel that a new energy is whipping our backs, forcing us to go on when in truth we are very near the end of our tethers…

Experience…

This evening I pay dearly for having got cold during a pause. I'm done in, I've a bad head-ache, I only want one thing; to take refuge in my sleeping bag to find a little warmth and to restore my health.

Monday, 12 January (Day 70)

Descent into Hell

We start off, laboriously. For a quiet day without incident.

But can one be laborious here?

Towards noon the sky in the distance is getting cruelly dark. Soon, it's as black as ink. That's clearly does not presage anything good. We compromise, we use the smallest sail. Like sailors the world over, who can see the worst coming, we hope that the squall won't be too severe…

Of course… In less than an hour it's sheer torture. We can't see a thing, we have to wait for each other all the time so as not lose sight of one another. Simply catching your breath requires an extraordinary expenditure of energy. The raging snow gets in everywhere; it infiltrates and whirls around in the hood, it steams up the mask so that we have to try to clean it all the time. Finally, the mask goes into the pocket and we go on with our faces bare to the cruel elements. The wind must be blowing at more than 50 km/h. It takes away your breath, until you feel that you are suffocating.

I believe that, if we have been able to keep going today, it's partly because of the terrain. For the first time since leaving the Pole, it is beginning to change, which means that we are at last approaching the mountains. We saw the first nunataks giving access to the Mill Glacier, then the terrain began to descend in successive waves. Some small craters and hillocks appeared. After seven hours of suffering, when we are trying to decide whether or not to continue with this descent into Hell, Dixie's ankle decides for us. It had been swollen for several days. Now he simply has to rest it.

That said, we have at any rate covered just under 47 km. But I'm pessimistic. While mending the equipment in the tent, it dawned on me that today I had done nothing but cope with the moment in hand, grit my teeth against falling over, heading towards the south-west… That's the way things happen on adventures like this; the carrot at the end of the stick, always keeping your objectives in sight, like yellow post-it notes stuck on the fridge door. Right now, the notes for the day are: kill time, avoid falling over and follow the right course…

The rest is no longer important. I have definitively acquired the conviction that nothing can stop us now. I repeat that to myself all the time. In 70 days we have covered 2,754 km of which almost 2,500 were under sail. How am I going to be able to live without them after the expedition?

Things are pretty bad. We never stop thinking about getting to the Ross Ice Shelf, which should be our moment of salvation. That's probably the reason why we have been able to proceed despite the storm.

Today, my digestion is not like it is at other times. Breakfast is decidedly too heavy, but we have to make the ritual sacrifice to morning fat to compensate for the small amount of food we ingest during the day. What a foul taste! It weighs on the stomach. Imagine a packet of cereals mixed with olive oil that's been diluted with hot water. Next time we ought to use sesame oil so that the taste is better! The more diluted it is, the easier it is to swallow. But the polar diet prescribes as little water as possible so as to get the most out of its nutritional elements. Outcome: the ration makes a really unsavoury mixture, like gruel. Disgusting! To conceal the taste of this mixture as much as possible, I embellish it with little squares of chocolate (one does one's best) and then I quickly drink a cup of coffee. Trying to think positively, I tell myself each morning, (despite the fact that I have the impression of taking in nothing but calories), that I'm putting the finest possible oil into my engine.

As far as my physical condition is concerned, it's no luxury either. My head is cold, I've got a headache and earache and my neck hurts. For me the head is the thermometer of the body. What's more, one of my ankles is swollen, and I can feel some severe contractions running across my back from having had to luff for so many hours. While we glide, my hands are literally frozen. I wonder how it is that we haven't had any first-degree frostbite. It must be said that the position we have to adopt for luffing is totally unnatural. The whole body – arms, head, torso, legs and feet – is completely twisted for hours on end.

Tuesday, 13 January (Day 71)

"You're Still Alive"

This morning's short period of calm made us think we could proceed under sail again.

How can one be so naïve as to think that each time we get up, the day ahead will be better. I actually believed that the excesses of *El Nino* would be to our advantage!

To sum up: we had been able to cover 16 km nonetheless, by fooling around with the 6 sq.m. sail, but the game became too dangerous. The wind was so strong that we had to keep the full sail close to the ground – definitely not hoisting it up, with the attendant risk of being carried off. Even so, that didn't stop us being lifted off the ground on a couple of occasions. Not as high as Dixie went when he had his accident in the early days of the expedition, but definitely a few centimetres in any event.

We could certainly never properly recount moments such as that, because the torments that we have to endure are really from another world. How can you describe the

On several occasions they were forced to unravel the knots in the cordage of their sails, which had become caught in the sastrugis.

feeling that at any moment your hands are going to be ripped off with the sails? How can you describe the sensation you get when your torso, after an entire day of being twisted out of shape, won't go back into its proper position? How do you define the various degrees of trembling in the legs? How do you make people understand that, above and beyond all this torture, the only things that kept us upright on our skis were the fleeting apparitions telling us; "You're still alive…"?

The wind is raging at more than 75 km/h; after 8 km, we decide to stop. The driving snow is so strong that everything will be white inside the tent.

We have only covered 22 km and we are 50 km to the east of the entry-point into the glacier. I have no illusions (there at least is something positive); it'll be a few more days before we reach it. If the weather in the Trans-Antarctics is the same as here, it must be snowing there a great deal. So how much time will we need for getting down the glacier and reaching the Ross platform?

To reassure myself, I remind myself of the accounts of the expeditions that have previously ventured into these mountains. They have all had to put up with very variable weather conditions.

Overleaf: The new traction sails are so effective that they have opened up new avenues of exploration.

A typical view of an Antarctic blizzard: building up of a bank of driven snow, in a diffuse light.

At the approach to the Sør Rondane Mountains, on a calm, clear day. In order to repair the damaged sledges, they first had to empty them completely.

The last crevasses at the exit of the Ski-Jump (an ice fall named by Roald Amundsen in 1911) of the Axel Heiberg Glacier.

On the Axel Heiberg, the snow was so deep that we had to force through passages along which we later took the sledges.

Overleaf: The Antarctic is the biggest desert in the world. The interplay of light effects create a surreal and ceaselessly changing atmosphere.

When the wind was too strong, they were forced to advance on foot, pulling their sledges along behind them.

We deviate far too much with our power-kites. A spectacular fall during the storm drives me wild. I refuse to allow myself to wallow in such feelings; so I avoid getting angry with myself. Instead, I imagine some carefully elaborated fantasies. For example, that a cloud or a huge satin sail comes to envelop me with gentleness, with lightness like a fairy's kiss.

Let everything go. Don't resist. Falling is nothing other than allowing the earth to exercise its magnetic force. Calm down. Consciously. Finally, chase away all ones enemies with a deep, deep breath.

Before taking to the road again, I wonder to myself whether our endurance is without limits or whether the moment will come when we hit rock-bottom. Already, the head wind is too strong, and the struggle is exhausting. Going on is useless. It is with much difficulty that we finally succeed in mounting the tent.

For the first message of the evening, we switch the Argos to the position: A0 − B14 (big bliz-zard with halt, storm conditions). This way, HQ will know that the weather is seriously dete-riorating.

Sunday 18 January (Day 76)

In the Antechamber of the Cosmos

The good weather is suddenly back two hours after we set out. In a few minutes, we witness a veritable apotheosis. The Antarctic has just unveiled itself, like a giant curtain rising to give us the impression of at last being able to catch sight of the primeval mountains. There's no doubt about it, it's an immaculate conception. Creation in its purest form. A sensuous whiteness that says it all… Snow, at rest at last. The blue print of the world.

First we see Mount Don Pedro emerging, and then the impressive Fridtjof Nansen Mountain comes into sight.

We need a another two and a half hours to reach the head of the Axel Heiberg Glacier. The spectacle deployed there is extraordinary. Worthy of a description by Dante. The way from Hell to Purgatory traverses, he says, a steep and perilous mountain. But where are the angels sent by God to help one overcome the obstacle?

Far away, the cirrostrati are already arriving, there's no time to lose: we must get as far as we can into the glacier before the bad weather returns. We must flee as quickly as possible the cataclysm that's about to hit us.

FLEE!

The central part of the first break in the slope doesn't seem to have any crevasses. Without stopping to think, I allow myself a little fun. Sitting on the sledge, I hurtle off down the 350 metre powdery slope that is between us and the intermediate basin…. Magnificent; the Antarctic is sliding past me at 30 km/h.

Mt Nansen at the entrance of the Axel Heiberg Glacier.

Intoxicating…

There is only one seat in this open air theatre and I have paid a lot of money to sit in it. The mountains unwinding before us are as they were when they appeared on earth several hundred thousand, perhaps millions, of years ago. In the same place, even.

Astounding…

I only have a few seconds for this fabulous journey; then suddenly powdery white snow arrives, the landscape darkens, I have the impression that if I touch the mountains with my fingers, they will evaporate and resume the gaseous state that was theirs a long, long time before…

Giddy…

No doubt about it: to spend time in this way among the Antarctic ice and to measure oneself against the winds, comparable to those sweeping the surfaces of far off planets, is to treat oneself to a visit to the antechamber of the cosmos.

Unforgettable…

I'm in the process of living what will without doubt remain for all time one of the most precious moments of my life. Alone in this powder! Quick, catch the seconds, pack them with beautiful images before sending them to my personal realm of the beyond so that they become moments of eternity.

Tobogganing on the Axel Heiberg Glacier! Dipping my forefinger into the snow so that it too makes its little furrow.

Oy oy. Be careful… Not there… Slowly…

A bit of a fright. Arriving at full speed at a place where the slope gets suddenly steeper, I have neither the time nor the means of slowing down or stopping to check the nature of the way ahead after rebound. At moments like this, to hell with rationality, one prays to ones guiding star.

On into the void. Phew, it passed……..

Dixie, the wiser of the two, hasn't followed me.

From here on, it's downhill, and we launch ourselves into a cocktail of rockfaces, of rocky protuberances and blue ice. Far away, the Ross Ice Shelf. On a steep slope, Alain sat himself on his sledge without compunction and disappeared at breakneck speed. Throughout the expedition, we have paid attention to the slightest detail. Dementedly, even. Then, suddenly he's out of control, launching himself headlong into a descent into hell, without even warning me. After a few seconds he disappears as though swallowed up by the slope, which, just a few hundred metres away from where we are, curves downwards and gets steeper still.

Fine… But what am I supposed to do? I have to decide quickly. Either I follow him, or I zigzag. During our crossing of Greenland, I remember that a certain spot not far from our destination we also started to do some high-speed tobogganing like that, lying flat on our stomachs on the sledges.

But here, out of prudence, I choose a safer way of descending. One hour later I join up with Alain at the foot of the slope. After 10 hours of progress, we are swallowed up by about a metre of snow.

Turning round to survey the slope that I had just hurtled down, which I must admit has a serious incline, I can't stop myself imagining Amundsen and his people. I know that they came this way. But how on earth were those supermen able to climb up this part of the glacier with their equipment and their dogs? A mystery...

Hang on, here's Dixie.

The furrow that I've made is about 50 cm deep. The sledges seem to be floating on a white sea...

We've been on the go for more than twelve hours.

Feeling our way, we stop a few metres from the first great crevasses of the ice-fall to the east of Don Pedro, roughly at the same place where Børge was trapped one day last year.

Taking off our skis to mount the tent, we sink up to our waists into the snow. It isn't easy to move in conditions like that!

It starts to snow a little, the silence is heavy and padded. In the distance, we can hear avalanches crashing down the slopes of Mount Nansen. Their dull explosions remind me of 1994, during one of my attempts on Everest. I was trapped in a little tent above the icefall on the west coomb. For 48 hours, avalanches were thundering down the Nuptse and the west ridge; we were between two huge crevasses and the wind caused by the avalanches almost carried us off. Here, luckily, we are some 6 km from the sides of the glacier; I know that we're not in any danger. However, it's snowing so hard and the visibility is so poor that there's no question of going on. There are too many crevasses all around us. Assessment of the day: we have progressed 32 km and descended by about 1000 m in altitude.

Setting up camp in more than one metre of snow on the Axel Heiberg Glacier.

Monday, 19 January (Day 77)

Full Rehearsal...

Have I ever seen so much snow fall over such a short period of time? A further 20 centimetres have fallen during the night. As we can't see further than a couple of metres, I already know that we are trapped. It's the 11th day of forced halt.

So as to notify HQ, Dixie switches on the beacon (AO-B7): "halt, because of bad weather".

No matter what happens, we won't be reaching McMurdo before 30 January. So I'm going to have to borrow money to pay the insurance premium, which after that date increases from $1,500 to $49,500 per week...

Forget about it! With everything we have to contend with, it's better not to have ones head cluttered with such preoccupations.

A whole day inside the tent...

What do we do at times like this? We kill time. Tidying the bags, the tent, the sledges. Checking the state of the equipment. The sails, the suspension lines, the traction lines, the PC, the batteries. Doing a little sewing: the clothes, the gloves, the sails. Diving into a book or into deep thoughts...

As we are progressing in a dangerous area, we take advantage of this prolonged halt to review, one more time, the procedures to be adopted and the tasks to be carried out in the event of one of us falling into a crevasse. When we go into difficult areas we are roped together. We each have at our waist an ice axe, two ice screws, a mini pulley, a mini self-blocking clasp and two cords so that we could climb up, the length of the rope, in the event of a fall.

Outside the light isn't good and the danger of the crevasses prevents us from going on. Alain and I talk about home. Of our home (he designs the kitchen, I choose the decoration). We recreate the world, we waffle on about the meaning of life, we discuss our respective passions.
It's still snowing, and I have the impression that it's snowing the world over.
Like yesterday, I have forgotten to do my yoga exercises. What negligence!
Good, so as from today I've decided to be even stricter with myself and to find the time during the day, come what may, for the minimum of stretching exercises and meditation. Daily relaxation is something that I cannot neglect...

This evening it's Dixie's turn to prepare the soup: cream of vegetable, one of the three varieties that we brought with us (mixed vegetables, peas and broccoli). It's his favourite.

I prefer the cream of broccoli... Soup-time is an important moment. It's an opportunity for a hot drink, to be able to feel the heat of the bowl between the hands. We have formed the habit of imbibing the liquid, in turn, each slurping as

Blizzards prevented the Expedition from advancing during eleven days of the crossing.

noisily as possibly, vying with the other to demonstrate how truly delicious it is. This is a variation on an Asiatic custom that I picked up during my Himalayan peregrinations, and it has become a kind of ritual for us on expedition.

Tuesday, 20 January (Day 78)

In Amundsen's Footsteps

Get up at 19.30 – we're still on GMT but we now proceed at night. We have to make progress at all costs. No matter what the conditions.

As we can't see anything and the snow is getting thicker all the time, the most extreme prudence is called for.

What should we do? I suggest that we go on a reconnaissance without the sledges. In fact, it's impossible to pull them over such terrain anyway. Given the weight, they sink too deeply into the snow. We have to rope up. In the event of falling into a crevasse – and there are many of them around – Dixie can hold on to me, because I'm in front. The terrain is horrible, and unpredictable. The skis bury themselves at each step, which is normal because it has snowed so much, but we never know whether any sudden subsidence is due to the freshness of the snow or to the presence of a crevasse. The exquisite sensation of walking through a minefield.

With skis on our feet, roped together and without the sledges, we try to force a way alongside the crevasse near which we have been installed since the day before yesterday, but we sink in up to our knees. What's more, the strip of snow on which we're proceeding seems to be getting narrower and the terrain is giving way more and more beneath our feet. It's too dangerous: after 750 metres I decide that we should turn back.

A zone of crevasses under Mt Don Pedro on the right bank of the Axel Heiberg Glacier.

A pause before taking on a field of crevasses.

Planning the route on the Glacier.

Crossing the central part of the Axel Heiberg Glacier.

The descent of the Axel Heiberg was perhaps the most difficult part of the Expedition, but possibly the most picturesque.

The yellow bands across Mt Nansen. An avalanche is in progress in the centre of the picture.

Views of the Axel Heiberg Glacier.

It must be said that the crevasses here are really impressive. One could easily place a gothic cathedral inside them, but we really have no wish to end our days at the bottom of one of them.

How quiet it is suddenly. A deathly silence has just settled over this corner of the Antarctic. Heavy, unmoving, cold, frozen…

While retracing my steps, I have an idea. Why don't we make a special path for the sledges? If Dixie skis close by my side, we can together make a furrow nearly 60 cm wide, just enough to get them through. Shall we try? So, we try out the theory, skiing side by side. The result? The D system for the sledge trail works quite well but takes too much time. The 750 metres cut a while ago were covered in three and a half hours.

We stop. We'll have to wait for the weather to become more clement. We do some filming… After two hours, the cold attacks us. We have to put up the tent and have a little something to eat. It's midnight.

Seven hours later, we are playing cards while waiting impatiently for the dawn, when the fog finally clears. The seracs at the foothills of the Don Pedro Christophersen (one of Amundsen's sponsors) are coming slowly into view. Good grief! We have to go that way…

As far as establishing the itinerary to follow to the Axel Heiberg Glacier was concerned, we had only two reliable sources at our disposal (apart from studying aerial photographs with a magnifying glass). These were the writings of Roald Amundsen, and information from Børge Ousland, who was one of the first explorers to take this route after Amundsen. During one of my visits to him, in the suburbs of Oslo, he had advised me to steer as close as possible to the seracs, which we can see a few hundred metres from where we are now.

En route. Even though visibility is better than it was, we stick to the same technique: roped together and sledgeless. I attempt to force a way through this crevasse riddled snowfield. No problem, I'm in my element, dare I say.

Two hours later, the sun appears, which facilitates the tricky reconnaissance of this part of the glacier, that we have to cross following a gigantic S–shaped path. We have just covered about 3 km, to reach the point known to polar explorers as *The Triangle*. It is situated halfway up the glacier, between two ice-falls. We now have to go back to get the *pulkas*, taking care to mark our way as best we can. Three hours later, back at *The Triangle* again, we start our descent towards the edge of the platform.

The atmosphere is like in a fairy tale, the weather, perfect. The rays of the sun turn the snow phosphorescent. Avalanches are crashing down on all sides, like streams of white lava. It's all the more impressive because their back-wind is all around us and almost succeeds in licking us. On the left of the photo, Mount Nansen with its yellow strata, and on the right Don Pedro, with its blue seracs: the picture is sumptuous. A place just crying out for the IMAX treatment. Dixie and I feel our energy increase tenfold. We're going to need it for negotiating the rest of the descent, for the snow is both deep and soft.

It's seven in the evening on this Wednesday, 21 January. That means we've been working for 23 hours. Suddenly, going round a crevasse, I come to a halt. Leaning on my ski sticks, far in the distance I can make out the Ross Ice Shelf! At last! Above it, an oceanic sky. I've been waiting for this moment for hours, weeks, months and years. I surrender privately to this spectacle and can't prevent a few tears of happiness.

I now know that we're going to succeed. The Pacific Ocean is there, in front of me. And "only" some 1000 km away, the ice floe is waiting for us. Even though we are not yet at the end of our adventure, we can in future say that we have just crossed the Antarctic...

A few hours later, we are on the lower plateau of the glacier, at just under 1,000 metres of altitude, at the foot of the last ice-fall that Amundsen christened *The Ski Jump*. Standing there, it's obvious why he gave it that name. Some 86 years on, it hasn't changed perceptibly.

We continue our descent for a few more hours before setting up camp, at the very place that Amundsen stopped to find a way through the glacier. *"On 18 November 1911, we halted to find a way of getting away from these giant chaotic crevasses all around us. Enormous blocks of ice, gigantic abysses and colossal crevasses are blocking our way... Pretty difficult to find the way ahead, but after 5 hours of reconnaissance, Hanssen and Bjaaland have managed to find a path that is reasonably practicable."*

It's already 22.30. We've been going for exactly 27 hours.

Barely three days ago, we were at more than 3,000 metres altitude.

Camp is set up at the foot of the Ski Jump.

Thursday, 22 January (Day 80)

The Black Hole

A complete white-out. The sky has disappeared. I'm not yet aware of it, but we won't be seeing any more of the mountains that we have just crossed. We can't see anything any more. Nonetheless, we decide to weigh anchor, so I get out the compass to set course for the southern end of the *Zig Zag Bluff*, a small pass some 60 km to the north. This is the pass which leads out of the glacier; it should enable us to avoid the last field of crevasses before the ice-shelf.

The terrain is rising again, the skis go in about 20 cm. Even though the snow is sticking and the sledge is heavy, I feel that it is now a part of me. In fact, for a long time now we are as one, it and me. As though this implacable continent had decided to recast the straps, harness, shafts, clips, *pulka* and man in one mould. There are no longer any constraints between these various elements. Nothing but sensitivity, understanding, co-ordination, respect and harmony. The problem is that this metamorphosis is not a constant. When it presents itself, like this morning, it must be grabbed with both hands to take advantage of the energy it releases. It's thus that I feel deep inside me, or I should say deep inside the yoked team, an unheard-of power being born that hurtles me headlong into the battle against the elements. It's impossible to lose fights like that.

This morning something inexplicable is happening to me. I can't get started. The slightest gesture is an enormous effort. I literally have to drag myself along. The pulk is an even more cumbersome burden than usual.

I'm struggling a long way behind Alain. My body is the same consistency as a wet rag doll. I don't want to go on anymore, no more ambition. A great emotional instability seizes me.

Last night, I had a frightful nightmare where I looked on, powerless, as my two and a half-year-old baby (my second son) fell down a huge concrete staircase... Now, I'm frightened... A panicky fear that I haven't given enough love to those closest to me. I suddenly can't control myself. Overwhelmed by waves of nostalgia, wanting to cling to my past, to my youth. Powerless, in the middle of a black hole. What on earth am I doing here?

I stop and sit on my sledge, in tears...

I yield without formalities to this destabilised Dixie, and when we call a halt for the first time of the day, I tell Alain what's happened. He understands...

In fact, I gave myself one hour, no more, to put an end to this negative influence on our progression. One has to accept emotions as they come, and above all not try to fight them. Negotiate with them, discuss, and then get free of them by visualising success...

Little by little, I come to the surface. For the rest of the day, I'm wondering what could have caused all that. Could it be excessive tiredness? Could the crisis have been provoked by the flow of powerful impressions that I had yesterday, contemplating those overwhelming natural splendours? Has a safety valve given after eighty-four days of an expedition that is becoming a bit long? Dixie, get a grip. Make your tracks, nothing else. Push, pull, struggle, for hours on end. It's no good my pulling with all my strength, stretching my muscles as far as they'll go, I know that we will make faster progress if I let Alain do most of the work. From now on, he is charged with making the tracks. We walk for nine hours, proceeding with great difficulty over this sloping terrain. My heels are on fire. I no longer even think about the pain. When we stop at 19.30 this evening, we have, despite everything, covered more than ten kilometres.

Friday 23 January (Day 81)

Above the Void, Inch by Inch

The same weather as yesterday, same snow, same work. This morning the temperature is hovering around −3°C and the snow is more viscous than ever. I make tracks for eleven whole hours, with a short break every fifty minutes. I can't see a thing. Despite the compass, I constantly have to correct my course. I soon can make out some vague blue transparent shapes in front of me; blocks of ice or crevasses? Hard to say. I have the impression that they are still a long way off, but without warning, I 'm right on top of them (it's always the same in a white-out – there's no way of judging distance). Horror! The stick plunges through the snow, plunges still further without coming up against ice: they are indeed crevasses. I advance with caution, I'm in more than 40 cm of powdery snow. No way of fathoming what lies beneath my feet. The terrain suddenly gives way…

Start of a zone of large crevasses.

Bloody hell, I'm right in the middle of a covered crevasse without even realising it.

I hold my breath… Needless to say, my heart is pounding wildly… Hold my breath, make a sign to Dixie to wait for me. I have the impression that, on my right, the ground is giving way even more steeply. "Careful, Alain, careful…" Slowly.

First push my ski forward, gingerly feeling out the terrain, make myself as light as possible, avoid brusque movements. Then I realise that I'm not roped up. Already, as a reflex I recapitulate what I should do if I fall… First, ask myself if my course is perpendicular to the crevasse or not. If yes, I should throw myself forward. If not, I have to choose to force myself to one side. How many times have I lived through similar situations in bad weather? I know that it only needs a few days of blizzard for the gaping jaw of the crevasse to be entirely covered with a thin layer of snow. Naturally, with time this film gets thicker, harder, stronger and more solid.

Thinking about the recent storms that have been beating down on the region, I realise that the "snow bridge", which I'm clearly in the process of crossing, could have formed only yesterday or the day before. In which case, I've got no chance of getting out of this. It's crazy what flashes across the brain in such blinding moments. Nothing surprising in the fact that just before dying you can find the time to see the whole of life flash before your eyes.

At each step, my stick goes in up to its hand guard, I hold my breath, I proceed even more cautiously, until the moment when I feel the bottoms of my skis change direction, straighten out and start to go up again. *"Come on Alain, one more go, make yourself light, light, and you've reached the other side of the crevasse."* That was *not* a good moment…

Dixie catches up with me and we continue our journey. I surprise myself several times by shouting, even screaming, to accompany the effort and to tug the sledge out of this snow. At each pull, I feel my hips being lashed, my heels are on fire from bending forwards, my hands can't hold the ski sticks any more. They hurt, and I can feel that they're paralysed. My fingers are like pieces of wood. On the edge of despair, I surprise myself with inward laughter: the proud! It's the circle of pride! Dante had warned us about it. The first circle of purgatory is the circle of the proud. How could we have dared to think that the Antarctic would surrender so easily? Following the course of the Divine Comedy, the end can only be getting nearer. Strengthened by this thought, we go on: one step, then another, and another…

It's 19.30, and we've been on the road for eleven hours. We won't reach the pass today.

It's the tenth day of foul weather. Børge Ousland took only two days to cover the distance to the end of the Axel Heiberg Glacier from the Ross Ice Shelf. How did he do it so quickly?
This evening I feel a little overtaken by this adventure, which seems to want to take us far further than I had imagined. Outside, a light wind is picking up. For five days it had left us.
I go to sleep thinking about the sails; they've been folded in the bottom of the sledges for nine days now.

Saturday, 24 January (Day 82)

Burning Eyes

It snowed abundantly all night long. This weather really gets you down. I make tracks like an animal in 40 cm of "fresh" – seeing virtually nothing at all around me – until we get to the *Zig Zag Bluff* pass. After which, the terrain starts to go down again. There's no doubt about it, we've got to the other side. A few more hours march and to my right, I can see the areas of crevasses at the foot of the glacier. Behind us, everything is black, we won't be seeing the Axel Heiberg again, nor the mountains that we have just crossed. It's incredible.

Ten more kilometres to the Ross platform but we're staying put for today.

In the evening, I see that my hips are bleeding. The effort of these last few days has been almost superhuman. My heels are in intense pain. Let's hope for a little wind to give them all a bit of a rest.

Armed with a video camera, I retrace my steps to take advantage of the better light. I stay behind a little to let the impressions intensify. For the last hour I've been advancing virtually blindfold as my eyes have been literally burnt by the ultraviolet rays. I know that I shouldn't have done it, but today I allowed myself to ski without goggles (I hate wearing goggles). A big mistake. An error that costs a lot. Because even if at times during the day the cloud cover cuts out the sun, the ultraviolet rays are unaffected…

Around 4 o'clock in the morning, I begin to feel some stinging in my eyes and under my eyelids. Before the final halt, I have to blink more frequently to moisten them; keeping them open is increasingly painful. When we are finally in the tent, I use the drops that Alain gives me. That helps… But I can't stop myself from keeping my eyes closed (or else I cry), so I have to feel my way around to find whatever I'm looking for. It's not funny, in any event…

After the Argos ritual, I can at last lie down. Before going to sleep, I wallow in the music of Andreas Vollenweider.

Sunday, 25 January (Day 83)

Snow-quakes

The Ross Ice Shelf has a funny welcome for us. We thought we had finished – or nearly – with trouble and misfortune. With the difficulties of the road as well.

Wrong: the bad luck continues.

First of all there is this end-of-the-world atmosphere which augurs nothing but ill; the clouds are low, grey, then black, full of darkness and ill omen. How threatening!

On the Ross Ice Shelf the situation is so dire that on the night of 4 February, Alain and Dixie consider food rationing and a forced march to McMurdo.

Far to the north, however, where we are heading, the sky is clear and cloudless. This contrast gives the impression that we are travelling in a huge corridor, gripped in a vice. The snow, is dull, the mountains invisible, the light colourless, the silence oppressive. Something serious is about to happen... Soon after we leave we are faced with a stretch of ground that is particularly difficult to negotiate; immense sheets of snow, formed by the wind and seemingly resting on a bed of air, what we call in mountaineering jargon *"wind sheets"*. Whenever you put a ski on them, they cave in a few centimetres (or more) and giant cracks cover their surface like flashes of lightning. At the same time, this sudden subsidence is accompanied by a series of dull explosions, coming in waves one after the other, from the point of impact to the outer limits of the shattered area, some fifteen to twenty metres away.

I would relish the spectacular nature of these snow-quakes if it weren't for the fact that I'm obsessed with the realisation that from now on we are navigating not on *terra firma* but on an ice-floe, and that this tongue of ice is literally bristling with crevasses, each one more murderous than the last.

At each mound, I can't prevent myself automatically lifting my head to survey the terrain around me to check whether I'm in the middle of one of these blasted traps. Not very restful, as you can imagine...

Which God do we have to worship to finally obtain something? Dance the dance of the wind, perhaps? For that's our only hope, and it's become a genuine obsession. As for "El Nino", who should, theoretically, be giving us a hand... It's not yet a question of despair. Almost. More and more handicapped by my eyes, I'm reduced to seeking Alain's tracks blindly with my skis, feeling my way to the left and to the right all the time. I'm proceeding by touch, if you please... Fortunately, as the tracks are deep in the snow, I can feel through my skis, without having to open my eyes, if I'm slowing coming out of them or if I'm following the correct path.

But we are not of the same build, and so I'm having trouble doing this properly. Finally, I find a position that is both efficient and comfortable: my right ski in the track of the Alain's right ski, and my left in the track of the left hand runner of the sledge.

I count up to ten, than I open my eyes for an instant. Up to twenty, and I open them. One minute, and I blink… When I rub my eyes, it's even worse. We go on like this for hours… I have to admit it, today, everything looks black to me (it needs to be said), and I suddenly wonder whether the Argos messages have been getting through. We certainly know that it was working wonderfully, as was confirmed by consulting the web-site and our contact with Michel at the Pole, But since then, nothing. And if they don't receive any more news? Will Michel trigger the rescue service? I can already see an aeroplane coming to find us, even though we haven't asked for it…

Monday, 26 January (Day 84)

"A Piece of Cake!"

The snow is getting a little harder, the skis are only going in a few centimetres and the wind makes a few fleeting appearances as though to let us know that it hasn't forgotten us. Far ahead of us to the north, the weather seems to be fine. My companion has a great deal of pain in his eyes. I'm feeling nervous, but I don't know why.

Recently we've been talking less and less to each other. As though, we need to immerse ourselves in solitude to prepare for an important struggle.

In any event, we have come to a critical point in the adventure. When we left the Pole, we definitely had some wrong ideas about how relatively easy it would be to make progress on the Ross Ice Shelf. Børge had assured us that he had had excellent snow and wind conditions here, apart from a few days of white-out. *"A piece of cake!"*, he had even said during our conversation last summer. But "the cake" that we are currently tasting on this platform of floating ice is very different from the one the Norwegian apparently tasted last year in the same place. Of course, one year is never quite like another in the Polar Regions. However, the enthusiasm that accompanies the preparation of a project of this size can lead one to forget that each venture is unique and that nothing is ever comparable.

Tuesday, 27 January (Day 85)

Iron Discipline, Hellish Discipline

The wind got up at about three in the morning. We were lying in wait for it, the little b……! It was blowing about 20–25 km/h and in the right direction; ideal for the kites. Renewed hope for eating up the distance. It's snowing and visibility is roughly zero, but that doesn't dampen our enthusiasm. On this flat terrain we soon learn to fly by automatic pilot, like sailors accustomed to risking themselves on the frozen seas.

The pain in my eyes is hardly getting any less and blinking is still difficult. I'm still angry with myself for having taken off the goggles the other day.

If one hasn't experienced such an adventure oneself, one can't imagine the discipline required to bring it to a successful conclusion. Everything is discipline, in fact. While on the move, besides the mandatory wearing of goggles, there is a whole host of other rules that have to be obeyed. For example, putting sunblock on the skin of the face every hour. If not, sunburn is guaranteed. Or, making sure of taking off a layer of clothing when you begin to sweat, otherwise a thin film of ice covers the inside of the jackets, which consequently become like cardboard. Another obligation. In the tent each evening, when adding water to the saucepan: although the temptation is to take the snow right at the entry of the tent to avoid having to get dressed and go out again, you must take it from further afield as the slightest impurity (due to the frequent comings and goings, or to the stove) can cause stomach upsets. Another one. Mending the sails: you cannot simply pay attention to the places where they have given way; it's essential to check all the seams and all the lines.

They are, in a sense, a series of little safeguards that you surround yourself with all the time. If, in order to avoid getting out the spade and digging in the ice, you fail to put enough weight on the sail as you set off, there is the risk that you may see it depart before you manage to rejoin the sledge. In short, attention must be paid to every little thing, and one must never take the easy way out. Seen from this viewpoint, living such an experience is a famous education for the will.

When I had my accident at the beginning of the expedition, I was able to overcome the pain as a result of a series of little exercises of self-control. First, by telling myself that without a doctor, without any rest, there was nothing for it but to go on. Fate had so decided; I had to grin and bear it, convincing myself all the while that it was, after all, possible to withstand the pain through will-power and reflection. After several days of such mental gymnastics, I began to control the pain, and the reflex defence mechanism of always looking ahead without complaining became automatic. At that moment, the day is won... After all, character-forming is very much a part of the reason that I let myself in for such nightmares. Fire to forge the steel.

Ten hours later, we've covered 101 km. This evening, the tension of the last few days has evaporated to be replaced by good humour; the wind is making the tent canvas shiver, which seems to be saying that it wants to stay.

Morale soars sky high. Just five or six days more at the same rhythm and we will finally have completed our crossing of this damned desert.

I find myself dreaming, thinking of all the people I love. Oh to be at home again! A tender kiss for each one of you.

Thursday, 29 January (Day 87)

Without Tracks, We're Flying Blind

Yesterday, little or no notes, no wind, 15 km on the counter. I forget… On the stock exchange of emotions, the shares have plummeted, just as they had previously soared.

Tonight, however, the wind got up. A small wind. Aeolus yawning,…

We have to move quickly to take advantage of the slightest breeze.

The terrain is flat, but frightful. We're gliding on a crusty snow that gives way unevenly beneath our skis. We have to do balancing acts and luff to keep going in the right direction.

After eight hours on the road, Aeolus wakes up at last. As always on this continent, when one sees a "plus", you must tell yourself that the "minus" can't be far behind. This time, it's the visibility that drops following the change of wind. No matter, we go into overdrive (the plus) but it's freezing weather (the minus). Naturally, we're making good time (the plus), but we have to be careful all the time because on several occasions already today we have lost sight of one another (the minus). And so on, and so forth…

Sailing today is not easy. Skiing for the most part behind Dixie, I try to follow his tracks. But I can't always make them out in this fog. They are only two thin greyish lines on the ground that the white of the snow quickly disperses.

When I can't find them right away, seconds turn into minutes. One moment I think I've lost them, and that I'm going in the wrong direction. Then, that I've cut across them without noticing. When I haven't seen either Dixie or his trail for a while, say a quarter of an hour, I set off in the other direction to cover the same ground and try to find them. The effort I have to make to keep my eyes fixed on the snow like a maniac, so as not to lose sight of those two lines…

Now and again, it's Dixie who halts, worried that he can't see me when he looks back. It should also be said that today we have negotiated a large area of crevasses indicated on the map. They weren't all that wide, but we had to be careful nonetheless. It must be ghastly to be lost on this continent! On fourteen million square kilometres of ice.

In short, today was another kind of hell.

To go into the wind as much as possible, that's the order of the day. Not only do we have to pull constantly on the sail, but, given its lateral position relative to the direction in which we're heading, we also have had to put up with the rubbing of the harness on our hips. With the pain in the ankles and back as a bonus. In fact, the whole body is exposed to the tugging of the sail, and it gradually goes numb as the hours of sailing go by.

Another problem we're facing now, under sail, is dehydration, as it's difficult to stop for a drink while we're on the move. It's vital to take in sufficient fluids in the mornings and evenings, in the form of tea, coffee, soup, an extended meal or simply melted ice.

The fog suddenly parts, just as we are navigating in a huge area of crevasses indicated on the map. To proceed across open terrain is of course less dangerous, but it doesn't stop the worrying impression that we are exceeding certain limits, that we're going too far, that we are on the point of doing something stupid, like digging into our reserves in this way when it should be reserved for a truly critical situation. What's more, it seems that everything is happening whether we want it to, or not. Evidently, we are not entirely masters of our own destiny…

One or two hours later, it's not important, the white-out is back. Shutting us up straightaway in its invisible white cage. The maddening fog that removes all possibility of resting the eyes, of fixing on to something. Quite simply, you can't see a thing. Nothing. Proceeding under such conditions is so destabilising that after a while I can feel the sharpness of my vision being impaired. When I fix my eyes, to relax them, on the shapes and colours of my immediate surrounds (in fact the only things that I can see), I realise that for a brief moment everything is out of focus…

I don't know why, but I've been looking at my watch more frequently than usual. During the last hour's gliding, I think I must have looked at it every five minutes, and the tension is mounting…

In my little notebook, I re-read in the evening a maxim left by my marathon partner (he has already been to the Antarctic Peninsula to run moreover) . "The human spirit is nothing if we don't test it, explore it, punish it and reward it. Focus, focus, focus…"

We have covered 80 km despite the rotten conditions. On the one hand, this result is satisfying. On the other, we never stop asking ourselves where the favourable winds that we were promised have got to.

In the evening, it begins to snow again, it is mild (-10°C) but we're cold, despite the hot tea. It's the sign of the deep exhaustion that's settling into the body and into the mind, but should we have expected anything different?

There is however no question of taking the slightest extra meal. It is already the 29 January and the terrible truth is before us; although there is not the slightest problem with shortage of food reserves, our days are now numbered.

Unconsciously, we were dreaming of finishing in style with a few superb days of sailing that we could add to the trophy cupboard. Never, throughout the crossing had we tried to break speed or distance records. But now, they are almost a necessity.

Monday, 2 February (Day 91)

And What if We Don't Make it?

The heavenly star has been shining for three days now and the wind has disappeared.

It's the middle of the Antarctic summer. It's fine, very fine… too fine. These are the finest days of the expedition.

The snow is sparkling with thousands of little suns, the sky as clear as crystal. Far off to the east, the Trans-Antarctic mountain range stretches as far as the eye can see. A superb panorama.

To think that we had expected this fine weather: it should have brought us a good katabatic, at least, that is what we were hoping. A gentle breeze, that would have lofted us along in our armchairs as far as the ocean. Once again, disillusionment sets in.

Progress was not as it should have been. Everything leads to that conclusion all the time. In the Antarctic, one has to live in the present. Not to worry about what will happen. Not to rely on past, overly ephemeral experiences. In this context, Dixie is quite right to be positive all the time. Never to say, "Today we only covered 21 km", but rather "the 21 km we covered today bring us nearer to the goal". It is preferable to immerse oneself body and soul in the tiny details of everyday life, to tie knots with the insignificant little details which help us to pass the hours, days and weeks. To learn each day, with the greatest humility, the immediate culture of the ice. To soften the present.

So much for theory. Practice is something else. After a quick calculation this evening in the tent, I reckon that we still have 667 km to go and that we only have twelve days worth of victuals in the sledges. To be sure, there are a few additional rations hanging about here and there. But reality imposes its own rules: if you divide 667 by 12, even say by 15, you still have an average of 44 km per day. What if we don't make it?

Just one detail: since yesterday, the amount that I have to pay for ANI to guarantee the logistics in the event of an accident rises to $7,000 per day. Curiously, although that thought has been stressing me out for weeks, I hardly think of it any more. We'll see how we can deal with that problem later... What's essential now, is that we get ourselves out of here. 10 hours of sailing later, 101 km further on, despite a halt of two hours for lack of wind.

Alain wakes me up at 2 o'clock in the morning; he insists on our having breakfast already to avoid having to stop at about 8 o'clock. I can't get the gruel of fatty cereals down, and I doubt whether the wind is strong enough.

We are obliged to march all day long in a state of half-asleep. After a short rest, we'll try to turn night into day. The wind is back in the evening, we gather up our belongings, and just as we are ready to leave it drops again. It drives you mad! The terrain however is so perfect, so seductive, that we can see ourselves flying in a straight line right to the target.

I would never have thought that I would still be on this ice on 1 February. I would have loved to wish Happy Birthday to Thijsje on 8 February, and above all not to miss Saint Valentine's Day.

Tuesday, 3 February (Day 92)

At Jeannine's...

Weather very overcast, poor visibility, -13°C, wind less than 7 km/h. We make the most of it by sleeping a little and get up at 8 o'clock. Night departures are now a thing of the past. Even though time is pressing, we must nevertheless sacrifice ourselves to the ritual of organising the sails and the suspension lines, and replace the worn-out ropes. It only takes ten minutes, or so. The white-out sets in and we leave for 6 hours of march, using the compass. I feel relaxed, though tired. Very tired. What's more, every time I bend or lean forward, my head spins and I see thousands of stars. That tells you everything.

It might well be very bad weather, but morale is good and the jokes abound. During the halts, we find ourselves more and more frequently at table at our imaginary Jeannine's, with Dixie drinking a *Ciney* and I a *Duyvel* (Belgian beers) as indeed one of the Argos codes indicates[24]. So a short day today, but we'll try tomorrow, come what may, to do at least 10 hours so that we can tell Michel, via the Argos, that there's not too much to worry about; the machines are in good shape, very good shape, even.

Wednesday, 4 February (Day 93)

A Forced March

No matter what the conditions of the day may be, we have to carry on. Make progress.

And so we walk, we make progress: two hours, four hours, six hours, with a bad headwind. After ten hours on the road, we set up camp. Apparently, it's routine, like every day. The actions follow one another, always in the same sequence. The poles, the double roof, the position of the sledges,......then the evening meal...

Something is bothering me, however. The excellent humour, which led us yesterday to go and have a drink at Jeannine's, was perhaps only pretence at merrymaking, a means of self-defence. It's hovering in the tent like a false atmosphere of relaxation, which is concealing a much harsher reality; we're not progressing quickly enough. With our habit of expecting Aeolus every moment of the day and night and telling ourselves that tomorrow will be better, it could well be that in a short time from now we will be up against a *fait accompli*. If we don't ration the food, we are running the risk of serious problems. Extremely serious problems. If we don't make plans for a possible forced march, the same thing.

I thought about this a while back while we were proceeding, after having reviewed all the parameters of this final stage of the adventure; the dwindling rations, the remaining distance, the weather conditions, the approaching winter, our strength will certainly one day, betray us. Although no definitive conclusion is to be drawn, and my confidence in the future remains intact, I have to admit that I had a pretty sombre picture before my eyes.

What's surprising is that Dixie admitted to having had the same thoughts.

Today, during the marching and during the halts, I am doing nothing but calculating the prob-abilities and the averages. Discounting the final 35 km that we would cover come what may, even crawling on our stomachs (I'm talking about the final 35 km before McMurdo), there are still 497 km to go.

The most than we can do each day is 25 km, given the conditions that have been with us for a week (and which are not going to improve as the austral winter approaches). So a maximum of ten hours' march each day with good visibility and good terrain. Perfect! That makes 20 days, e.t.a. (expected time of arrival) 25 February.

But do we have enough food rations? Mentally, I reorganise all the meals. There is only one solution: to cut them in half. I mean one packet instead of two every two days. I don't think that that will be much of a problem. We can afford to be under-nourished for a while, and there is always the surplus of breakfasts that we have been putting to one side throughout the cross-ing. This clearness of thought leads me to a frightening conclusion; if the wind doesn't get kinder, it will have to be the forced march. In the evening, I show my calculations to Alain.

– "Alain, I did some probability calculations a moment ago", he said during the meal, as though opening the most mundane topic of conversation. Take a look…"

– "What, you too?"

– "What? You've thought about what might happen? You've also foreseen a forced march?"

– " "Foreseen", "forced march", that's putting it a bit strongly, but I have briefly analysed the situation, yes… Not very encouraging, is it? In any event, it seems to me that there are decisions that need to be taken."

Throughout this expedition, I've been ready for anything, taken everything on the chin. And on this evening of 4 February, I accept with the same phlegm and determi-nation that from now on we're going to have to ration the food and set a daily quota of distance that must be achieved, come what may.

First measure: as from tomorrow, we ration. We are going to spread a single day's rations over 48 hours. However, to reduce the shock to the system, we decide to allo-cate a supplement and to add the leftovers from the breakfasts that we've been saving for two months (in all, more than ten kilos of food).

As far as the tackling the distance is concerned, we would rather for the time being establish a time limit: ten hours a day. Luckily, Dixie and I are of the same opinion (we tell ourselves that the wind will come one day to get us out of this); we prefer to march more slowly and cover less distance than to damage our feet, our heels and our ankles by forcing ourselves to eat up the distance at any price.

Here's an initial calculation: there are 20 days of food rations left and 500 km to cover. What's the solution?. This means that in all we have to do 25 km per day. According to this schedule, we will arrive at McMurdo on 24th February. I seem to recall that the base "closes" four days later, on the 28th (which would mean that no outside travel would be possible, neither by air, nor by sea, for the personnel continue their work, of course). That leaves a margin of four days.

Not great, but we'll have to live with it.

Because it's the time for balance-sheets and forecasts, I throw in for good measure the nice little noughts for the insurance: 24 days times $7,000 equals $168,000.

Situations such as these call for navigating between two seas, holding your breath in the dark depths and gasping for breath when you resurface, without really knowing why.

Right now, I'm deep down there. No more insurance, no more aeroplane, no more ships. I don't give a damn for all these problems... We're in it up to our necks in any case. Furthermore, Scott, who camped not far from here on the 3rd of March 1912 on his return from the South Pole, encountered the same problem (some consolation). He wrote in his logbook; *"Everything is against us... This morning, however much we pulled with all our strength, for three-quarters of the distance covered today the wind was very violent, so much so that we were incapable of moving the sledge. The surface of the glacier, until recently excellent, has since been made execrable by a thin layer of flaky crystals that stick too firmly to the underlying layer for the breeze to be able to sweep them away. These grains of ice cause an insurmountable friction against the runners. May God have mercy on us, hauling is impossible in such conditions. We're keeping up the appearance of being in good spirits, but what each of us is thinking within himself is not too difficult to imagine..."*

At times, one has to plumb the depths to find the strength to get back up.

Before we went to bed, all this ended in fits of laughter. No panic, lads. If we have to spend the winter blockaded at McMurdo, so OK, we'll spend six months blockaded at McMurdo. Where's the problem?

Sunday, 8 February (Day 97)

Seventy-two Hours of Madness

Given the circumstances, I've written nothing since last Thursday. For these last three days, a truly crazy wind has swept down upon the expedition, literally and figuratively.

Let me recapitulate. On Wednesday evening, the perspective of a forced march was evoked and even envisaged, based on a series of realistic calculations and hypotheses. It could be said that, although the turn of events didn't unduly worry us, we didn't conceal from ourselves the fact that our troubles were far from over.

On Thursday morning, the silence weighed heavily at breakfast. We were both no doubt reflecting on the previous evening's conversation; I think that Dixie and I were both secretly hoping that the wind would have got up during the night. No question of it. This morning, it's the contrary and the sky is leaden. The bad luck continues. It has its effect. Our movements are slower, we look at each other less frequently, our mood is more morose and our bodies more weary.

But, it was written somewhere in the annals of the Antarctic that Thursday 5 February would be a day like no other. Marked with an asterisk. One hour after we rose, and were preparing to strike camp, the wind dropped, then began to blow from the other direction. So surprised were we, that, at first, we couldn't believe it.

 – *Dixie? The wind… it's changing, isn't it?*
 – *We'll see…*
 – *Do you reckon it's for this morning?*
 – *Not too fast, old man…*

Thirty minutes go by and it settles in at about 12 km/h, coming from behind. Suddenly, the preparations slow down, the movements are more precise, we move as though in a film in *slow motion*. We have the impression that we have to adapt our behaviour, camouflage our movements and make ourselves very small so as not to upset the precarious balance that has just settled on this corner of the continent. A brusque gesture, a word out of place, we think, and everything could topple over. That's the state of mind we're in!

At 9 o'clock, nothing has changed; we set off under sail. Two hours later, the GPS shows that we have covered 30 km. The conditions don't change. The snow is good, the wind steady… Without saying a word, we press on…

Towards 13.00, the counter was displaying 62 km. In the middle of the afternoon, a new count: 100 km had been covered.

During the halt, we were of course not claiming victory, but I suddenly felt lighter. Fatigue gives way to a certain light-headedness; above all don't let's interrupt this fantastic cavalcade.

A bar of chocolate, a few crumbs from the rations at the bottom of my pocket, and we're off again, even though the fog has come to shuffle the cards. But no white-out is going to stop us. As there is very little difference between night and day at this time of year, we suddenly decide that for this year the night of 5th February will no longer exist.

At around midnight, when we do not for one moment entertain the idea of setting up camp and are still flying along like angels, the digital screen reads 196 km. I yell out:

 – *Hey, Dixie, what do you reckon? Shall we stop for a little longer than usual?*
 – *Why not…*

It's extremely cold, and 15 hours of non-stop gliding at −25°C and at 13 kilometres per hour is pretty tiring; we set up the tent to prepare our picnic and hot drink. Just the inner tent, so as not to waste too much time.

Take stock, quietly, say nothing, so that nothing comes to disturb the balance. The fleeting moment of a while back now seems like the very finest china. An exquisite

Rotten terrain, deep snow, numerous falls before the final dash to McMurdo.

moment where one begins to believe that everything is going to be alright, but one can't quite believe it. The idea that we're on the verge of pulling off a huge exploit crosses my mind for an instant, but we won't savour that instant too quickly. It's not yet done. We are a bit like athletes in a cross-country race who are giving their all to achieve a possible new world record...

We are both convinced that today will be decisive. I would even like to say solemn... It's becoming increasingly clear that our fate is in the process of being decided. Take advantage of this fine spell (that's saying a lot because visibility is down to 50 metres) and continue this mad race against the clock, against the winds, against the bad moods of the Antarctic; one mustn't think about that any longer. It's now or never.

Is it night-time? Is it day-time? I've no idea.

We are gliding in silence towards the culmination. We have just found the missing pieces of a three-month-old dream. Of course, as the hours unwind and the time goes by, a certain weariness descends. Fatigue hacks at the kidneys. And my legs, where are they?

"*They Kill Horses, Don't They...*" The older ones among us will remember that film depicting some impoverished couples, who, in order to win the meagre prize offered by a group of swindlers, dance without stopping for days on end until there is only one couple left. They were turned to jelly on the dance-floor and it was only by some miracle that they stayed upright. Staring wrecks, spent, swapped for a few green notes. Perhaps we aren't yet total wrecks, but it's clear that, just like them, we are working tonight to the finish. No matter what happens, we're going to melt into the wind just as long as it deigns to blow on this corner of the ice-shelf.

5 o'clock in the morning and the Antarctic wakes up. Hold on! I hadn't noticed. We're still gliding as though in a dream. We're heading straight for McMurdo but at the same time, everything has stopped. Something has to freeze in any event for us to be able to go on like this...

Dixie, the GPS?

It's fine. Come on. We must tell ourselves that every 25 km behind us is one day saved… At the moment, I daren't count. 6 or 7 perhaps.

Friday, 6 o'clock in the morning…

Good, so we must get rid of this beguiling torpor. The risk of falling asleep is getting too great. For that, we must make up jokes; naturally that's not too easy.

The cold can be a powerful soporific. At high altitude, in the death zone of 8 000m, mountaineers who die frozen sleep peacefully; a few moments before death, they probably experience an instant that transforms the cold into a nice warm blanket.

Since we set out yesterday morning, I feel that here too the cold is capable of sending us to sleep, even if we're progressing at 15 km per hour. To avoid that, we turn to childish games. Cross too closely in front of the other, creep up behind him to surprise him and unbalance him with a little push, or get in front to interfere with his course, bring your sail too close to his, as if to tangle them up together, or come up alongside, pulka to pulka, to give him a fright. In short, anything to keep one awake…

At each halt, it's the GPS obsession. How many? 18 km in the last hour. New calculations, new sums. The results of the little needle give us some of its strength! It's incredible, we've been standing up for more than 20 hours and we're speeding along like ice-skaters…

At each halt, we set another goal. Not at the beginning of the day, but in the afternoon, when we realise that the wind is stable and that there's a chance of it remaining so for a few more hours. First halt of the day after 10 hours; there we decide to do five more hours. After which, we put the tent up for a pause of two hours. 196 km covered. During the stops, I have to run and jump about because they're freezing…

Eight in the morning… For a second, I have the illusion of seeing the mountains, without knowing if I can really see them or not; it's a magic moment.

Now the distance record is within our grasp. For some time, the weather has been fine and we can think only of that. Not only do we have a furious desire to beat it, and even to go on to do 300 km, but just thinking about it keeps us awake and gives us renewed strength.

So, we're winning on all counts.

Towards nine in the morning, Aeolus needs a rest, just as we do. We practically fall asleep on our skis. It's with trembling eyes that we consult the GPS screen: 79°827' latitude south, or a distance of 271 km in a straight line! On 9 January 1996, Børge Ousland covered 226 km; the record for the longest distance covered in the Antarctic in 24 hours (without motor) has been beaten. We have been going exactly 24 hours and 30 minutes.

This time, there is no longer any doubt. McMurdo isn't far. The expedition is saved…

In setting up camp (it's about ten in the morning on Friday 6th February), we realise that we are exactly 40 km from the spot where Robert Falcon Scott and his two companions set up their last camp, on 29 March 1912, before the tragic outcome of their expedition. He wrote then: *"All the time, we have kept ourselves ready to set off for the stock-pile, some 12 miles away, but outside there are still thick whirlwinds of snow chased by the storm. We must now abandon all hope. We'll hold on to the end, but we're becoming progressively weaker; death can't be far away. It's frightful, I can't write any more…"*

Despite the emotion brought on by this flash-back, we're impatient to announce the good news to HQ. As we are at more than 79° latitude and the Inmarsat satellites are adjusted to 80°, there's a fair chance that we'll get through. As long as the batteries haven't suffered too much.

Feverishly, as one can be at times like this, I get the equipment out. It's ringing but Michel isn't there. It's his answering machine. Next, I try the cellular phone of Baudouin Remy. I know he follows our doings very closely, and that with Sigrid at Compaq, he is one of the nearest to HQ.

– *Hello, Remy?*

– *Yes?*

– *It's Hubert here. We just done 271 km… In one go…* (it's crazy to think that one can call a mobile phone in Belgium from the Antarctic like this…)

– *What? How many?*

– *271 km in 24 hours 30 minutes… Do you realise?*

– *Your position, please, before anything else…*

– *Yesterday, the wind got up and…*

– *No, old friend, your position first…*

– *OK, wait, it's 79.827 E,……*

– *No, please wait officer, I'm on the line to the Antarctic, it's important.*

– *What? Hello, hello, Remy?*

– *Don't go away Alain, I'll be right back. It's like this officer,………*

Slapstick exchange. What on earth is going on? Baudouin was in fact in his car when his mobile rang. As the main road on which he was travelling (Avenue Brugmann in Brussels) has few parking places, he stationed himself momentarily on the pavement to note down our position. His hurry was born of the fact that we hadn't sent any Argos messages since Wednesday evening, and that at HQ it was "Action Stations!". I had in effect forgotten that one of the conditions of the expedition stipulated that after 30 hours without contact, the rescue procedures had to be triggered… He was badly parked when a policeman – one of those fine moustachioed Brussels cops – came to knock on his window. *"I'm talking to the Antarctic, officer, one moment please…"*, he said to the representative of law and order. Thinking that he was making fun of him, the latter was not amused. *"Get out of your vehicle, if you please…"*. But on the other hand, there was a certain Hubert who was telling him important things and the line was in danger of being cut at any moment. Finally, Baudouin pretended to comply, saying to Alain that he would call him back in a second, moved his car to park it further along, just as badly… So then the moustache saw red, and still not believing that there were two hare-brained Belgians who had gone to the Antarctic on the line, he threatened Baudouin and wrote four offences in his note-book; refusal to obey, using a mobile phone while driving, parking on the pavement and insulting an officer of the law. While throwing in an extremely menacing *"You'll have me to deal with…"* Remy told me that things were later sorted out at the police station.

Friday 06 February, 18.30. We've slept for 4 hours.

Dixie is first up, and outside to take a look around. The wind has picked up speed again; we must leave as soon as possible.

Four hours later, we're again on the boards with the 21 sq m. The cold is burning, the limbs are hurting, the degree of consciousness is falling…

White Antarctic litanies.

All that fades away before the performance that we are in the process of achieving. Towards 4 o'clock in the morning, we have swallowed up a blessed 140 km. We are only 130 kilometres from McMurdo. As an evil snowstorm brews up, spewing 60 km/h winds at us, we decide to stay put for the day.

Mustn't exaggerate. Rest must come before everything…

This day is becoming a crazy day. Where will it end?

At this moment, everything is going well for us. I make the most of this respite to try out a trick that I had thought of before we set off. It's for slowing down the sledge, (like for example when we have to wait for each other) without having to engage in the delicate manoeuvre of lowering the sail. I sit down on the front of my pulka, make myself comfortable, make sure that the skis are properly parallel on either side, and that they are both exercising equal pressure.

And, forward…

Good heavens, it works! Oh if only I had tried this trick earlier! I take out the GPS to check on my speed: I'm doing 15 km/h!!! Perhaps we have an idea here to be developed for our next crossing of the Antarctic under sail…

If one counts our 4 hours of sleep, that makes it now nearly 72 hours that we have been on our skis. It's become too dangerous; we can't allow the slightest blunder now that we are so close to the goal!

Oh how nice it is to do this kind of addition: 271+ 140= 411 km under the belt since Thursday morning. It's an unbelievable success…

Saturday, 7 and Sunday, 8 February (Days 96 and 97)

After the days of doubt, the hours of folly, after the torture, comes the enjoyment.

Today the snow is less hard. As if we were gliding on a carpet. It's very nice not to hear the dry and almost metallic rasping of the runners on the ice. In fact, it's a little like skiing in cotton-wool, with just the rustling of the wind in the suspension lines for company.

I was so relaxed that I found myself plucking the lines of the sail as though they were the strings of a harp. Moreover, I did manage to produce a few notes of music, as they

were so taut in the stron[...]   [...]vas possible to
amuse myself in this way[...]   [...]aving had my
fists clenched for more t[...]

   This time, we had to r[...]   [...]We start again
in the middle of the nig[...]

   The wind is relatively[...]   [...]ctics, we have
to luff. A hard but beau[...]   [...]ring these last
few days, has issued us w[...]   [...]r pace. We are
convinced that we have[...]

   There is nothing mor[...]

   The Pacific Ocean i[...]   [...]icans must be
expecting us. Belgium t[...]   [...]Michel, Baudouin and the rest; suddenly everything is agreeable chaos.

Today I've had the impression from time to time that my head was spinning. Can the ice cause intoxication in the way that deep water can? Of course not, I'm raving. It's the beginning of the end that's giving me the bends. Nothing else…

What a beautiful Antarctic night this is! Especially with the outline of the Mt Erebus volcano displaying its curves on the horizon.

Just before setting off we hear the sound of an engine! It's ANI's Twin Otter flying overhead. "Good God", I say to Alain in a panic, "they've come to find us!". Bloody hell, what's going on? Can our safety no longer be guaranteed? Hasn't the extra days' insurance been paid? How far will the Network go? Stories are told that when there are financial problems, ANI is prepared to send one of its Twins to pick up the bad payers. Wherever they may be. But, it's nothing like that. The pilots make big signs and pass low, over our tent. Alain reckons that the firm is taking advantage of the plane's being on stand-by, under contract to us, to do a little extra business with the people at McMurdo.

This human contact brings us a little nearer to the goal, in any case. We are now like horses that can smell the stable. That doesn't prevent this Sunday from being a very hard day. We have to stop every quarter of an hour on account of the raging gusts of wind (at least 60 km/h). That obviously slows us down: not only because of the stoppage time itself, but also because each time we set off we have to get the machine going again, reconstruct the movements, find the best position for the sail and adjust the suspension lines… In short, it's as though we had to pay our final bill before checking out of this world of ice, by repeating once more, the most difficult movements that we've made up until now.

The evening reward, for once, is not the bowl of hot soup in the hands, but Mount Erebus and the Mina Bluff – which we know from books. They are taking shape before our eyes. Before going to sleep, Alain confides in me, "I'm dead tired. This final sprint is very hard…"

This Sunday, nine hours forty-five minutes after setting off, we have bitten off a further 97 km! Which puts the South Through the Pole 1997–98 Expedition just 46 km from the goal. Not too bad…

We are certain that it will all be over within two days, but we still have to be careful, because, as luck would have it, the final approach to McMurdo is pock-marked with crevasses.

As I slip into my feather bed, I can't hold back a few tears; I can't bring myself to believe that in three days we have covered a trifling 508 km, or a daily average of 169 km. To think that on Wednesday evening we were making plans for a forced march and were convinced that we were entering a life or death situation!

Monday, 9 February (Day 98)

With only a Voluptuous Solitude for Company

To accomplish the final thrust, our departure must be relaxed. Above all no panic, the stakes are too high. How many adventures have ended badly because the desire to be done with it was too great and mistakes were made in the rush?

Here are this morning's conditions: banks of driven snow, a very strong wind, visibility 20 metres. Our sledges, which protect the tent from the prevailing winds, are once again buried in snow like during the good old days up on the plateau.

As we set off, a real storm gets up. It would have been too good to end under a blue sky! Nonetheless, with the gaps in the clouds and the snow letting the sun through from time to time, we are treated to an unforgettable sight. The problem is that we don't have much time to enjoy it, because we have to luff (and almost lose our balance) since the gusts of wind are coming from the wrong direction. What's more, the snow is deep, which often makes us lose our balance. How many time have I fallen over this morning, with the sledge finishing up on top of me, the suspension lines tangled up with my skis? I'm convinced that, years from now, when I recall the Antarctic and times like the ones we are living today, I will wonder how we managed to make the crossing in such storms. It's very simple: in two hours we have covered only 17 km!

Suddenly, no more wind. We stop. Half an hour after the flat calm, the wind gathers speed again. We too, at the same time: it's to be one of the finest moments of the expedition. For these hours are perfect; an ideal wind, a temperature that is almost mild, an excellent, cushioning snow, good ice underneath, perfect gliding on a soft terrain, without mishaps, in a straight line, elegant, above all efficient, the sun now and again putting in miraculous appearances, the 21 sq.m. behaving better than ever, and then, to crown it all, the joy of experiencing this moment with only a voluptuous solitude for company...

While trying to find my centre of gravity, I let myself lean backwards until, completely upside down, my head touches the snow, and so I discover the countryside from an angle that is, to say the least, original...

A few hours later, we come into an area of crevasses that has a bad reputation. It's the one shown on the map under White Island. Thanks to fleeting moments of brighter weather, the first signs of Antarctic civilisation come into sight. Some black rocks on the horizon indicate Castle Rock, the hill separating McMurdo from the New Zealand Scott Base. Of course, Dixie and I are searching the horizon for the famous Mount Erebus. We were told that because of its 3 000 m, we couldn't miss it, but, like Sister Anne, we can't see anything coming. The sky is still heavy and the clouds are clinging to the mountain.

It must be said that we haven't too much time to look into the distance, because the squalls are incredibly strong. They almost flatten us to the ground before throwing us forward once again, for a few dozen metres. As soon as we learn to make the best possible use of them and virtually fly over the powdery snow, they quieten down as if by magic. At that moment, their momentum carries us forward a short distance, exactly like a water-skier letting go of the line and sinking gently into the water. As for us, we sink gently into 40 cm of fresh snow!

> *What a fabulous sight up in the sky! They are like frayed white ribbons moving lazily in procession over our heads. When one looks at them one can yet again feel the omnipotence of the wind.*
>
> *Since yesterday afternoon, we have been faced with snow that is too deep. When the wind was fairly strong, we could glide over it, but when it blows in great gusts, it's just not possible.*
>
> *As visibility is zero, why should we obstinately want to glide at all costs?*
>
> *And yet, I can feel that this a moment of great joy for Alain. I can see him dancing with the wind in the powdery snow, pulled by the big sail. What a pleasure to witness him savouring such moments of joy in this way.*
>
> *We film a little, while being careful about the crevasses.*

We finish the day on foot. What should we do? Go on to the end at the base? Or plant our tent for the last time so as not to leave this implacable universe too quickly? We opt for the second solution. We are certainly burning with impatience to get in touch with our loved ones and we also have a wild desire to bring things to an end, no matter what kind of welcome the Americans may give us. I also think that before starting on a new life, one must gently extract oneself from the former. It's a bit like the single-handed round-the-world yachtsmen who often are afraid to cross the line at the end of their voyage. I know already that my actions in the tent this evening, even if I know them by heart and have done them a hundred times before (and that's pretty accurate as we are on the 98th day of the expedition), will have a quite different significance; they will signify a great victory while at the same time taking leave of a part of myself.

It is 5.30 GMT, when we make camp for the last time.

Dixie announces a veritable orgy of cheese as the aperitif. After the meal, a few games of cards to punctuate an evening of indispensable banality. I say banality because there are now three figures enthroned in my head – a 98 day crossing, 3,924 km covered of which 3,340 km using our sails – which will become, for a long time, a very long time indeed, the substance of my dreams.

Tuesday, 10 February (Day 99)

McMurdo's Apple

Even on this last day, the wind leaves a lot to be desired. It's going to be ski sticks that get us going today. The last few kilometres, the last moments of dialogue with the ice, the wind and the sledge…

Almost at once, a vehicle with caterpillar tracks draws near. Steve Dunbart welcomes us warmly. Head of the rescue team at McMurdo, he had set out to meet us yesterday; but as with us, the storm and the lack of visibility had stopped him.

We have a chat and that does us good. In short a liberation, a foretaste of victory. But we have to stay calm and suppress our emotion. There are still a few kilometres left to cover. Crossing the airport runway, we shake a few hands and somebody offers us an apple, an ordinary apple. What happiness! A little further on, a veritable four-lane motorway begins; marked out with a multitude of pennants that are going to lead us to the Scott base. We cover the final 7.5 km on foot. It starts to snow. For the last time, we have to struggle against a strong wind, but we no longer feel the cold, the squalls or the snow; the sledge has become a part of us. I know already that I'm going to miss all that terribly. I feel a lump in my throat. I'm overcome with emotion.

For a brief moment, I imagine the reunion with all the people that I love. I speak to one, to another, fall into the arms of a third, a fourth. Thank you, thank you. Everything is confused, and I can't prevent a few tears. It's now that the emotion is at its strongest, and I know this because I have experienced it so many times. Afterwards, everything will be so different. I take off my goggles and take down the hood of my jacket; I want to feel for one last time the snow whipping my face and the violence of this nature overwhelm me body and soul.

Through the fog, we can make out the black mass of Castle Rock. It's the end of the crossing. "We've done it!!".

I try to remain realistic and to avoid being too emotional. When we distinguish through the curtain of fog the group of people waiting for us, I suddenly realise that this is the end.
I have a last look at the expanse of ice that has carried us throughout all these days. A final thank you to the nature that I love so much. The welcome is exactly what we need. Simple and warm. We fall into each other's arms. What an adventure! We take off our skis for the last time. At each moment, I try to realise that it's over, "gedaan", "fini"! A short interview is granted to AP (Associated Press) and soon, a digital photo wings its way to the Internet and to our website, to be seen everywhere in the world. The equipment is loaded on to a lorry. Steve tries to play the good guide, but I'm not listening, I'm not there. Alain and I shake each other's hands without saying a word.

We enter McMurdo; a town in the Antarctic! An impressive sight.

We are welcomed very officially by Al Sutherland, the head of the NSF in McMurdo. While congratulating us on our success and enquiring after the state of our health, he explains to us the constraints to which he has to submit in order to make us welcome. In all, we are entitled to a hot meal and a shower. Because we were aware of this regulation, we don't make anything of it. That doesn't mean that there isn't some-thing strange and surrealistic about the situation, however.

So we can have a shower, wash our clothes, put them out to dry in one of their hangars, and undergo a medical examination. After which we are invited to have a meal in the canteen.

Al offers to put a little country retreat, some 7 km out of town, at our disposal free of charge while we are forced to wait to go home. This aluminium box, referred to here as "Silver City", resembles some of our distress shelters in the Alps. It will serve as our lodging until we can board an ice-breaker bound for New Zealand, in two week's time. Al's an honourable man, and he believes that we haven't much food left, so he puts some freeze-dried products and other food, at our disposal. During the day, we can of course come back into the town and circulate as freely as we wish…

Here we are already thrown into another adventure. For McMurdo is one of those incredible little towns at the ends of the earth. Equipped with state-of-the-art

After ninety-nine days and 3924 km Alain Hubert and Dixie Dansercoer arrive at the American Base at McMurdo Sound.

scientific laboratories and possessing impressive logistics, this base is a veritable tool of scientific work at the disposal of the international community.

The people here reserved an extraordinary welcome for us, in any case. Since we left the South Pole, some have been following our progress on the Net. They confirmed to us that these weather conditions have been the worst for almost ten years. During the days after our arrival, everything is focussed on repatriating us, but it's not that simple. There is nothing certain either about the date or the means of transport. Having missed the 2 February rendezvous with the ship, we are embroiled in a logistical nightmare, trying to find a way home. There is the possibility of an ice-breaker in a fortnight's time. Some (were they joking?) even suggested that we might be spending the winter here. The press, our sponsors Compaq, the family, the friends, all are like cats on a hot tin roof.

Will we really be able to rest, to let ourselves go, to begin to relive the best moments? How to describe and recount them? How to organise the first smatterings of adventure stories that will be demanded of us, but at the same time begin to make room within ourselves for others, for family and friends?

In the uncertainty and difficulty of the situation, friendships and complicity develop. How could we forget the visits of some to our retreat, or the meetings with others on the street corners of the town, the fresh bread in the lower lab, the little cakes from the kitchens, the helping hands and the long conversations in the hangars with the rescue team and in the office of the base's doctor, Ralph…

Finally, following an agreement between the Belgian and American authorities, we are graciously invited to embark on a US Air Force aeroplane bound for New Zealand.

Wednesday, 18 February

A Taste of Eternity

At Christchurch, the Belgian Consul was waiting for us. A very warm welcome which relaxed us after all those diplomatic-scientific complications. In the evening, we join up again with an old friend of Dixie's and … Belgian beer. Conscious of what awaits us in our country, they offer us today a final escapade on the west coast of the island. Let's dive in the Pacific.

Far away on the horizon, there is a white and black land, a lost continent of great importance, a continent of incredible challenges, with its imaginary landscapes, its incomparable dialogues, its human beings who attach themselves to it, trying to decipher the past of our planet in order to describe its future. There is a part of us there. Dixie and I look at each other. We understand. Beyond the horizon and somewhere within us.

A little tourism – off to meet the penguins with the chief medic from McMurdo.

To clear our minds, and prevent our muscles going rusty (they are not yet acclimatised to this new way of life) we happily accept the offer of a trip on foot up the mountains at Arthur Pass. Since we left our host behind some way before the summit, we will be departing with a new nickname: *The Belgian mountain goats.*

The tension begins to rise. Tomorrow, we are to leave for Sydney and then Singapore, Amsterdam and Brussels. In a few hours, we will regain our territories, our daily lives and our affections. We will then have to undertake the other side of the adventure; trying to share this immense richness, this intimate strength and this sense of urgency that has been bequeathed to us by this fabulous continent.

Our crossing lasted 99 days. For us, now, it seems like an eternity. But, it was a only little stretch in the thread of our existences, and it will only be a flash of lightning in the great book of the world. There are many coincidences, or should one say similarities? One hundred days, nearly. Exactly the same period as the first crossing of the Antarctic 40 years ago. What their cohort of motorised vehicles, backed by continuous re-supply, had been able to accomplish was matched by our sails flirting only with the strength of the wind. A century of days for a centenary, a story to salute once more, the intuition of Adrien de Gerlache on the grandeur of this continent.

A hundred days finally for the hundred songs with which Dante marked out his Divine Comedy, an eternal call to human adventure.

Celebrating the success of the crossing at Christchurch in New Zealand: nothing beats good Belgian beer.

NOTES

(1) The Argos codes utilised by the expedition are based on the principle of sending messages (pre-defined by the user) by transmitters to instruments stationed on two NOAA satellites (National Oceanic and Atmospheric Administration, a branch of the United States Department of Commerce. These instruments then re-transmit the messages towards earth, either in real time when they are in the proximity of a receiving station, or after having recorded them. On the ground, the stations transmit the data to the Argos centre which carries out the required processing (calculating the position, for example) before sending the results to the users. As the expedition had taken with it two beacons, each comprising 16 positions (of which one was for distress), it had 225 information codes at its disposal. Other than data concerning the progress and the state of health of the two men, each morning the Argos codes communicated the position of the expedition with an accuracy of between 1000 and 150 metres.

(2) "Nunatak" is the name given to a rock or group of rocks which emerge from the ice.

(3) "Polynya" derives from a Russian word meaning "lake". Polynyas are large expanses of open water, which remain unfrozen amongst the winter sea ice.

(4) As the Antarctic ice flows inexorably towards the coasts, a few centimetres per year at some places, a few metres per year at others, the site of the former King Baudouin bases – one built in 1957–58 and the other in 1961–62 – is also moving slowly closer to the ocean. As they were also becoming progressively embedded in the ice, it was thought that at one and the same time they were being drawn closer to the coast and would eventually be carried off by an iceberg. Two years ago, the Belgian Professor Hugo Decleir, flew over the site and managed to establish that a gigantic crevasse was now occupying the space that was formerly inhabited by the Belgians.

(5) This diet had begun with a thorough cleansing of the human system; grapes and water for a whole week. For further information about the polar diet, please see the relevant appendix.

(6) Three communication techniques were used for getting in touch with HQ; e-mail (laptop), telephone via a sophisticated transmitter-receiver based on the geo-stationary Inmarsat satellite system (active up to 80°S), and the Argos beacons that transmitted the coded messages to HQ each morning and evening.

(7) Patrick Nassogne is a multimedia producer who is passionate about kites. It is partly thanks to him that the sail now marketed as "THE INTEGRAL" – the 21 sq.m. – was able to be developed and built.

(8) In order to be able to deal with the largest possible number of Antarctic winds, three different sized sails were developed for the crossing: 6, 12 and 21 sq.m. See the appendix on traction kites.

(9) What the Americans from the Amundsen-Scott base called "Belgian chocolates" were simply a dietary supplement tailored to the specific needs of the two men each day. See the appendix on the polar diet.

(10) "Katabatic" winds have been observed at all latitudes of the world. They are caused by cold dense air drawing down from the plateau to the coast. Nowhere else are they as violent as in the Antarctic.

(11) At the moment there are no regular commercial air or sea links between Antarctica and the other continents. There are numerous tourist cruises to the continent – especially departing from Punta Arenas for the Antarctic Peninsula. For its departure from McMurdo, the expedition was counting on the arrival of an ice-breaker coming from New Zealand.

(12) The Laboratory for Environmental Glaciology and Geophysics (LEGG) at Grenoble is a research unit run by the National Centre for Scientific Research (NCSR). It is made up of several teams studying climate, chemistry and glaciers. They also develop models of the evolution of certain objects of the solar system (comets, frozen satellites, certain small planets) and studies of the physics and behavioural mechanisms of the ice.

(13) Edgard Picciotto, who is 76 years old, was one of the most active of the Belgian Antarctic researchers. He was notable for being the first to have conceived of a method of measuring (based on the isotopic composition of the ice) the accumulation rate of precipitation on the ice cap, particularly in the most remote part of the Antarctic. He was also taken on by the Americans in 1966 to manage the 2nd phase of the Queen Maud Land Traverse.

(14) The scientific mission has two objectives: observation of the physical characteristics of grains of snow (from pits dug to a depth of 1.5 metres) and the collection of snow samples for isotopic analysis. For further details, please see the appendix on the scientific mission.

(15) The Antarctic region between the Sør Rondane Mountains and the Amundsen-Scott base is a zone which had only been explored once before during the Queen Maud Land Traverse, from 1955 to 1957.

(16) The katabatic shelf is a phenomenon of climate.

(17) Because of the importance accorded to the rise and fall of the ocean levels and its possible link with the melting ice (global warming), the study of the dynamics of the Antarctic ice cap is a major concern of hundreds of researchers throughout the world. For further information on the glaciology and dynamics of the ice cap, please see the book "L'Antarctique et la Belgique" by Michel Brent (Editions Labor, Brussels, 1997).

(18) A "Mindsurfer" is somebody who lets his mind wander gently and with the necessary detachment over his day-dreams, ideas and memories.

(19) The Belgian researcher and specialist in atmospheric dynamics Hubert Gallé (Georges Lemaître Institute of Louvain-la-Neuve) agreed to the use of his mathematical model on the Antarctic winds for simulating their characteristics (strength and direction) for the whole of the trajectory followed by the Expedition.

(20) The Pole of Inaccessibility is the place furthest removed from the Antarctic coasts. The station there was established by Russian scientists at the time of the International Geophysics Year (IGY) in 1957–58.

(21) In 1959, the Americans and other countries involved in IGY organised an international conference to agree on the future international management of the continent. The twelve nations participating in this meeting were: Argentina, Australia, Belgium, Chile, France, Great Britain, Japan, New Zealand, Norway, South Africa, USA and USSR. These countries constituted what was to be known for a long time as "The Club of 12". The treaty that was signed was named the Antarctic Treaty. The very foundation of Antarctic management established the status of the white continent permanently. Its essential objectives were and still are: the freedom to explore the Antarctic; the pursuit of international research; and the utilisation of the land and its resources for exclusively peaceful ends. Signed at the height of the Cold War, the Treaty was welcomed by the international community as an historic event.

(22) Created in 1950 by the United States Government, the National Science Foundation (NSF) is an independent government agency charged with the promotion of science and engineering through scientific programmes. Its annual budget is in the area of $3.3 billion (1996), which covers some 20,000 research and educational projects. Cost for Antarctic amounted in 1995 to approximately $196 million.

(23) As the magnetic variation is important in the Polar Regions (in the Antarctic it can vary by as much as 100°), it is essential to know it if one is to make use of compass readings. Today, all GPS manufacturers have introduced magnetic variation data into their machines.

(24) See Note 1 (Day–2) for information on the Argos codes.

www.antarctica.org

By Michel Brent

"Hello, Michel? I've decided to create a web-site for the expedition. A site that will explain the adventure in all its details – its genesis, its technological innovations, the story of the traction sails, etc – and which will also talk of the centenary of the *Belgica*. It will tackle the subject of the scientific mission and above all will follow day by day our progress on the polar icecap. Are you interested?"

August 1997. Just two months before the departure date, when the final preparations were in full swing, and I was finishing my book on the Antarctic and Belgium, Alain Hubert decided to create a web-site! "No problem about the design of the site", he confided in me, "It's Carl Beeth – a young computer graphic artist, computer scientist and Belgian webmaster of Swedish extraction who will be taking care of that aspect of the work. As for you, all you have to do, initially, is to draft the copy for the various sections. Afterwards, during the expedition, you will just have to write a few words once or twice a week on the progress of the expedition…"

In the 10 years that I have been taking care of the "communications" side of his great adventures, Alain and I have always been in agreement about pushing things as far as possible in this area. When he entrusted me with the first press folder on Everest, I was convinced that beyond the information about the project itself (climbing the North face, at the time), we also had to provide as much information as possible about this Himalayan myth for the journalists, information that in general is not easy to find. I recall that the folder contained more than 60 pages and that my colleagues seemed to be pleased with the result. We had proceeded in exactly the same way when we had prepared for the North Pole expedition in 1994.

This time, we were up against something even bigger. After flirting with the idea of short and snappy sections, as is the general tendency for most websites, we reverted to our first idea: don't withhold information from the public and always go for quality. One month later, the copy for the site was ready; it would lead surfers not only through the history of the continent and a summary of its links with Belgium since the wintering of Adrien de Gerlache in 1898, but also into the many and varied aspects of the SOUTH THROUGH THE POLE 1997–98 expedition. At the other end of the world, somewhere on the west coast of America, a computer professional was busy re-writing these pages in computer language.

Once the body of the site had been written, we still had to work out how the day to day tracking of the expedition would be reported. "A few words once or twice a week" is how Alain had put it. Everyone who followed the expedition on "antarctica.org" knows that it was nothing of the kind, and the "antarctica.org" did a great deal more besides simply following the progress of the two stooges. At the beginning, however, I was asking myself a whole host of questions: who will be interested, via the Net, in an expedition which will be crossing what is basically the same kind of landscape for 4,000 kilometres? What will I be able to recount about an adventure that will have the same scenarios every day, or almost? What meaningful copy will I be able to produce from basic information consisting of just two letters followed by two numbers and a few laconic words, as for example "A8–B9 = white-out all day long", the only means of communication with HQ that the two men would have once they had passed the 80th degree latitude south?

We should first consider what had happened between the opening of the web-site (on the same day as the departure of the expedition) and the publication of the first homepages on 22 November 1997 (19 days after Dixie and Alain had left the site of the former King Baudouin bases). If surfers were unable to follow the suspense of the first weeks (storms, blizzards, problems with the sledges, etc) it was because everybody had been caught short. Alain and Dixie were preoccupied, Beeth was working away in his corner of the world without a great deal of communication, and Patrick Nassogne (the multimedia producer who initiated the web-site) was having a holiday in Africa. I had realised that the programme I had developed to enable me to send my copy directly to the web-site was not working. Certain things were clear: I needed to learn immediately the rudiments of the HTML language, together with the people who were managing the Internet site, or the site would be completely devoid of interest. I further realised that if their progress was to be spiced-up with a hint of suspense, I would need to "hatch" something every day, not once or twice a week as Alain had envisaged. On 17 November, the Belgo-Swedish computer graphic artist would come and initiate me in the art of Internet languages.

Since then, with practice, all these hieroglyphics and other codes have become familiar to me. At the time, as a beginner, they filled me with dread. My fear was all the stronger because Beeth had gone back to the United States and I found myself on my own faced with the many things that had to be done to update the homepages. Before he set out, Alain had left me the telephone numbers of some computer friends who were ready to help me if the need arose. Which is how I met Frédéric Sepulcre from the Ardennes, a management consultant engineer who was to take over the Excel spreadsheets for the daily logarithmic calculation of the positions received each morning from Toulouse via the Argos satellite system; daily distance, daily running total, distance remaining until the South Pole and until McMurdo, overall average, among others.

Initially somewhat doubtful about the idea of involving the largest possible number of people in a step by step adventure of this kind, I came to realise that "www.antarctica.org" was going to be able to present itself as a genuine daily newspaper of the expedition. I decided to run it in the manner of a journalistic chronicle – with contributions from polar region specialists, the explanation of certain phenomena that are only to be found in Antarctica and the necessary rigour for the drafting of the copy.

The first communiqué was published on 22 November, that is to say the 19th day of their journey, under the title *"Camping at the foot of the Sør Rondanes"*. Until then, they had covered 163 km and were involved in the ascent of the Gunnestadt Glacier with mixed success. The opening of the framework site had an immediacy about it and a climate that induced suspense. There were, in effect, weighty uncertainties hanging over the fate of the expedition – at least that's what Brussels was thinking. The first: even though the sponsor had accepted the principle of resupply, this had to happen before the end of the month (of November), because that is when Blue One's Twin Otter, which was to have brought the new sledges to the area, was due to return to Patriot Hills. The second: on this continent as elsewhere, there are always uncertainties about the weather, which can keep planes on the ground for days at a time. The third: the two men had chosen not to wait where they were but to keep going. The Twin Otter has a limited range, so we were genning up on the distance between the tourist station and the course of the expedition. And that wasn't all: the satellite communications, which until then had been good – when Alain telephoned me I could hear him as though he was in Belgium – were getting worse. Towards the end of November, the expedition could not even get in touch with Blue One any more, and one morning I learnt from the Adventure Network International (ANI) staff that the radio exchanges for finalising the re-supply arrangements had had to take the incredible route of "Antarctica-Belgium-Antarctica". Incredible! It was down to me to give the green light for the Twin Otter to leave, for the pilot needed to know whether the ice where the two adventurers were at the time was suitable for landing. Remaining worries: while Alain and Dixie continued to make progress, the C130 which should be bringing the sledges was blocked in South Africa by bad weather. To conclude this unsettling little picture, I learned that the sledges had been received by a local company, and not by Anne Kershaw (the ANI representative) and instead of being safely stored in some private place, had been provisionally dumped in a hanger at the airport. In a nutshell, I was far from convinced about the final fate of the expedition.

So those were the circumstances surrounding our first steps towards the "antarctica.org" communiqués. Suffice it to say that the small space on the homepages at my disposal was soon to become far too restricted for my liking. *"Don't make the copy too long,"* Beeth and Nassogne had advised me during my apprenticeship, *"people get bored very quickly on the net..."* I quickly decided not to follow it blindly; if events so warranted, I wouldn't hesitate to extend the copy by several screens.

Once again, events proved me right: on 30 November, I received an Argos saying *"Serious accident Alain"*: it was the incident of the CO poisoning from the MSR stove that wasn't working properly from the start. We had the feeling that bad luck was really playing its part: the C130 still couldn't take off from South Africa, the Twin Otter was committed to an unavoidable schedule, Alain had fainted, Blue One was trapped in a blizzard, the new sledges were left unguarded in an airport hangar of a town with the worst of reputations for security and theft… Then we had to add a telephone message from the Argos people to this weighty atmosphere to the effect that, on Monday 1 December, there was a general power cut in the premises of the NCSS (National Centre for Space Studies) and that until further notice no codes would be reaching them… Coming precisely at the moment when the resupply should be taking place, the news was not particularly well received.

With hindsight, I believe that all these events served to popularise "antarctica.org". Thousands of people, whether they were sympathetic to the endeavour or not, visited the site to see how things would develop. Public interest is aroused when things go badly – as everybody knows – or when there is bad news to digest in front of the TV. The site was a bit like the private telly of the expedition, and what's more, information appeared their first, before being sent to the Press…

The suspense could have been even greater, because I did not disclose everything on the website. The Twin Otter left Blue One on Monday, 1 December, without the pilot having received any information either from HQ or from the expedition itself. I was to learn later that they had a mission to fulfil in the general direction of the expedition's itinerary, and that they had decided to make an attempt at resupply, the weather conditions being at last favourable. Then some six hours later, Blue One rang to say there was no one at the camp nor any tracks. Normally there would be no cause for alarm. But in view of the previous problems there was good enough reason to be worried. I have to admit that I endured several hours of anguish. Their position finally reached HQ via Argos, and, redirected, the Twin Otter was able to find them 11 km further away and unload the replacement sledges.

Another fairly dramatic event was going to make "www.antarctica.org" well known: Dixie's accident the day after the re-supply. It was Friday, 5 December, the Argos messages was the code A8–B5 *"Serious accident Dixie"*. *"Panic in the Antarctic"* was to be my headline for that day, after receiving fresh news via a satellite link with Alain, who explained to me that Dixie was suddenly lifted off the ground by his sail, had fallen back heavily on to the ice several times and was suffering from severe pain in the ribs. The accident caused a big stir in the Press and "antarctica.org" benefited from the fall out of the incident. The fact that the daily newspaper, Le Soir, mentioned the site address in its supplement published in connection with the "Last Continent" exhibition also helped to make the expedition's Internet pages well known; since the end of November, surfers had started to write to tell me their impressions. Apart from the teething troubles of the early weeks which received a fair amount of (totally justified) criticism, opinion was unanimous: to my utter astonishment, they thought the site was superb!

Towards mid-December, even though I did not yet have any information concerning the number of visitors to the site, it seemed to me that it had reached its cruising speed and was now playing its part in providing information for the general public. A final visit from Carl arriving from the United States brought me definitively up to speed not only concerning the three pages that I had to look after, the Homepage, the Daily Reports Archive and the Daily Progress Table, but also with the cross-references triggered from the hyper text. Be that as it may, communication with the expedition, by telephone or by e-mail, was becoming increasingly rare: it was true that the batteries had endured a cruel test at the time of the re-supply operation and that this energy source had to be preserved. On the other hand, the two adventurers were slowly approaching 80°S, beyond which the Inmarsat satellites were of no use.

As far as the daily updates were concerned, I was therefore obliged to restrict myself to the three or four Argos messages that came in each morning. As they arrived in code *"A1-B6: on foot with crampons"* or *"A3–B0: unavoidable crevasse area"*, for example, and they were more and more limited to figures showing the rate of progress, I was obliged also to read between the lines. Did Dixie recover from his brief spell off the ground? Radio silence. Were the successive equipment breakages (traction sails, sledge shafts, stove, etc) impeding progress too much? Mystery. The morale of the troops? Another unknown. How had they taken these successive time losses when the first parameter of this adventure, at least if it was going to be successful, remained, as ever, their rate of progress? I didn't have the faintest idea. One morning, I got the Argos message *"A8–B0: Dixie, problem digesting grub"*; but the next day, not the slightest reference to the excessive fat in the diet. How should I transform this information into accessible language? By circulating hypotheses and by making, for example, a report on the polar diet developed by Alain Hubert and Arnaud Tortel, a French dietician.

On 26 December, they were some 700 kilometres from the South Pole when I received the following Argos message: *"A13–B10: unexpected encounter explained later via e-mail"*. This was the opportunity I had been looking for to introduce an interactive element into the web-site and which gave me the idea of organising a little competition, the "South Pole Contest": it was a question of asking the visitors to provide their interpretation of this brainwave. Following which the winner (I assume that we will learn the answer during their stay at the American base at the Pole) would receive from the expedition's financial partner a small symbolic gift, on this occasion a jacket stamped with the expedition logo. For a few days HQ was inundated with e-mails, and so that the surfer could experience the same pleasure as I did in discovering the avalanche of responses, I decided to publish them in full on the web-site. Some disclosed a genuine interest in what they could have encountered: a weather balloon, a barrel of fuel, an American flag, dust particles coming from a volcanic eruption, relics from an earlier expedition, a piece of a satellite, an abandoned polar vehicle, a meteorite, and so on. Others on the other hand were merely whimsical: a bottle of Coca Cola, a bird, Madonna's knickers, a refrigerator fallen from an aeroplane, an unidentified gliding object called Father Christmas, some tourists, a used condom, a penguin's egg, a plastic palm tree, a skeleton, a nudist camp, Tintin in Tibet, a Playboy magazine, an inflatable doll …

This little competition enabled me if nothing else to get an idea of the "antarctica.org" audience. What was most encouraging was that the adventure of the two Belgians was being introduced as a subject in the schools, and the teachers seemed to be taking advantage of the event to initiate the youngsters into Antarctic matters. I remember in this respect a response sent by a French school situated in the magnificent mountainous region around Chartreuse. How was it that these people, these French who are normally so chauvinistic, came to be interested in an adventure by Belgians? That's part of the flamboyant mystery of the Internet.

While the "South Pole Contest" was in full swing, the two Belgians finally arrived at the South Pole. The first contact with HQ took place on 3 January at 19.20; Alain's voice, breaking up from interference, reached me via Patriot Hills which had to act as an intermediary between the American base and Belgium; I could only just make out that the two men were on good form, that there was no question of giving up and that they would shortly be on their way again.

The next day, imagine my surprise when, opening the homepage, I saw a photograph of Alain and Dixie inside a greenhouse looking at some basil leaves. How could that have been accomplished? The enigma didn't last long; one of the technicians at the base had taken the photograph and had immediately sent it via modem to our webmaster, Carl Beeth. He had then done the rest without telling me. Even though I was by now completely familiar with Internet matters, I still found it staggering that barely a few hours after reaching the South Pole after covering 2000 km of Antarctic ice, a photograph of the two men could be seen in this way by tens of millions of people throughout the world. In the same way that I found it incredible (before they had gone beyond 80°S) that I could just press twelve digits on the HQ's telephone for it to ring in the tent, for Hubert to pick up the receiver and for me to hear his voice as though he were in the neighbourhood. When technological progress titillates the brain in this way, I never stop thinking about the moving and dramatic telephone conversation, from the south summit of Everest (8,748 m) in 1996, that the famous mountaineer Rob Hall had had with his wife who had stayed behind in New Zealand. Trapped up there by a frightening storm, with neither tent nor oxygen nor food at a temperature of −70°C, he had made use of the Inmarsat satellite links, just like the Belgians, to tell his wife who was seven months pregnant that everything was OK, when in fact he knew perfectly well that he would never be coming down again.

On the site, it was a veritable stampede. Close friends and others wanted to examine this photograph and take stock of the two men's physical condition. Opinion was unanimous; apart from two big hairy beards, their skin wasn't even flaky, they were not looking too thin and the smiles on their faces said a great deal about their condition. And then there was the e-mail that we received two days later, Monday 5 January, which was also quite explicit about their determination to go on to the end of the project.

My dear Michel,

It is 11a.m. on this 62ⁿᵈ day. We have been given an extraordinary welcome and so we have decided to stay 24 hours at the Pole.

We want at one and the same time to rest a little and to discover the base. The people here are very nice. They invited us to dinner, to hold a little conference in the cafeteria, which was something of a success and people were extremely interested. After which, we were allowed to go into the "computer" hut. Which is how we were able to find the web-site. It's superb. You are one hell of a support for us.

Something else: the Americans here have seldom seen guys in such good health (the two expeditions that arrived here yesterday and the day before were not in such good shape). Unlike them, we have no frostbite or other sores. Dixie has fully recovered from his fall. Just our hands are numb at night and in the morning when we get up because of the handles of the kites that we have to grip for hours at a time each day. We have certainly lost some weight but gained some muscles. For, just think, when the wind is behind (bravo Gallé) and therefore often weak, we have to make continuous figure-of-eight movements to make progress. That requires an enormous amount of effort.

But I have to tell you that the sail is incontestably the key to the success of our expedition (our thanks to Patrick, it's quite unbelievable!). As you know, we had to make use of the small winds despite a very, very difficult terrain. At around 150 km from the Pole, the ice became easier but the snow heavier. Before that, during the entire crossing of the plateau, it was nothing but sastrugis fields followed by sastrugis fields. We even found some that were 70 cms high. Awful!

We've had days of 7 to 8 hours of sail without stopping, without drinking, urinating (even) as we go along and nibbling at the chocolates that we had in our pockets. We had to make progress and make up for lost time. In the end, everything has worked out well.

We will arrive in McMurdo towards the end of January, that's for sure. Weather conditions should be favourable. It's a pity that we didn't have better terrain, if not we would have literally brought the house down. We haven't tried to put in very long days; we wanted first and foremost to be certain. But you should know that in any case we ride every day and in every weather. I mean by that that the two Belgians, are good, very good, very, very good!

Don't think that kite-flying here is a pleasurable pastime in the way that it is in Greenland, for example. It's very, very hard. I'm only beginning to realise the audacity and madness of our project. Our team is well run in and together now.

Again 100,000 thank yous to Compaq (please forward) for the new sledges. Without them, nothing…

And now for the definitive Belgian story; we had covered 2,200 km on the icecap and when we got here we overshot the Pole by nearly 6 km without realising. I have to say, in our defence, that visibility was terrible and that we were following some pennants, which we thought were leading straight to the installations. If we hadn't seen a C130 land in the fog (we thought at first that it was a bird), I believe that we would have done a few more kilometres without being aware of our mistake. In which case, perhaps we would never have arrived here. Who knows? But the fog cleared away and the wind dropped. So it was on foot that we rejoined the base, four hours later.

We deposited the scientific samples and collected new bottles. As far as the gear is concerned, it's in perfect condition, even if we have to spend ages maintaining it. It's a bit like competitive cars. We sleep very little – at most 4 to 6 hours a night. One of the managers at the base has offered to lend us a Sony digital camera to replace those that were broken. Please, ring home for me and give everybody a kiss from me and wish the children well for the exams (ditto from Dixie).

Big kisses all round and it will soon be champagne time.

Alain

Despite having been resupplied on the way, this was the first big success for the expedition. This visit to the Pole was reassuring for their friends at HQ. Since they had held a conference and had been able to send an e-mail, this meant that the restrictions imposed by the official Antarctic authorities were intended more as a brake on the enthusiasm of people who believe that the continent is an easily tameable adventure playground, rather than a desire to hinder the progress of people undertaking something serious on this land at the end of the world.

One week after the arrival at the Pole, I decided to give greater emphasis to the interactive side of the web-site. I have to say that by now I was convinced that the site was of interest to a large number of Internauts which is why I launched Operation Welcome. Everybody who wanted to could write to me to have their messages passed to the two Belgians just as soon as they set foot in McMurdo. My purpose in organising this operation was two-fold: to allow as many people as possible to express themselves, and to procure for the two adventurers the finest possible reward. I also offered my apologies to the visitors for not having had the presence of mind to ask Hubert what the object that he had found on the ice on 26 December had been. So the two operations "South Pole Contest " and "Operation Welcome" would be running in parallel until the end of the expedition.

From the first week of January until their arrival at the beginning of February, suspense on the site grew. First there was a flood of mail; we received more than 500 messages of congratulations and several thousand competition entries. Then there was the chaotic progress of the two rogues when they left the Amundsen-Scott station.

The Argos was used less frequently from 20 January on: instead of the four to five usual messages, I was only getting two or three. All saying more or less the same thing: rotten weather, and once they were on the ice shelf they had to proceed on foot in 50 cm of heavy snow. By reading between the lines, I begin to realise that they were really suffering and that excessive tiredness was beginning to effect their actions. At least, that was how I interpreted the reduction in the number of messages on the one hand, and on the other, the shortening of the transmission slots. The distances covered were calculated by Frédéric each day and they too were far from encouraging: 2 km, 18 km, 16 km, 15 km. They were in fact so worrying that I got in touch with the NCSS at Toulouse to double-check that the Argos was working properly.

On 3 February I only received one code: *"gliding problems, snow changing"*. One day later and they are again faced with a white-out and the Argos mentions problems of balance. The next day, Thursday 5 February, Toulouse transmitted nothing. Not the slightest message on my PC in the morning; no, they hadn't received anything from the Antarctic, yes, the satellite retransmissions were working normally. Keep calm: they had to sleep, perhaps they were in a terrain that was so bad that they had neither the time nor the desire to signal, and in any case they would show themselves again that evening. At 20.00h, still nothing. A little before midnight, I called the night shift at NCSS: beacons 194 and 195 have remained silent. The same Argos silence Friday morning.

Now the situation was more complicated. One of the most important orders for the expedition stipulated that, if HQ received no Argos message for 30 hours at a stretch, the rescue operation should be set in motion. As the last message received was at 23.00 on Wednesday, 4 February, it was now 33 hours since HQ received any news. The situation was not yet critical, and I remained discrete as far as the Net was concerned. In less than three hours, everybody who had a part to play in a possible rescue operation had been notified. As for the time being there was no reason to suppose anything fatal had happened.

At about 14.00, I discovered a message on the answerphone from Baudouin Remy, the director of the film about the expedition, whom Hubert had called after having tried to reach me. He explained that the two men had not had time to switch on the beacons because they had just covered the incredible distance of 271 km in the space of 24 hours! On to this was grafted the comic story of the cop giving Baudouin a hard time (see Day 96 of 8 February). Since the latter had received the call on his mobile phone in heavy traffic, he had not taken the trouble to park properly and had informed the officer of the law that he was in contact with the Antarctic! An excellent day for the Net!

As the final dénouement was drawing near, the journalists were no longer satisfied with the daily press releases issued via Compaq. They were getting in touch with HQ direct. Some rang me, others paid a visit. All wanted to weigh up the chances of success for the expedition. But none of them understood that the word "foresee" was not in the Antarctic dictionary. Which is how I came to evoke the possibility of the two men being trapped in McMurdo for the austral winter. It was an interesting experience to find myself on the other side of the fence answering questions instead of asking them.

As I wanted to keep the people at McMurdo informed of their progress and to redirect there the messages of congratulations, I was wondering how to get in touch with that base. One had to move quickly so I needed a name, an e-mail address, perhaps a telephone… We searched high and low without success. Then suddenly on the evening of 28 January an e-mail appeared from a photocopy repairer based at McMurdo! He wrote asking if we would like him to take some photographs of them as they arrived? A miracle! I replied and informed him of my plans. Two days later, after having received the first official green light, he sent me the details of the electronic address that the expedition was going to be able to use during its stay at McMurdo. I was already imagining the majority of my colleagues using this incredible facility for interviewing the two men without interruptions. At this point, I got to know – still via the network – several technicians and scientists who were working down there; all were following the progress of the two men with great interest. The most astonishing thing about all this correspondence is that I noticed that most of the people were upset that the American authorities had laid down such strict orders for private expeditions that came their way ("one shower, one meal…"). One wrote to me saying, *"Many of us here having been trying to get these rules changed. But that's not easy because of bureaucracy everywhere. Are we not all guests of the great Antarctic nature?"* The euphoria didn't last long. On 4 February, I received a polite e-mail from the head of the base, who had been informed of what we were up to. In ten lines, he tells me that the base was under the direct control of the American government and that is was therefore out of the question, as we were not part of an official research programme, that we should avail ourselves of activities such as the opening of an e-mail address. Even if I understood this reaction and was obliged to respect it, I will treasure the undying memory of those few days conversing with strangers at the other end of the world, who greeted with enthusiasm both the fabulous exploit of the two Belgians and the manner in which the adventure had been tracked on the Net.

It was someone from McMurdo who informed me their tent had been spotted some 15 km from the base. In a few hours time, we would certainly be getting some news. On "www.antarctica-org" I of course disseminated the information and had the surfers experience the arrival almost in real time. On Tuesday evening, I gathered together at HQ the most loyal adherents of the site; in a temperature of −5°C and under a star-sprinkled sky, we drank champagne and awaited the call from McMurdo. At 3.45 on Wednesday the 11th, Alain rang to announce the victory. He informed me also that on their arrival they were led to an uncomfortable cabin located outside the base and that the official welcome had been fairly cold.

Three hours later, the RTBF called HQ to ask whether it would be possible to have one of the two men on the line for their early morning broadcast. Alain, who I had asked to be on stand-by for the media, agreed. Which was how, at 8 o'clock in the morning, the time when the audience is at its greatest, the first "live" interview from the Antarctic took place. Disappointed by the hospitality that they had been accorded, Hubert couldn't prevent himself from replying to the journalist – who was specifically asking him about the welcome – that if the Belgian Political Science Authorities had not "spat" on his expedition, things would certainly not have transpired in the way that they did.

A short explanation is called for here. During 1997, having already received the scientific support of the Laboratory for Environmental Glaciology and Geophysics (LGGE) at Grenoble, Alain Hubert had approached the Belgian Political Science ministry in the hope of acquiring official recognition from the authorities of his country. But since, in their eyes, this expedition did not qualify as one of the international scientific programmes on the Antarctic, he was given the brush off. The scientific nature of the project was recorded, but nothing more. This decision did not in any way interfere with the preparations for the expedition, nor with its implementation. But a more favourable response would have facilitated relations with McMurdo, spared the two adventurers from having been put up in some crude barracks and perhaps made possible an earlier departure on an official C130.

That was all well and good, but the word "spat" was let drop. And everybody heard it. Three hours later, a fairly bitter fax arrived on the desk of the Minister responsible for Political Science. Drafted by a Belgian researcher who had been personally advised of the situation the day before the speech, it expressed his indignation that his department had not been able to benefit from the media impact created by South Through the Pole 1997–98 for enhancing the value of the research that the country was conducting in the Antarctic domain for the public at large. An internal polemic followed; yet again, the workings of a stuffed-shirt bureaucracy were conflicting with public common sense. Between the radio and television interviews given by HQ and the daily updates of the Internet site, I was following this exchange of correspondence with the greatest interest; it's not every day that a sporting venture attracts the attention of the political luminaries.

At this juncture, the Belgians remained confined to barracks. They were *personae non gratae* as far as official flights to New Zealand were concerned and of course had no idea when they would be able to leave the continent. At HQ, it was battle stations. If we didn't act fast, we would have to wait for more than a month before seeing the two adventurers return to their country on a tourist ship arriving in New Zealand on 8 March. All the fans got busy. Some approached the Palace, others the military attaché at the American Embassy, still others the country's political authorities. The Press from their side, while telling the story, naturally recounted this hospitality aspect. The RTBF interviewed the Minister in charge; two days later, the daily newspaper Le Soir carried the story on its front page; La Libre Belgique on its page 2; the Flemish newspapers also were carrying this astonishing story. In short, for two days there was a general outcry.

We didn't have to wait long for the results of this mobilisation: Friday, 13 February in the afternoon, a press release was issued by the cabinet of the Federal Minister for Political Science. It announced, in the opportunistic style that is customary for this type of literature, that the exploit has been very favourably received by public opinion as well as by the scientific establishments and stipulated that the Minister "*wishes to add his voice to the congratulations directed towards our two compatriots who have accomplished such an exploit of physical endurance, courage and willpower but who also spared the time and their resources to bring back snow samples that are to be analysed by Belgian and French research institutes…*" A few hours later, during the customary Friday meeting of government ministers, the subject of the Antarctic expedition was brought up: I learnt later that the exploit of the two Belgians had given rise to gibes of every kind.

However, public opinion had definitely been alerted, and that is what made things happen. On Saturday morning, the McMurdo authorities came to find Hubert and Dansercoer to escort them to official lodgings in the town. Twenty-four hours later, they were invited to board an American Airforce Hercules C130 to rejoin the Christchurch military base in New Zealand. The legendary American hospitality was brought out at the last moment to save a very bad situation.

Even though this great adventure was now over, we decided to make "www.antarctica.org" live on for a few more days, so as to enable the heroes themselves to draft the homepage of 13 February and to provide for as many people as possible the opportunity of expressing their opinions on what Belgium had just undertaken, one hundred years after the historic wintering of Adrien de Gerlache. Just beneath the surface of all these messages, one could sense in any event that an exploit such as Alain Hubert and Dixie Dansercoer had just achieved had awakened a deep sense of belonging to the human race. Not the man with his materialistic and brutal profile on the eve of the 21st century, but the man who still understands the meaning of words such as "free", "imaginary" or "outstanding".

Between 22 November 1997 and mid February 1998; "www.antarctica.org" received more than 400,000 visits. Most of the 'hits' came from Belgium, but there were calls from Botswana, Chile, Kenya, Malaysia, Indonesia, Nepal, New Zealand, Honduras, Russia, Uruguay, South Africa and of course Europe in general and the United States. Between 1 and 15 February, the United States Government visited the site on 231 occasions. At the time, "antarctica.org" was ranked as one of the 5 best Belgian sites and one of the 3 best temporary sites. The volume of material transferred was 1.4 giga, of which almost 30% was in text. At the beginning of December 1997, the site was voted "Site of the Week" by T-Zine, the weekly news letter of *Tijdnet*.

APPENDIX 1

POWER KITES FOR TRACTION

Although the kite itself is several thousand years old, its use in traction is more recent. Marco Polo wrote in the 13th century of fishermen off the isles of Samoa, who used kites to power their canoes along the waters of the Pacific Ocean. In Europe, it was only towards the end of the 18th century that the first kites made their appearance as a means of traction. In 1826, the Englishman, William Pocock, invented a kite-powered *calèche*, a sophisticated vehicle that could travel both in the wind direction and against it. In 1903, his compatriot, Samuel Cody, demonstrated the stability and efficiency of the kite in crossing the Channel on a boat powered by the device.

However, for the Expedition, the most important breakthrough came from the work of the American engineer, Francis Melvin Rogallo. In 1948, he designed the

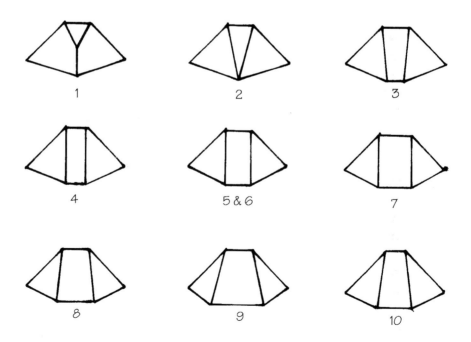

Sketches of the NASA Parawing (NPW) by Francis Rogallo, 1957.

The greater speed reached with the traction sails (or power kites) was 45 km/h. The greatest sustained rate of advance was 100 km in 3 hours. No one has ever travelled at such speeds before in the Antarctic.

first kite not containing any rigid structures, known as the "Rogallo Flexikite". It consisted of a flat, flexible sail, where the aerodynamic lift was provided by the airflow over the curved surface formed when it was deployed, and where the shape was dependent on the attachment of the cords in a specific order. The assembly would capture the wind in such a manner as to create a very distinctive curvature.

Rogallo, the pioneer of free flight, was for several years in charge of the aerospace department of NASA, studying the landing systems of space capsules, at sea and on land, for which he conceived numerous wing profiles. One of these, the *NASA Parawing Rogallo*, inspired the design of the power kites used on our expedition.

This design failed to arouse sufficient interest and no trials were carried out. This elegantly simple concept was rapidly abandoned in favour of the parafoil: a wing containing cell like structures (ram-air cells) which was invented shortly afterwards by the Canadian, Domina Jalbert. This parafoil was to be at the origin of the modern directional parachute, and later the para-glider.

In the field of traction on skis, on the other hand, it is more than probable that the credit should go to the German, Dieter Strasilla who, from 1961, had adapted the parafoil for riding up snowy slopes, thus creating the new sport of para-skiing. This type of parachute, with its "*skywing*" bar, was initially adopted and developed in Europe, and would be used for the first time on the polar ice by Udo Krieger in 1988, to celebrate the centenary of the fabulous crossing of Greenland in 1888, by the expedition led by Fridtjof Nansen. In this form, or in the other, already more efficient form of the *Quadrifoil* (the boxed structure, attached to four lines, with two control handles) parafoils began to be used in some polar expeditions, in Greenland, the Antarctic and elsewhere.

The type of wing profile that we had already been using for several years on expedition would not however suffice for the successful crossing of the White Continent. The excessive weight and large surface area of conventional kites and parafoils, as well as our intention to use several different sizes of sail (each corresponding to a different

During breaks Dixie sometimes tied his sail to his skis.

type of wind) led us, along with the firm *"Blue Iguana"* in Belgium, to design a single membrane foil, instead of the classic wing with the ram air cells, previously used on ice and snow.

While leafing through the sketchbook of Francis Melvin Rogallo, we discovered the profile called NPW5. It was the fifth version of the NASA ParaWing. Dated 1957, it was to give birth to the new traction sail, which we had conceived of, and developed: we baptised our unusual bat-like wing *"L'Integrale"*.

The shape, the material of the sails, the attacking edge, the cord attachments were all designed to take into account the specific needs of the expedition. The principal criteria were: to optimise the lateral traction curve (it had to be raised, and as linear as possible); to avoid vertical traction; to reduce the weight to a minimum; and to stabilise the horizontal traction component, by slowing down the sail.

The design and fine-tuning of the power kites took some 400 hours of work. The testing was carried out in various locations: on beaches, on alpine lakes, and finally on the Greenland and Antarctic ice caps. We used entirely novel materials, which shortly after the start of the expedition, went on the market. The sail fabric consists of a particularly light and tear resistant polyester, which is attached by a large number of synthetic fibre lines, which are in turn attached to four thicker lines, which are then attached to the control handles. Two of these thicker lines are connected at one end (through the network of finer lines), to the front end of the sail, or its attacking edge, and at the other to one side of the control handles. The other two lines, connected to the network of the trailing edge of the sail, are attached to the opposite end of the control handles.

For the expedition, we used sails of three different sizes (6m^2 12m^2 and 21m^2) which allowed us to deploy the sails at wind speeds between 6 and 55km per hour. We could thus sail 50°into the wind, according to the type of snow encountered. Managing the lines, which link the pilot to the fully expanded sail, is extremely uncomfortable due to the cold, and the marked irregularity of the terrain. To make this simpler we reduced the length of the lines to 15m at low wind speeds, and about 12m for the higher winds.

When the wind speed is too low, the pilot has to manoeuvre the sails, in order to optimise their "window of flight", and thereby increase the effective wind speed, allowing a speed of between 4 and 6km per hour. However, when under full sail, it is possible to reach up to 45 km per hour.

The new sail "*L'INTEGRALE*", which comes in three sizes, constitutes an additional and original new aspect to the research into the techniques of transport over ice. This traction sail thus opens up new perspectives for future sporting, and scientific expeditions onto the ice caps, or other white spaces of our planet.

Ongoing research into sail technology aims to improve and develop the sail materials, design and construction, in order to provide better and improved features. These technological advances are aided by the feedback from on the ground testing by expeditions, which is incorporated into the development process.

No doubt, better and better sails will be available in the future.

Untangling sails and undoing knots was the recurring theme of the crossing.

APPENDIX 2

THE SCIENTIFIC MISSION

Just over 100 years ago, in 1897–98, the *Belgica* expedition, during its over-wintering in the Antarctic, managed to complete an entire year of scientific observations. Today, the Antarctic Continent finds itself at the centre of the debate concerning the future climate of our planet. The future of man on Earth depends to some extent on the behaviour of the cooling mechanism of our climate machine, made up of the continental ice cap, and the surrounding austral ocean.

In the big debate being conducted at the present time on global warming, (whether or not this is connected to the increased emissions of greenhouse gases), the Antarctic plays a fundamental role. The Antarctic ice cap is a reservoir for 90% of the fresh water of this planet, and the injection of even a small proportion of this water into the oceans, following even a minor rise in ambient temperatures, would modify the global sea level. In addition, the Southern Ocean could play an important role in the absorption of atmospheric CO_2.

Due to the geographical isolation of Antarctica, there are regions there that have been virtually undisturbed for millennia, and deep ice core samples reveal precious information on paleo-climatic conditions. A major part of the glaciological research being conducted on the Continent today focuses on the big question: Is the volume of Antarctic ice increasing or decreasing? An understanding of the underlying processes would give valuable insight into the future evolution of the World climate, and the effect of this on the level of the oceans. This enormous block of ice, suffice it to say, is not about to melt. It is, on the other hand, in a state of continuous flux under the influence of physical processes, which are important to understand.

Falling in the form of snow, precipitation accumulates little by little on the surface of the continent. This snow is progressively transformed into ice, which under the influence of gravity flows gradually to the coast, where it is finally, after several hundreds of thousands of years, discharged into the sea. This continent is also plagued by the most violent katabatic winds on earth. A joint French and Belgian research project demonstrated recently that these winds carry a not insignificant amount of accumulated surface snow to the ocean.

How will climate change cause the wind patterns at the surface of the Antarctic to be modified, and how will the snow cover react? The Antarctic shows in some places a tendency to increased snow falls. Will it continue to follow this trend or will it reverse?

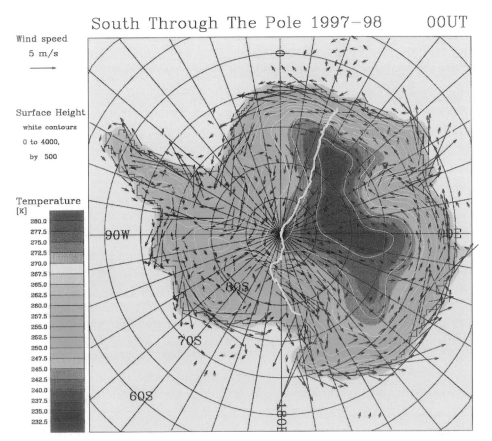

South Through The Pole 1997–98   00UT

Wind speed
5 m/s

Surface Height
white contours
0 to 4000,
by 500

Temperature
[K]
280.0
277.5
275.0
272.5
270.0
267.5
265.0
262.5
260.0
257.5
255.0
252.5
250.0
247.5
245.0
242.5
240.0
237.5
235.0
232.5

Using mathematical modelling techniques, the physicist Hubert Gallée simulated the principal climatic conditions that the Expedition would encounter.

The length of the vectors indicating the direction of katabatic winds is proportional to their speed. The surface temperature is represented by a colour coding (scale in the bottom left-hand corner of the diagram), and the altitude by the white lines rising in steps of 500m.

The early reaction of the snow cover, under the effect of the violent winds which blow around the coastal regions, may allow scientists to rapidly detect such a reversal. In order to know more, it is necessary to identify the factors influencing the evolution of the polar snows.

The first objective of the scientific mission of the "South Through the Pole 1997–98 expedition", in one of the least frequented regions of the Antarctic, addresses this. The project carried out on behalf of the Laboratory of Glaciology and Environmental Geophysics (LGGE) in Grenoble (working in collaboration with the Belgian scientist Hubert Gallée of the Institut Georges Lemaître of the University of Louvain-la-Neuve) is part of research aimed at improving our knowledge of the mechanics of the process, using mathematical models. The measurements taken in the field along with information provided by satellite will contribute to the greater understanding of the processes.

The Antarctic observations involved the digging of one metre deep pits in the snow (in order to cover several years of snow accumulation), at 150 km intervals across the Antarctic plateau. The aim of this was to obtain stratigraphic, temperature and snow density data, as well as details of the size and shape of snow crystals. These observations and the various measurements of the physical characteristics of the snow at different depths required the macro-photography of snow crystals by an original process developed in the context of the Expedition.

This line of research is linked to the European project on the observation of snow-fields lying on the polar ice-caps, known as "Polar Snow". This project brings together many well know research institutes specialising in this field, namely the University of Barcelona; the BAS (British Antarctic Survey), the CEN (Centre d'Etudes de la Neige à Grenoble) and the LGGE (Laboratoire de Glaciologie et de Géophysique de l'Environnement, also based in Grenoble). In this, France plays an important role because all the data from Antarctica is collected and analysed in Grenoble. The observations carried out by our expedition in Queen Maud Land, are of particular interest as this area has been virtually untouched before. In addition, it is the area which has been selected by the European Community for deep ice coring, in the context of the EPICA Project, to reach levels which contain snow falls dating back much further than those accessible to the expedition. These deep cores contain important information on the evolution of the Antarctic climate.

The second research objective was the collection of samples of Antarctic snow for isotopic analysis. These samples contributed to the international project – 'ITASE' (International Trans Antarctic Scientific Expedition), directed by Dr Majewski of the University of New Hampshire in the United States. Briefly, the isotopic content of the snow (deuterium and oxygen) will depend on the isotopic make-up of the water, which evaporated from the ocean and then fell as snow when the clouds passed over the polar ice cap. The paleo-climatologists have been able to identify a virtually linear relationship between the isotopic content of the snow and the ambient temperature at the moment it fell on the collection site.

The samples taken, using a titanium sampling tube (50 mm in diameter and 1.50 m in length), were conserved at low temperatures, and transported to Grenoble for further analysis by the LGGE. The results will be fed into the ITASE database.

We managed to dig around 10 snow pits, collect over 600 measurements and observations, take 360 photographs and collect over 100 samples of snow from over 50 different sites in the course of our crossing of the Antarctic plateau. The weight of the scientific equipment, which we took with us was 7.40 kg.

APPENDIX 3

THE POLAR DIET

THE ESSENTIALS OF A POLAR DIET

Crossing the Antarctic, without resupply, requires a certain amount of research into advanced dietetics. There are three strict criteria that must be applied to foodstuffs to be used under such demanding conditions: they must be light, compact, and high in energy.

They must be light to keep the weight of supplies and equipment to manageable proportions. Similarly, they must be compact in order to reduce the physical bulk of the mass to be transported, and finally, they must be extra rich in calories in proportion to size and weight due to the intense physical effort that will be required to undertake the journey.

From the outset, the involvement of specialists, (in fields as diverse as "Sport Dietetics" and "Bio-engineering"), who examined not only the human nutrition aspects, but also the food technology, and packaging technology aspects of the problem, gave the expedition an additional edge. Due to the severe climatic conditions to be encountered, and the physical hardship imposed by the hostile terrain, the daily calorific intake required has to be in the region of 6000 kcal. Such a high level of calorie intake can only be achieved progressively to allow the body to adjust to the new foodstuffs (even where a pre-expedition diet has been introduced). For the 100 days of the expedition, the calorie intake was phased in as follows: Phase 1: 15 days at 4602 kcal/day; Phase 2: 20 days at 5 636 kcal/day; and Phase 3: 65 days at 6206 kcal/day. However, for the last phase, the ration foreseen for breakfast, turned out to be too large, and a total of 6000 kcal turned out to be sufficient.

With the objective of reducing total weight to a minimum, everything had to be done to combine a maximum of nutritional value, with a minimum of weight. To achieve this, the classic balance between the basic constituents of traditional foodstuffs had to be altered from 55% to 26% for starches; 12% to 8% for proteins; and 33% to 66% for lipids, (taking into account that one gram of fat provides 9 kcal of energy as opposed to 4 kcal for one gram of sugar or protein).

In order to optimise the efficiency of absorption of the foodstuffs by the cells in the body, a few rules had to be followed concerning the type of fat, proteins, and

191

starches to be used, as well as in the choice of fibres, and vitamin complements to be added.

FATS. Absorbed in large quantities, fat is stored in the tissues, forming a layer under the skin, and around the organs. These deposits are of prime importance, as under the permanent influence of the cold, they form an insulating layer under the entire epidermis, rather than only in the usual areas (stomach, hips and thighs). Among the fats, it is the polyunsaturated fatty acids which ensure the barrier qualities of the cell membrane, and reduce cellular dehydration. They must, therefore, be present in large quantities in order to limit the rate of fluid loss through evaporation and sweating, as this is responsible for the excessive frosting of clothing and sleeping bags in the severe cold.

PROTEINS. Indispensable for the construction and regeneration of various tissues in the organism, these have to be present in sufficient quantities (±1.3 g/ kg of body weight). However, the complementary nature of the different sources of proteins has also to be taken into account. Proteins derived from the same food group (cereals, or products of animal origin, or vegetables) are actually deficient in one or more essential amino acids. It is necessary, therefore, to insure that they are combined during a meal in order to establish a balanced diet.

SUGARS. Although excellent muscular fuel, as a rule, slow sugars must be favoured above fast sugars, in order to avoid hyperglycaemic peaks after a meal. However, during effort, the consumption of rapidly metabolising sugars (simple sucrose molecule type, like for example chocolate) is perfectly acceptable, as the body is working at full metabolic capacity.

FIBRES. Contained in milled cereals, in müesli and oleaginous fruits, these are essential to the proper functioning of the bowels, controlling the movement of ingested foods through the intestinal tract. It is important that the fibres be of proper biological quality in order to prevent poisoning the body.

VITAMINS, MINERAL SALTS, AND OLIGO-ELEMENTS. The necessary quantities were calculated with respect to the amounts already present in the foodstuffs making up the daily ration. Virgin oils are rich in lipo-soluble elements (Vitamins A,D,E, and K) and in poly-unsaturated fatty acids. Cereals, müesli, brown sugar, oleaginous fruits and pemmican would cover the daily requirements of vitamin B, mineral salts (magnesium, potassium) and oligo-elements (iron, copper, manganese, zinc, silicon, nickel and selenium). Cheese provides the necessary calcium. Even though there is sufficient vitamin C in the rations, it was still important to add another 1g per day, as it has a palliative effect, effectively replacing deficits of other vitamins, for a period.

CITRATES. These have an alkalising effect on the blood, as they are responsible for capturing acidic toxins (lactic acid and other by-products of muscular activity) and they promote the elimination of these in the urine. They also aid digestion by stimulating secretions from the liver and the gall bladder, and generally promoting the elimination of toxins. Finally, they help in maintaining the balance of intestinal flora.

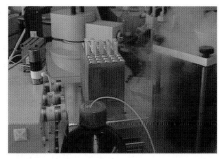

Laboratory preparation of anhydrous milk fat (AMF) at Corman.

Mixing AMF with cereals, before freezing.

Freeze drying the pemmican at the CER in Marloie.

Wrapping the daily rations at Bolloré Technologies in Quimper.

The final product.

THE PRINCIPAL FOODSTUFFS SELECTED

Listing the principal foods used in the daily rations, in function of the application of the rules of dietetics, is not done here merely in order to suggest the *best* combination for such an expedition (multiple possibilities exist according to taste) but rather, to briefly outline the types of foods which were chosen to build up the polar menu.

PEMMICAN. Inspired by Nordic recipes, this is a complex culinary preparation, based on meat, with carrots, leeks, celery, red cabbage, soya, bamboo, wheat flour, roast onions, black currant, sesame seeds, mustard seeds, wheat-germ oil, nettles, salt and pepper. Rich in animal proteins, not only does it have a pleasant taste, but it contains many essential vitamins and mineral salts. Very fatty, it also provides a good balance between various fatty acids, and contains a large quantity of mono-unsaturated fats.

AMF. Anhydrous Milk Fat (AMF) is obtained exclusively from dairy cream, or butter of the finest quality. No neutralising substance is added. It is processed by centrifugation, which permits the removal of water and non-fat dry matter. The low melting point of the milk fat (20°C) allows the required fluidity to be achieved at low temperatures. This is a very important factor to take into consideration, as during the expedition, the products prepared from this substance literally melt in the mouth. In order to reduce the melting point, it is necessary to increase the proportion of poly-unsaturated fatty acids (oleic acids), which improves the biological efficiency of the substance. Several flavours can also be added by a process of hydrolysis.

PROTEIN POWDERS. Developed from vegetable (soya) and animal proteins (eggs, and dairy caseinates), these provide the full range of essential amino acids, present in the appropriate quantities, and in a relatively low volume.

MILLED CEREALS. Each mixture is made up of a combination of two cereals selected from amongst the five types (buckwheat, oats, millet, triticale, quinoa) and the whole grains are crushed in a mill. There is no separation into flour, bran or germ. As with müesli, the glycaemic index of these mixtures is very low and they are rich in fibres. This is a "living" flour as time, heat and light have not degraded the vitamin, mineral salt, oligo-element and yeast contents.

MUËSLI. Prepared principally from a mixture of triticale, oats, wheat, and dried fruit. Triticale (*Triticum spelta*) is a variety of wild wheat, grown at moderately high altitudes, where the grain remains husked after harvesting. Despite having a lower calorific content, this grain is markedly more balanced and valuable than ordinary wheat, because it contains both starch and fibres, and is an important source of vegetable protein. It is also rich in vitamin B1. Müesli is also an excellent source of slow burning sugars and rates 60% on the glycaemic index.

OLIVE AND SESAME OILS. The choice fell on these oils because they are particularly rich in fatty acids ('omega -cis'). Cold pressed oils ensure that the diet contains a sufficient amount of indispensable unsaturated fatty acids.

CHEESE. Cheese is selected for its fat content (55 %) and because it is made from raw milk. It is a food source rich in fats and proteins of high biological value.

OLEAGINOUS FRUITS. A mixture of sesame, pumpkin, and sunflower seeds, linseed, walnuts, almonds and cashew nuts. These oilseeds and nuts rate very low on the glycaemic index, and contain a large amount of essential fatty acids (polyunsaturated).

SOUPS. These are essentially a source of glucides. The choice finally fell on three types of instant soup having high calorific value per kilogram of dry matter.

CHOCOLATE. Source of rapidly metabolised sugars, chocolate is retained because it has a powerful effect on the body, both by the release of sugars in the blood and through the positive psychological associations it has.

RAW SUGAR. This is unrefined cane sugar. Not only does it retain the sweetness of sugar, but it also contains the mineral salts necessary for its breakdown. The glycaemic index is 80%, as opposed to 100% for pure glucose.

COUSCOUS, POLENTA, PURÉE. The glycaemic index is a little high, but the energy content is significant. The consistency increases the bulk of the food ration, promoting a sensation of satiety. These foodstuffs, incorporated into the evening meal, are easily interchangeable according to the taste of each individual member of the expedition.

TEA. Polar beverage par excellence. (Without sugar). Tea is rich in theine, which like caffeine, tends to act on the kidneys and the subrenal glands, producing a stimulating effect which is temporary in nature. However, tea has its own anti-theine device, the tannins. The tannins can bind to the molecules of theine, but for this effect the tea has to brew for a while. In addition, these tannin-theine complexes act as powerful anti free radical agents, which promote the elimination of toxins produced by muscular effort and the digestive process, from the body.

HERB INFUSIONS. Taken in the evening, these help the body to replace vital fluids, and affect the person in various ways, according to the plant extracts contained.

LEADING EDGE FOOD TECHNOLOGIES

Weight is the principal limiting factor in an expedition of this type. In the 106kg of equipment and supplies packed into each sledge, the 100 days worth of food supplies represented 60% of the total weight. Certain novel techniques were used to maximise food value with a minimum of weight and space occupied.

FREEZE DRYING

Freeze drying combines the virtues of dehydration and cold treatment. The fresh product is frozen at very low temperatures (-40°C), and then is placed under vacuum, and is progressively heated in such a way as to cause the ice to sublimate (go from solid to vapour, bypassing the liquid phase). The technique has the enormous advantage in that it preserves the aroma, the taste, the essential characteristics, and all the biological value of the raw material. The water content of foods is a particularly troublesome characteristic, but the use of industrial freeze drying technology permitted the expedition to slice 10 kg off the total weight of foodstuffs to be carried.

PACKAGING

The aim of the research into novel packaging techniques was to find a way of reducing the total weight, without jeopardising the ability of the packaging to withstand the conditions, and the ability to conserve the foodstuffs for the duration of the expedition. Before being organised into daily rations, the different constituent, had to be wrapped in a thin thermo-retracting film of a thickness of 19 microns, formed by the co-extrusion of 5 layers of poly-olefins. The film is entirely recyclable, and can resist extreme conditions. This process was carried out on an industrial scale.

FRACTIONATION OF ANHYDROUS MILK FAT (AMF)

The fractionation of the milk fats allows one to influence the characteristics of the anhydrous milk fat. Fractionation of fats is a physical process which breaks down emulsions into their constituent parts. It is the only process of modification of physical properties used on milk fats. The operation is based on crystallisation, which takes place in vats, where the milk fat is subjected to cold, while being continuously agitated. The crystalline phase (the stearic fraction) is separated from the liquid phase (oleic fraction) by filtration. Applied to milk fats, which melt at 32°C, it is possible to prepare fractions with melting points ranging from 10°C to 44°C. This is one of the major innovations of the expedition, as the use of AMFs as a constituent of the daily food rations allowed us to develop our famous "pralines".

ONE OF THE THREE DAILY RATIONS DURING THE EXPEDITION

Basic components	quantity (g)	carbo-hydrate (g)	protein (g)	fat (g)	calories (kcal)	(%)
Breakfast						**1,438 kcal**
Muesli	80	56	7	7	317	5.6%
Raw sugar	20	18	0	0	70	1.2%
Freeze dried pemmican	80	0	15	59	593	10.5%
Sesame oil	30	0	0	30	270	4.8%
Protein (powder)	10	0	9	0	36	0.6%
Mixed ground cereals	40	29	5	1	144	2.6%
Coffee (caffeine free)	4	2	0	0	8	0.2%
Tea (bags)	6	0	0	0	0	0.0%
Lunch pack						**2,816 kcal**
Oilseeds and nuts (mix)	110	9	17	59	637	11.3%
Mixed ground cereals	70	51	8	2	252	4.5%
AMF	80	0	0	80	719	12.8%
Raw sugar	30	26	0	0	106	1.9%
Chocolate	150	93	10	47	830	14.7%
Cheese	48	0	15	24	271	4.8%
Dinner						**1,382 kcal**
Freeze dried soup	40	31	2	6	185	3.3%
Freeze dried pemmican	50	0	9	37	371	6.6%
Olive oil	40	0	0	40	360	6.4%
Mash potatoes or couscous	60	50	6	2	242	4.3%
Mixed ground cereals	30	22	3	1	108	1.9%
Oilseeds and nuts (mix)	20	2	3	11	116	2.1%
Herb tea (bags)	2	0	0	0	0	0.0%
Weight	**1,000**	389	109	405	**5,636**	
Total ration in calories		1,556	437	3,643	5,636	
%		27.6%	7.8%	64.6%	100%	

APPENDIX 4

EQUIPMENT LIST

SHARED EQUIPMENT: 45 KG

1 tent (*Lowland*)
1 snow shovel (*Black Diamond*)
2 ultra light ice-axes (*Charlet*)
2 x 30m dry rope – diameter 6mm
2 snow brushes
1 kevlar box for the burner: 30cm x 30cm,
    with ventilation hole for air supply
1 complete burner (*MSR Whisper- lite 600*)
1 saucepan, with integral double wall (*Olicamp*)
1 saucepan for melting snow
1 bowl for snow
4 special plastic containers for the fuel
    consisting of 46 litres of mineral oil (*Coleman*)
First–aid kit, urinal, etc.

REPAIR AND REPLACEMENT MATERIALS: 11 KG

1 complete burner kit (*MSR whisper lite 600*)
1 supplementary accessories kit for burner, joints, etc.
1 lighter, some water-proof matches
5 rolls of sticking plaster (*Strappal*), epoxy resin
1 metal saw
1 file for preparing skis
assortment of nuts, bolts, screws, washers rivets,
2 repair patches for inflatable mattresses (*Thermarest*)
steel wire of various diameters
safety pins, strong thread and mending needles
complete sewing kit, with various threads

2 multifunctional clamps
2 pairs of synthetic self adhesive skins (*Pomoca*)
kit of accessories for repairing ski bindings
replacement cables for ski bindings
200m of fine cord, 3 and 4 mm diameter
4 small carabiners "*mousquetons*"
3 sails. 6m², 12m², 21m² complete with handles (0.55 kg, 0.95 kg, 1.50 kg)
sail repair kit: tape, thread
small pieces of aluminium tubing for repairing the tent frame
small voltmeter and electric wires

PERSONAL EQUIPMENT (PER SLEDGE): 2 x 34.5 KG

1 complete sledge
1 pair of skis with the same bindings as for walking, (*Dynastar – mountain*) for sailing
1 mattress *Thermarest* –single thickness
1 simple closed cell foam mattress
various bags for storage
1 sleeping bag (prototype – *Lestra sport*)
1 down jacket, (light & waterproof – *Rab*)
2 under trousers and 2 polo-neck sweaters in polar light.
1 pair of under-socks
1 unbreakable thermos flask (1.8 l)
1 bowl, 2 spoons, 1 pen knife, 1 insulated cup
5 pairs of thin socks
5 pairs of vapour barrier liner for the feet
1 pair of thick warm socks
4 pairs of fine gloves
1 pair woollen mittens
1 pair of wind-proof over-mittens
1 pair of mittens in wind-proof polar material
1 pair of sun glasses – polarised
1 face mask with storm protection in rigid plastic
1 simple storm mask (*Poullioux*)
2 balaclavas in wind-proof polar material
5 under-shorts
toiletries
1 small bag for carrying daily food rations
toilet paper
log books, revolving pencils, etc.

1 mini-disk reader, mini-disks, lithium batteries
2 books, playing cards, etc.

NAVIGATIONAL AIDS: 0.6 KG

maps, sketches, set-squares
2 GPS (*Garmin III*), lithium batteries
1 compass (*Silva* type 15)
1 altimeter (*Thommen*)

COMMUNICATION AIDS: 13.6 KG

1 portable computer (*Compaq Armada 4110*) with lithium batteries
1 satellite transmitter-receiver (*Magellan, microcom M*), with lithium batteries
2 beacons (Argos) with pre-coded messages
1 universal distress beacon

AUDIO-VISUAL EQUIPMENT (PHOTO AND VIDEO): 6.4 KG

1 *Nikon* FM2 body, 2 lenses and skylight filter
1 *Contax* T2
40 rolls of film for slides (100 ASA) wrapped in cellophane
2 video cameras *Sony* DCR PC 7E, 1 wide angle
3 sets of lithium batteries (3xLSH20)
20 digital video cassettes
1 tripod

FOODSTUFFS (100 RATIONS, WRAPPED): 209 KG

15 x 4602 kcal + 20 x 5636 kcal + 65 x 6206 kcal (details given in the table in Appendix 3)
vitamins and food supplements
individual and bulk wrapping for the food packages

SCIENTIFIC EQUIPMENT: 7.4 KG

1 titanium ice-sampling column (length 150cm, diam.50mm)

100 plastic sample pots
1 mini- titanium ice-sampling column (length: 30cm)
1 spring balance
2 thermometers
1 *Anena* snow grain reference table
1 magnifying glass
1 note book, various accessories
1 complete system for macro-photography of snow crystals
1 saw

Personal Effects (Carried on the body): 12.5 kg

1 pair of polar shoes with inner shoes (*One sport-Millet*, prototype)
1 pair of fine socks
1 pair of warm socks
1 VBL (vapour barrier liner)
1 pair of trousers attached to the shoe with velcro (*Francital*, prototype (*MP+*))
1 jacket (with one way membrane)
1 jacket in polar-200
1 item of under clothing in polar- 100
1 wind proof balaclava in polar material, with fixed nose protection
1 pair of glasses (*Pouilloux-Vuarnet*)
1 pair of under-gloves in polar
1 pair of woollen mittens
1 pair of wind proof over-mittens
1 traction belt (*Petzl*, prototype)
1 pair of ski sticks (*Swix* – expe.)
1 pair of skis (back-country) with adhesive skins
1 small compass on the jacket
1 anemometer (*Sky-watch*)
3 carabiners
1 mini blocker (*Wild country*)
1 pulley
2 ice screws (*Charlet-Moser* in titanium)
2 thin ropes diam.5mm (for crevasses)

APPENDIX 5

PREVIOUS CROSSINGS OR ATTEMPTED CROSSINGS OF THE ANTARCTIC

1911–12: WILHELM FILCHNER

The German explorer Wilhelm Filchner undertook an expedition to ascertain whether the Ross and Weddell seas were separated by a land bridge or were in fact joined by a frozen sea. Once the expedition material had been landed, the ice floe on which the expedition had set up its base broke free. With great difficulty the men managed to save barely enough supplies to allow them to build another cabin, higher up and further inland. They were obliged to remain there the whole winter, but did not manage to complete their perilous attempt.

1914–17: ERNEST SHACKLETON

The first attempted crossing of the whole of Antarctica, on foot, was undertaken by the Irish explorer, Ernest Shackleton. The attempt failed because his ship, *Endurance*, was trapped in the advancing ice of the Weddell Sea. The epic journey of the 22 men who attempted, after this terrible setback, to reach first Elephant Island, then South Georgia is one of the best known in the history of the conquest of Antarctica.

1957–58: VIVIAN FUCHS – EDMUND HILLARY

Successful crossing by Vivian Fuchs, in 99 days, using snowcats. Organised on the occasion of the International Geophysical Year (IGY), the expedition was supported by ultramodern equipment (20 tonnes of material, transported by six vehicles equipped with caterpillar tracks). The equipment included 20 re-supply depots, material for building cabins *en route*, light aircraft, and a support team under the direction of Edmund Hillary (of Everest fame), which started out from the other edge of the Continent (the Ross Sea) to meet up with those who had started out from the Weddell Sea.

1980–81: RANULPH FIENNES

Part of the undertaking of the British adventurer, who got it into his head to go around the World via the Poles, North and South. This journey entailed crossing the Antarctic by skidoo. Ranulph Fiennes, Charles Burton, and Olivier Shepard left the South African base at Sanae heading for the South Pole, en route for the American base at McMurdo. It was the first successful motorised attempt, without outside assistance. It took 67 days.

1989–90: SJUR MØRDRE

A Norwegian team using dog sleds; was the first to open the route from Berkner Island to McMurdo, and was re-supplied twice. This was the last expedition to use dog teams in Antarctica due to the new environmental rule adopted in the following year, which restricted access to Antarctica for non-native animal species.

1989–90: JEAN-LOUIS ÉTIENNE AND WILL STEGER

The French doctor Jean Louis Étienne and the American explorer Will Steger, accompanied by four other explorers, using dog-sleds and aerial re-supply, managed to make the longest successful crossing of the Continent, from the Antarctic Peninsula to the Russian Station at Mirny (Wilkes Land), passing by the South Pole. This journey of 6,400 km was completed in 213 days.

1989–90: REINHOLD MESSNER

Reinhold Messner and Arved Fuchs crossed the continent of Antarctica in 92 days, with aerial re-supply, from the Ronne Platform to the Ross Sea, a journey of 2,400km.

1992–93: RANULPH FIENNES AND MIKE STROUD

Fiennes attempted another crossing of Antarctica without re-supply, from Berkner Island to McMurdo, this time accompanied by Mike Stroud. They were forced to abandon the crossing on the Ross Ice-shelf, only 500 km from their goal. This journey was the subject of the book "*Mind Over Matter*", which became a best-seller.

1995–96: BØRGE OUSLAND

The Norwegian adventurer Børge Ousland, in a solo attempt, succeeded in reaching the South Pole from Berkner Island, without support. Heading off to complete the crossing to McMurdo, he was forced to abandon the attempt shortly after having passed the Amundsen-Scott base.

1996–97: MAREK KAMINSKI

The Pole, Marek Kaminski, left from Berkner Island to make a solo attempt at crossing Antarctica. He had to abandon the attempt at the South Pole, after 53 days on skis, having covered 1,400 km.

1996–97: RANULPH FIENNES

Attempted solo crossing, without re-supply from Berkner Island. He was forced to abandon after 15 days, due to ill-health.

1996–97: BØRGE OUSLAND

Børge Ousland managed the first solo crossing of the Antarctic without re-supply, on foot, by ski and using parafoils. From Berkner Island to the Ross Sea, he covered 2,845 km in 64 days. His route is shorter than that taken by Alain Hubert and Dixie Dansercoer.

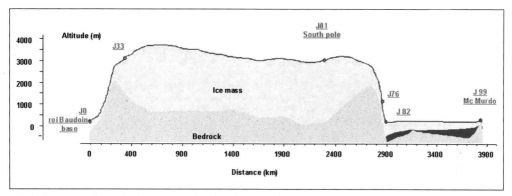

Vertical section through the route taken by the Expedition, showing the proportional thickness of the ice cap and the underlying rock strata. The "J" points indicate the progress of the Expedition.

Alt. 2800 m

J 76

J 77/78

Alt. 550 m

J 80

J 79

J 81

Route taken by Alain and Dixie across the Axel Heiberg Glacier to reach the Ross Ice Shelf. It is virtually the same route as that taken by Amundsen in his successful attempt to reach the South Pole in 1911.

ACKNOWLEDGEMENTS

If the wind filled our sails to carry us across Antarctica, to all those whose blew up the wind behind us, and whose breath carried us along on our way, gently, forcefully, intermittently, continuously, tenderly and watchfully, and without whom our project would never have taken off: we thank you all, even though we do not mention you by name:

Catherine, Julie, Martin, Gaëlle, Emilie, Jasper, Evelyne and Thijs; our families and friends, for having swelled the sails of our hearts; Eric Janssen, and all his team, for having that unshakeable faith in us and in our venture; Michel Brent, for his unflagging enthusiasm, his constancy, his critical sense and his priceless gift for co-ordination. Philippe Sohet, for his unconditional complicity and for the pertinence of his remarks; Philippe Lecomte for his discreet presence, and his support during the genesis of this adventure; Jorge Cordova for always being ready to face any test; Denis Dupont for his thousand and one interventions throughout the preparation of this expedition; Frédéric Sepulchre for his support and for the precision of his calculations of the daily co-ordinates of our progress; Arnaud Tortel, our wet nurse in dietetics; Baudouin Remy for his intelligence and his tenacity in the communication of the event; Hubert Gallée for having shared his remarkable mathematical model with us; Patrick Nassogne for the ingenious way he helped us to devise our revolutionary sails.

And our sincere gratitude, to all the others who helped us along our way:

ADD Ice, Embassy of the United States of America to the Kingdom of Belgium, ANI (Adventure Network International), Colette Astorgue, Carl Beeth, André Berger, Berghaus, Robert Biston, *Boloré Technologies*, Cécile Boly, CAB (*Club Alpin Belge*), Valérie Caroll, CER (*Centre d'Economie Rurale*), *Cherbai*, CLS (*Collecte Localisation Satellites*), Alexander Colhoun, Philippe Coppe, Corman, Daniel Dalemans, Claude De Broyer, Eddy De Busschere, Gaston de Gerlache, Leo de la Barra, Philippe De Meurers, Michel De Wauters, Hugo Decleir, Marc Depauw, Claude Deroanne, Pierre Dillembourg, David Dixneuf, Marc Dumont, Pierre Dumont, Steve Dunbar, *Dynastar, Embelco*, ESIEC (*Ecole Supérieure d'Ingénieur en Emballage et Conditionnement*), *Euroculture*, Faculté Universitaire des Sciences Agronomiques de Gembloux*, Famenne-Plastics, Fofo, Francital*, Joel Franka, Al Gilbert, Didier Goetghebuer, Herman Hannon, André et Nadine Hubert*, Icelandair*, IGN (*Institut Géographique National*), *Institut d'Astronomie et de Géophysique Georges Lemaître* of the UCL (Catholic University of Louvain), Japan National Institute of Polar Research, Nighat Johnson-Amin, Kalaallit Forsikring, Marek Kaminski, Kariboe,

Anne Kershaw, *KLM*, René Küng, *La Compagnie des Bains et Douches*, Louis Lange, Laurent Réfrigération, Benoit Lejeune, Lestra Sport, Philippe Levêque, LGC (*Laboratoire de Génie Civil* of the UCL), LGGE (*Laboratoire de Géophysique et de Glaciologie de l'Environnement*), Drew and Diana Logan, Jac Loosveldt, Bob Lowenstein, Lowland, Henriette Luycks, James R.Maddren, Pol Maréchal, Joel Martin, Eric Martine, Xavier Martineau, the scientists and administrators at McMurdo Base, Mireille Mercaez, Karl-Josef Metzmacker, Martial Moioli, Jean-Marie Nicolas, Maurits Nieuwling, NSF (National Science Foundation), Chantal Ochelen, *One Sport*, Borge Ousland, Bernard Pascat, Frank Patteyn, Colonel Pepermans, *Petzl*, Edgar Piccioto, Christian Poncelet, Jean-Pol Poncelet, Pouilloux, *Ralston Energy Systems (Benelux)*, Remi Revellin, Marino Roberti, Rottefella, Luc Schuiten, Mike Sharp, SID (*Service de l'Information de la Défense Nationale*), *Silverscape, Sonal, Sony, Starpole*, Greg Stein, Jerzy Surdell, *Sygma, Televox*, Jacques Theodor, Colette Thiry, *Travelpro*, Frank Tyga, US Geological Survey, Yves Van den Auweele, Sophie Van den Bogaert, Katelijn Van Heulekom, Van Hopplynus, Jean Pascal van Ypersele, Marc Vanthornhout, Ida Verlinden, Ralph Warren.

The 'South Through the Pole 1997–98' Expedition was accorded the Patronage of His Majesty, King Albert II of Belgium

Photographic Credits

Edgar Piccioto © ULB Department of Earth Sciences and the Environment, p. 100.
Denis Dupont: pp. 7, 10, 193.
Jean-Marie Nicholas: p. 11.
Michel Brent: pp. 8, 9, 35, 47, 58, 82, 89 (top), 108 (top).
Alain Hubert and Dixie Dansercoer: all the other pages
Sketches of the Rogallo NPW profiles: archives Francis Rogallo: p. 184.
Aerial photograph of the Axel Heiberg : US Geological Survey: p. 206.
Map developed from the Scientific Committee for Antarctic Research digital map of the Antarctic

BIBLIOGRAPHY

Australian Surveying and Land Information Group, *Carte générale de l'Antarctique*, stereographic Polar projection, scale: 1:20000000 at 71° latitude South, Australian Antarctic Division, 1996.

Berger, A., *Le Climat de La Terre, Un Passé pour Quel Avenir?*. De Boek Université, Bruxelles, 1982.

Brent, M., *L'Antarctique et La Belgique*. Labor, Bruxelles, 1997.

Byrd, R., *Pôle Sud*. Grasset, Paris, 1935.

Cook, F., *Vers le Pôle Sud : Premier Récit avant la Découverte du Pôle Nord*. Flammarion, Paris, 1902.

Etienne, J-L., *Les Pôles*. Arthaud (Collection La Nouvelle Odyssée), Paris, 1992.

——, *Transantartica, La Traversée du Dernier Continent*. Robert Laffont, Paris, 1990.

Fiennes, R., *To The End of The Earth: Transglobe Expedition 1979–82*. Hodder and Stoughton, London, 1984.

Fogg, G.E., *A History of Antarctic Science*. Cambridge University Press, Cambridge, 1992.

Fogg, G.E., and Smith, D., *The Exploration of Antarctica, The Last Unspoilt Continent*. Cassell Publishers Ltd, London, 1990.

Fuchs, V. et Hilary, E., *Rendez-Vous au Pôle sud*. Presses de La Cité, Paris, 1959.

Gallée, H., *Simulation of The Dronning Maud Land Katabatic Wind Regime*. Université Catholique de Louvain, Louvain-la-Neuve, Belgium, sd.

Gallée, H. and Schayes, G., *A Three Dimensional Atmospheric Mesoscale Circulation Model for Katabatic Winds Simulations*. Université Catholique de Louvain, Louvain-la-Neuve, 1994.

Gerlache, A. de, *Quinze Mois dans l'Antarctique*. Hachette et Cie, Paris, 1902.

——, *Victoire sur La Nuit Antarctique, l'Expédition de la « Belgica », 1897–1899*. Casterman, Paris, 1960.

Gerlache, G. de, *Retour en Antarctique*. Casterman, Paris, 1960.

Hubert, A. et Goetghebuer, D. (with the collaboration of Michel Brent), *l'Enfer Blanc, les Premiers Belges au Pôle Nord Géographique*. Labor, Bruxelles, 1994.

Huntford, R., *Expéditions d'Amundsen, Photographies retrouvées*. Albin Michel, Paris, 1988.

——, *Scott and Amundsen*. Weidenfeld and Nicholson, London, 1979.

——, *Shackleton*. Hodder and Stoughton, London, 1985.

L'Illustration, *Les Grands Dossiers de l'Illustration : La Conquête des Pôles*. Sefag et l'Illustration, Paris, 1987.

Landsing, A., *Endurance, Shackleton's Incredible Voyage*. Granada Publishing Ltd, London, 1984.

Laws, R., *The Last Frontier*. Boxtree Ltd, London, 1989.

Lecointe, G., *Au Pays des Manchots, (Récit du voyage de la Belgica)*. Scheppens en Cie, Bruxelles, 1904.

Lorius, C., *L'Antarctique, Continent de l'Extrême*. Denoël (collection Planète), Paris, 1991.

——, *Les Glaces de L'Antarctique : une Mémoire, des Passions*. Odile Jacobs, Paris, 1991.

May, J., *A la Découverte du septième continent*. Souffles, Paris, 1989.

Messner, R., *Antarctique, Ciel et Enfer*. Arthaud, Paris, 1991.

Östby, J., *Roald Amundsen*. Office de Publicité (Collection Traducta), Bruxelles, 1942.

Peisson, E., *Pôles, l'Etonnante Aventure de Roald Amundsen*. Grasset, Paris, 1952.

Reader's Digest, *Antarctique, la Grande Histoire des Hommes à la Découverte du Continent de Glace*. Sélection du Reader's Digest, Paris, 1991.

Scott, R.F., *Le Pôle Meurtrier 1910–1912*. Pygmalion, Paris, 1992.

Shackleton, E., *Au Coeur de l'Antarctique : Vers le Pôle Sud (1908–1909)*. Phèbus, Paris, 1994.

——, *L'Odyssée de l' "Endurance" : Première Tentative de Traversée de l'Antarctique (1914–1917)*. Phébus, Paris, 1988.

Skrotzky, N., *Terres Extrêmes, la Grande Aventure des Pôles*. Denoël, Paris, 1986.

Souchez, R., *Les Glaces polaires*. Editions de l'Université de Bruxelles, Bruxelles, 1988.

Victor, P-E. et J-C., *Planète Antarctique, Nouvelle Terre des Hommes*. Robert Laffont, Paris, 1992.

THE ANTARCTIC COLLECTION

The Exploration of the Sixth Continent

The Antarctic wastes have long held a fascination for man. This sixth continent was the last to be explored and its demystifying formed the stuff of legends. The tragic story of Robert Falcon Scott and the British National Antarctic Expedition of 1910–12 is known throughout the world.

The Erskine Press and Bluntisham Books have published a series of books dealing with the HEROIC AGE OF ANTARCTIC EXPLORATION. Some of these books are now out of print but nine recent publications are still available and fall into three distinct categories.

THE DIARIES

ROALD AMUNDSEN'S *BELGICA* DIARY

In 1897 Amundsen made his first trip to the Antarctic. This previously unpublished diary details his experiences on the ice which fed his ambition to be the first man to reach the South Pole.

214pp, hardback, jacketed, illustrated £24.95/$45.00

TRIAL BY ICE – THE ANTARCTIC DIARIES OF JOHN KING DAVIS

Davis was the foremost of the ship's captains during the Heroic Age and this journal details his dealings with expedition leaders such as Mawson and Shackleton.

248pp, hardback, jacketed, illustrated £29.95/$55.00

THE QUIET LAND – THE ANTARCTIC DIARY OF FRANK DEBENHAM

Frank Debenham was a member of the ill-fated Scott expedition and the main instigator, and first director, of the Scott Polar Research Institute – his brain-child conceived in Shackleton's hut at Cape Royds.

208pp, hardback, jacketed, illustrated £24.95/$45.00

THE FACSIMILES

TO THE SOUTH POLAR REGIONS – Louis Bernacchi

The story of one of the many smaller and privately funded early voyages – 1898–1900

364pp, hardback, illustrated £29.95/$55.00

VOYAGES OF THE *MORNING* – Gerald Doorly
The story of the voyage to relieve Scott's *Discovery* in 1904
288pp, hardback, illustrated £24.95/$45.00

WITH SCOTT – THE SILVER LINING – Griffith Taylor
Probably the most entertaining and amusing account of Scott's last expedition
506pp, hardback, illustrated £39.95/$70.00

THE TRANSLATIONS
VOYAGE OF THE *BELGICA*
Fifteen Months in the Antarctic – Adrien de Gerlache
The story of the Belgian expedition of 1897–99 and the first truly scientific expedition
256pp, hardback, illustrated £37.50/$67.50

THE SOUTHERN ICE-CONTINENT
The German South Polar Expedition 1901–1903 – Erich von Drygalski
384pp, hardback, illustrated £49.95/$90.00

TO THE SIXTH CONTINENT
The Second German South Polar Expedition 1911–13 – Wilhelm Filchner
304pp, hardback, illustrated £49.95/$90.00

The first English translations of two very important expeditions

These books are available through bookshops or direct from the publishers

ERSKINE PRESS, The Old Bakery, Banham, Norwich, Norfolk NR16 2HW

BLUNTISHAM BOOKS, Oak House, East Street, Bluntisham, Huntingdon PE17 3LS